A powerful feminist reconceptualization o
destroy our planet, our bodies and our life
the disastrous faces and forms of capitalis
colonization, globalization and a neoliberal denumanized system. But
the author does not stop here. Susan Hawthorne articulates powerfully
the feminist resistances around the world with the hope that 'mass
movements can recreate the world in new ways'.

—Farida Akhter, Nayakrishi Andolon, Bangladesh

This is the book that we have been waiting for! Susan Hawthorne
covers theoretical issues, critiquing the takeover of neoliberalism, postmodernism and anti-scientific ideologies. She examines the impact of
patriarchal industrialisation and classist oppressions on women's lives,
on humanity in general, and on the planet. Her easy-to-read style enables
everyone to follow her descriptions and analysis of present-day problems
and challenges. She defines the terms, and analyses how modern
patriarchy controls economics, controls and damages the planet and
Indigenous people and cultures. She highlights the patriarchal control of
medicine on people with disabilities and how the modern trans activists
are damaging lesbian cultures and lesbians. She writes about insisting on
access to safe, female-only spaces such as refuges and medical facilities.
She elucidates how patriarchy damages the planet, nature, and life for
everyone. Only by understanding patriarchy, and how destructive it is,
will we be able to address it.

—Alison Laurie, former Programme Director of Gender and
    Women's Studies, Victoria University of Wellington, New Zealand
    and long time feminist, and lesbian activist

Susan Hawthorne demands that we not only face the social and ecological
crises of our moment in history, but recognize their patriarchal roots.
Vortex makes clear the connections between these crises and does not
shy away from naming male dominance as a driving force. The book
reflects Hawthorne's impressive intellectual and artistic skills, bringing
the clarity of political analysis alive with her poetic language. *Vortex* helps
us understand how difficult it will be to meet these challenges and why it
is so crucial to do so immediately.

—Robert Jensen, Professor Emeritus, University of Texas at Austin

The global pandemic of Covid-19 has created the opportunity for nations and communities to take stock of where several decades of neoliberalism and the free market have taken us and to ponder — is there a way we can still save the planet? In this courageous and very timely book, Susan Hawthorne lays bare the links between seemingly disparate events and deeply embedded global directions, arguing we must resist if we are to live free, healthy, ethical lives as people and nations. This is a must read for thinking people in every country, and offers a radical feminist take on how to rebuild a future that respects people and the environment, and avoids the mantra to 'get back to normal'.

—Sandra Coney, writer, health activist and environmentalist

The current term 'intersectionality', with its focus on 'identity', has lost its ability to analyse 21st century patriarchy. *Vortex* is a tour de force committed to reversing this superficial analytical trend. Hawthorne powerfully explores the material effects on women and children, and on the planet which sustains all our lives, as we are differentially placed by the patriarchal bio-politics of neoliberal globalisation and capitalism.

—Heather Brunskell-Evans, philosopher and author of *Transgender Body Politics*

Photo credit: Susan Kelly

Susan Hawthorne joined the Women's Liberation Movement in 1973. She quickly volunteered at Melbourne's Rape Crisis Centre and was active in student politics. She has organised writers' festivals, been an aerialist in two women's circuses and written on topics as diverse as war, friendship with animals, and mythic traditions. She writes non-fiction, fiction and poetry and her books have been translated into multiple languages. She has taught English to Arabic-speaking women, worked in Aboriginal education and had teaching roles across a number of subject areas in universities including Philosophy, Women's Studies, Literature, Publishing Studies and Creative Writing. She is Adjunct Professor in the School of Humanities at James Cook University, Townsville. Susan has won awards in writing, publishing, the gay and lesbian community and in 2017 was winner of the Penguin Random House Best Achievement in Writing in the Inspire Awards for her work increasing people's awareness of disability.

Other books by Susan Hawthorne

Non-fiction

In Defence of Separatism (2019)
Bibliodiversity: A Manifesto for Independent Publishing (2014)
Wild Politics: Feminism, Globalisation and Bio/diversity (2002)
The Spinifex Quiz Book: A Book of Women's Answers (1993)

Fiction

Dark Matters: A Novel (2017)
Limen (2013)
The Falling Woman (1992/2004)

Poetry

The Sacking of the Muses (2019)
Lupa and Lamb (2014)
Valence: Considering War through Poetry and Theory (2011)
Cow (2011)
Earth's Breath (2009)
Unsettling the Land (with Suzanne Bellamy, 2008)
The Butterfly Effect (2005)
Bird and Other Writings on Epilepsy (1999)
The Language in My Tongue (1993)

Anthologies

Lesbian Poets and Writers: Live Encounters (2018)
Horse Dreams: The Meaning of Horses in Women's Lives
    (with Jan Fook and Renate Klein, 2004)
Cat Tales: The Meaning of Cats in Women's Lives
    (with Jan Fook and Renate Klein, 2003)
September 11, 2001: Feminist Perspectives (with Bronwyn Winter, 2002)
CyberFeminism: Connectivity, Critique and Creativity
    (with Renate Klein, 1999)
Car Maintenance, Explosives and Love and Other Lesbian Writings
    (with Cathie Dunsford and Susan Sayer, 1997)
Australia for Women: Travel and Culture (with Renate Klein, 1994)
Angels of Power and Other Reproductive Creations (with Renate Klein, 1991)
The Exploding Frangipani: Lesbian Writing from Australia and New Zealand
    (with Cathie Dunsford, 1990)
Moments of Desire: Sex and Sexuality by Australian Feminist Writers
    (with Jenny Pausacker, 1989)
Difference: Writings by Women (1985)

VORTEX

The Crisis of Patriarchy

SUSAN HAWTHORNE

First published by Spinifex Press, 2020

Spinifex Press Pty Ltd
PO Box 5270, North Geelong, VIC 3215, Australia
PO Box 105, Mission Beach, QLD 4852, Australia
women@spinifexpress.com.au
www.spinifexpress.com.au

Edited by Renate Klein and Pauline Hopkins
Index by Karen Gillen
Cover design by Deb Snibson, MAPG
Typesetting by Helen Christie, Blue Wren Books
Typeset in Minion Pro
Printed and bound by CPI Group (UK) Ltd, Croydon, CR0 4YY

A catalogue record for this
book is available from the
National Library of Australia

ISBN: 9781925950168 (paperback)
ISBN: 9781925950175 (ebook)

Contents

CHAPTER EIGHT

Breaking the Spirit of the Planet:
Climate Catastrophe   219

CHAPTER NINE

Sovereignty and the Spirit of Nature   249

References   257

Index   289

Acknowledgements

This book has been brewing for a long time. I began writing it in late 2017, but the research and reading has extended over 50 years, from my first gleanings of feminism. It is, therefore, not possible to thank everyone by name, but I am especially grateful to those who have challenged me over the years as it helps to clarify one's ideas and make one's arguments more convincing. I'd also like to thank those who have helped develop my ideas through support, suggestions for reading and including those whose books, articles and talks I mention here that have contributed to my thinking.

In October 2017, two publishers — one from Canada and another from Germany — were interested in seeing a shorter and updated version of *Wild Politics*. Once I started writing, the book changed shape and became a brand new book instead. I thank them for their encouragement and the impetus to update my ideas.

In 2018, I received a Residency at the Göll Writers House run by Nilüfer Belediyesi, Bursa, Turkey which allowed me two weeks of intensive writing. Those two weeks provided me with the overall structure of this book. In addition, I was able to stay in the village of Gölyazi which has existed since the fourth century BC when it was known as Apollonia. Thank you to all at the local council and to the librarians who welcomed us and helped us know more about the region, especially their fantastic libraries.

My thanks also go to my social media friends whose posts alerted me to new developments or to articles in the media I would not have seen. There are many fine ways to use social media for research as it is like entering a giant library with a maze of Borghesian stacks that can divert you or illuminate a dark corner.

Sincere thanks to radical feminists who have not only survived a long period of being dismissed and much attempted erasure, but who have also generated a great deal of hugely productive activism in all the areas which I cover in this book. I could not have written it without you.

Those who have worked with me on the book deserve enormous thanks as I crept slowly past one deadline or another. Thanks to Renate Klein, always my first and last reader, editor and reference queen; to Pauline Hopkins for her eagle eye and her textual clarifications; to Maralann Damiano who kept the administrative wolves at bay; to Rachael McDiarmid for a new Spinifex website and for her ability to promote radical feminist books; to Caitlin Roper whose knowledge of social media has taken this and other books out into the digital ether. Two early readers, Diane Bell and Robert Jensen assisted me in clarifying different areas of the manuscript. It is always a boon to have trusted readers. Thank you to typesetter, Helen Christie and to cover designer Deb Snibson for making the book look beautiful, inside and out. Sincere thanks to indexer, Karen Gillen for a clear index.

My thanks go to my partner of more than 30 years, Renate Klein, without whom this book would not exist. I extend to her my love and sincere thanks for everything. Finally, to the latest inhabitant of our household, Nala, a rescue dog; thanks for the laughter you have created even when confronted with final proofs.

Mission Beach,
September 2020

The Year of the Pandemic

The writing of Vortex was almost complete when the coronavirus pandemic hit. Such an important global event has to be accounted for because so many of the issues I cover in the book are connected to the fast-moving global spread of Covid-19. *Vortex: The Crisis of Patriarchy* has developed from my earlier work *Wild Politics: Feminism, Globalisation and Bio/diversity* (2002) and *Bibliodiversity: A Manifesto for Independent Publishing* (2014). Also relevant is my long involvement in the Women's Liberation Movement and other movements for social change including for ending racism and discrimination against people with disabilities and those in poverty. The speed of the coronavirus resembles the vortex, a movement spiralling down at increasing speed.

While there remain questions about the cause of Covid-19, several things are certain:

- Globalisation, free trade and the fast movement of goods and people ensured that wherever it had arisen it would move quickly to other places.
- Global systems of agriculture, forestry and fishing make it inevitable that the wild becomes a product for the consumer market in its own and other countries.

- The industrialisation of fishing, farming and forestry reduces biodiversity and weakens systems of survival of plants and animals, thereby affecting humans.
- Corporate pharmaceutical power has resulted in research that ignores biosafety measures.
- Deforestation destroys the habitats of wildlife, forcing them into closer proximity with humans.
- A throwaway planet is one in which necessary health products are manufactured in the cheapest markets, resulting in nations losing the ability to make their own products, thereby creating shortages and price gouging of necessary medical equipment.
- The #BlackLivesMatter protests that occurred in spite of calls not to participate were inspiring in ways that are difficult to encapsulate because people made their demands peacefully (on the whole), thoughtfully and with considered calls for changes that no decent government should ignore. That #BlackLivesMatter did not fully represent women is a matter to be explored elsewhere.

In this book, I examine the many ways in which the crisis of patriarchy has led to the pandemic along with a multitude of other negative outcomes for ordinary people. The result of the crisis of patriarchy is a war against the planet, its residents including humans, wildlife, plants and its environments, whether they be forests or grasslands, seabeds or sea trenches, mountain tops or deserts, snowfields or farmlands. The pandemic also brings into focus a range of other global events:

- The reliance on fossils fuels creates big corporate profits but leaves Indigenous peoples landless or with destroyed land, has long-term deleterious effects on farming land, rivers and underground water supplies, and contributes to climate catastrophe.
- In India, the sudden lockdown resulted in migrant workers having to walk home to their towns and villages because they had migrated to cities for work in order to survive, work which

dried up when Covid-19 hit. Previously, these workers would have stayed in their communities and worked there.

- The provision of healthcare has been removed from communities of people and instead put in the control of Big Pharma and the industrial medical system; those who work outside the system are frequently criminalised.

- The dependence of corporate patriarchy on slavery: the slave trade from Africa to the Americas; the enslaved conditions of Indigenous peoples everywhere; the enslaved conditions of women around the globe as part of the colonisation process and into the era of neoliberalism; the enslaved conditions of colonised peoples all around the world that continues under patriarchal corporate capitalism (Patterson 1982; Galeano 1973/1987; Guillamin 1995; Enloe 1983; Pateman 1988).

- The potential for large corporations that use the terms of free trade agreements to sue governments for loss of profits because of pandemic shutdowns. Patricia Ranald (2020) highlights the Investor-State Dispute Settlement (ISDS) procedures. Examples of government actions that could attract such suits include directing private hospitals to treat patients diagnosed with Covid-19; and building capacity to manufacture medical equipment. Both of these could cause losses to trade partners who might decide to bring such a suit.

- The dependence of patriarchal capitalism on wars which are counted as contributing to economic growth through the production of weapons of war, research into ever-more destructive weapons, the mobilisation of soldiers on ships and aircraft, the growth of prostitution near military bases and the opportunity to carry out experiments on military personnel and civilians on the use of drugs (Enloe 1983; McCoy 1999; Klein 2007).

- The continuing dissociation of bodies from reality and the intensification of technological interference in bodies. This includes microcolonialism, the move to reify 'bodies without women', cyborgs and disembodiment (Klein 1996, pp. 346-358), as well as dysmorphia and transhumanism (Bilek 2020f).

But the pandemic also offers some hope, some openings that might make the future better.

One immediate effect has been the reduction in air pollution in cities. The air over Hubei province in China and over Beijing and Shanghai cleared when the hard lockdown came into force in China. In Australia, cities previously choking on smoke from the bushfires also cleared. In India the night sky is currently clear enough to see stars. Pollution in waterways, too, has reduced in places as different as Venice and Delhi. As Arundhati Roy (2020) writes, "who could not be thrilled by the swell of birdsong in cities, peacocks dancing at traffic crossings and the silence of the skies?" And in the sea near me, there have been rarely seen dolphins and manta rays close to the shore. I read in the newspaper today that a kangaroo has been spotted in the Adelaide CBD; that cougars have wandered Chile's capital, Santiago, and in Haifa, wild boar have been seen in the streets. What is it that the animals know? Is the Earth letting us know that change is possible, if only we take the right path?

Prior to the pandemic, only Finland was considering introducing a Universal Basic Income (UBI). Some weeks into the pandemic the idea was being considered in Spain (Zeballos-Roig 2020). Government payments during the pandemic in Australia, New Zealand and the UK for example have resembled a UBI and it will be interesting to see the upshot of this.

It has brought into focus the importance of universal publically owned health systems. A push towards increasing privatisation of health systems is something activists should consider campaigning against.

The print editions of *Playboy* closed down and in Germany, Angela Merkel asked for the closure of all brothels; in Australia those in the sex trade who ignored a similar closure have been charged with a criminal act. Radical feminists have called for this to happen for many years. Abolition of prostitution and the closing down of pornographers has never had a better chance of coming to fruition.

While social distancing has been difficult for some (especially the poor and homeless) for others it has created new ways of coming together in driveways, over new internet apps and reducing the disconnection that is inevitable with so many constantly on the move around the globe. A greater appreciation for the local is a possible outcome. Interconnectedness can happen in many ways.

Deglobalisation, degrowth, decolonisation and deindustrialisation could all be considered opportunities for the future.

The closing down of nations around the world seemed unthinkable a year ago. Even the raising of unemployment benefits like Newstart in Australia was unlikely to occur. The second wave has created some different challenges and each wave that follows will bring new chances to create momentum for radical new ideas. Governments do have money for the common good when they make a decision to act. It is time for them to put the common good at the front, instead of the profiteering of corporations for the 'good' of a few individuals. Whether they will do it — and to what extent, and whether it will benefit women — remains to be seen.

Mission Beach, Queensland,
8 July 2020

We talk of Cassandra. Belief is as important as knowledge.
For what is knowledge if no one believes it?
There have been many times when destruction could
have been avoided, when the future was glaring at people.
That was the fate of Cassandra, though her ears had been
licked by a serpent, no one would believe her prophecies.

They laughed at her story of the wooden horse —
and the city fell. They laughed even as they died.

There have been many Cassandras. Many of us.

—Susan Hawthorne,
The Falling Woman
(1992, pp. 83–84)

Introduction

The last two decades have been a period of war, growth of patriotism, global financial crisis and deepening violence against women, against majority peoples whose needs have been violated and of growing crises for displaced peoples and refugees. They have also been a time of environmental vandalism and the triumph of the economy over the social, one of the consequences of which is the global pandemic.

The vortex that is the subject of this book seems to be getting ever deeper, swirling ever faster and wider, ever more out of control. The speed of the vortex has been made visible by Covid-19. The vortex of patriarchy encompasses the deep deceptions of capitalism at its worst where entitlement, consumerism and celebrity culture are held up as cues for happiness, while the world's majority live in dire poverty and where the environment continues to be plundered.

The vortex is particularly destructive to those who are caught in its empty centre, as are people with disabilities, Indigenous and poverty stricken peoples, the landless and refugees. Among all these groups are women who bear an unreasonable load of poverty and violence against them. Wars fought over resources and ideologies continue to attract young men as fighters for old men's dreams. The majority who are killed and maimed are women and children: they are collateral casualties.

The global structures are not just affecting humans: the planet, its animals and plants, glaciers, wetlands, seas and mountains, deserts and farmlands, forests and rivers are all feeling the effect of the vortex. Climate change, increasing rates of extinction and pollution of all kinds are among the environmental disasters of capitalism without compassion or conscience.

These constitute the crimes of neoliberal capitalist patriarchy. They are wars against all who live on the planet. We are at a crisis point.

A note on truth

We know from the history of fascist states and states at war that truth is an early casualty. Around the world, we are seeing a revival of 'strong men' in positions of political power who disregard truth. Donald Trump's survival of impeachment in 2020 is just one example. His ability to tell endless lies without blinking is remarkable in its audacity and it is demeaning of all who surround him and kowtow to him.

Thanks to political philosophers and writers like Hannah Arendt we understand that blatant lying is a known method of a successful propaganda machine. We remember George Orwell's Ministry of Truth in *Nineteen Eighty-Four* (1976) whose rationale was the spreading of lies that purported to be truth. We have seen the development within academia of a philosophy that insists that truth is relative or does not exist at all. Postmodernism has been the predominant philosophy in arts and humanities since the 1990s (though it began its climb in the early 1980s). I have read many of the key texts and still find them wanting. When it took over the humanities, no one imagined that it would also take over the sciences. The latest postmodern and queer inroad into science has been through the transgender movement. Consider the following:

In an ever-changing, incomprehensible world the masses had reached the point where they would, at the same time, believe everything and nothing, think that everything was possible and that nothing was true … Mass propaganda discovered that its audience was ready at all times to believe the worst, no matter how absurd, and did not particularly object to being deceived because it held every statement to be a lie anyhow. The totalitarian mass leaders based their propaganda on the correct psychological assumption that, under such conditions, one could make people believe the most fantastic statements one day, and trust that if the next day they were given irrefutable proof of their falsehood, they would take refuge in cynicism; instead of deserting the leaders who had lied to them, they would protest that they had known all along that the statement was a lie and would admire the leaders for their superior tactical cleverness (Arendt 1951/2017, p. 500).

And this, projected on the Ministry of Justice building in London in July 2018 (Linehan 2019):

Repeat after us, Trans women are women.

Or,

$2+2=5$

The relativity of truth is widely used by politicians. Australian Liberal senator, Jim Molan said on ABC-TV Australia in early 2020, "I'm not relying on evidence" as the basis of his position on climate change (ABC-TV, 2020). Here, the postmodernists and the neoliberal right-wingers show that they have the same colours. In spite of this, too many self-defined progressives have not noticed the alliance. An alliance that has been obvious to radical feminists for several decades (Brodribb 1992; Bell and Klein 1996).

A note on words

Words matter to me. As a poet and a woman interested in language, words matter. What they mean, what they signify and what they suggest. Monique Wittig in her book *Les Guérillères* writes:

> The women say, the language you speak poisons your glottis tongue palate lips. They say, the language you speak is made up of words that are killing you. They say, the language you speak is made up of signs that rightly speaking designate what men have appropriated (1971, p. 123).[1]

Feminists are facing a new round of male appropriation of language and political misuses of language. In this book, I use the word 'sex' when speaking about women and men, girls and boys. The word 'gender' is used only when I mean sex-roles — and mostly I prefer to use the term sex-roles over the term gender which has become increasingly misused in recent years.

The word 'identity' is also problematic. The term 'gender identity' is its most common usage, but it is also increasingly used in popular culture. If I say my identity is female, I am speaking about a biological reality. If I say my identity is Australian, that's not the only facet of me. Identity individualises people and disconnects the different parts that form people. My identity is neither solely Australian nor female, nor white, nor a person with a disability, nor lesbian, nor a member of the over 60 group, nor a rural person, nor a poet, nor any other aspect of my life. It is all of the above and more. Identity does nothing to help people join forces for a political purpose. If I imagine that I am a rich white man, will I suddenly become rich? The answer is obvious: No. Identity is no longer a useful political term because 'identity' dissects and disconnects us. It makes collective action all but impossible.

Because 'identity' has created a world in which the individual is at the centre of political positioning, it is difficult to call for collective action. The powerful have always understood the principle of

---

1   Monique Wittig's book was first published in French in 1969.

divide-and-conquer. It was used in the USA from the 1600s to 1967. There, the State of Virginia enacted laws against interracial marriage and in order to make it real created a multiplicity of words for speaking about African descent. Those labels included Sacatra, Griffe, Marabon, Mulatto, Quadroon, Metif, Meamelouc, Quarteron, and Sang-mele (*Scoop It* 2018). These were racist and oppressive laws.

We can see how this proliferation of labels has been picked up by the transgender lobby. The number of identities that are available to people, as discussed on social media, is around 50, each with its own flag. And it is not the commonalities of these identities, but the differences that are the focus, in just the same way the state of Virginia divided African Americans. When the oppressed cannot see what brings them together, they cannot fight against the oppressor.

The most usual claim is that feminists are to blame for everything, especially radical feminists who have been renamed TERFS (Trans Exclusive Radical Feminists) or SWERFS (Sex Work Exclusive Radical Feminists). But the power of radical feminists is wildly overstated. It reminds me of US fundamentalist, Jerry Falwell speaking about September 11, 2001. He said, "… the pagans and the abortionists and the feminists and gays and lesbians … You made this happen" (cited in Parenti 2002, p. 47).[2] Yet again we find a repetition of absurdities and falsehoods. I know of no feminist or lesbian organisation with access to aeroplanes to fly into buildings. I know of no radical feminist with the power or money attributed to her by the postmodern, queer, trans and sex work lobby. But, as I identify in each chapter, there are billionaire lobbyists funding the political organisations behind all those groups.

The language wars are alive and well among the lobbyists for prostitution. The war of words, once again, has been prompted by a postmodern neoliberal outlook in which the purveyors argue

---

2 For a longer discussion see my essay 'Fundamentalism, Violence and Disconnection' in Hawthorne and Winter (2002b).

that prostitution is work. So, they say, let us call it 'sex work' and then all will be well. Those who refute the term 'sex-work' have left the industry and are lobbying for laws that will, eventually, see the abolition of prostitution.[3] They have left the room in which they are told to say prostitution is work, when the evidence shows that it is violence against women: Women die, their mental and physical health is compromised and they often become homeless and socially isolated (Moran 2013; Norma and Tankard Reist 2016).

Some groups that have managed to work across significant and obvious differences are people with disabilities, Indigenous peoples and radical feminists. The reason is that they have collectivised across what binds them/us and approached it with an understanding of structural power and its systemic use against them/us.

The movement of people with disabilities is a movement made up of people with extraordinarily different needs: from physical disability, to disabilities of the senses, of the brain, of mental and social disorders. And I have seen some marvellous critical work in this field which I discuss in Chapter Two.

Indigenous peoples around the world are amongst the most marginalised and they too have been able to come together across borders of language and of culture to speak about their vision for the future, sometimes pragmatic, sometimes idealistic. These ideals for the future and changes in the present are based on a sense of commonality of structural experience. The colonisers, in the main, have used the same oppressive techniques and undoing them is necessary for a better life. These issues lie at the core of Chapters Four and Five. When it comes to naming Indigenous peoples I use the following rules of thumb: I use the word Indigenous when speaking of multiple groups, especially when referring to First Nations peoples internationally, in addition to using the term First Nations. In Australia, when referring generally I use both Indigenous and Aboriginal and Torres Strait Islanders. When

---

3   See Meagan Tyler's essay on the Nordic Model in Norma and Tankard Reist (2016).

citing an individual I sometimes refer to their country name or the name which they themselves use. Life is complex and sometimes naming conventions can be too.

Women are the poorest of the poor and radical feminists, because of their structural analysis of power, have joined together all around the world to fight against oppression in all its forms. Chapters Three, Six and Seven examine the specific crimes against women carried out by neoliberal patriarchal capitalists.

Key terms in this book

A vortex is a circular movement of gas or liquid. To visualise it think of water going down a plughole; think of the images of tornados — a spinning mass of air and moisture with an empty centre. In the former case it disperses material quickly into the unseen zone of plumbing pipes; in the latter case it is destructive and can smash houses, uproot trees and kill anyone in its path.

> Vortex: environment
> *a mass of air or water that spins around very fast and pulls objects into its empty centre*
>
> Vortex: literary
> *a dangerous or bad situation in which you become more and more involved and from which you cannot escape*
> (*The Cambridge English Dictionary* 2020).

In this book I am using the word in both the literary and environmental sense. The vortex has been created by neoliberal capitalist patriarchy. It has an empty centre because at heart it is nihilistic and only data and profit matter. It is in crisis and has been heading for the full impact of crisis for decades. The current crisis of shutdowns from Covid-19, the climate catastrophe, the environmental, health and economic crises resulting from these, is massive. Neoliberal globalisation created some of the catalysts from disconnected and intensifying levels of international travel, to the inability to make masks and medical equipment in our own countries, to the escalating levels of men's violence against women daily and globally, and increasing mass poverty. These and other ingredients contribute to the dire situation the planet is in at present. In this book I want to examine the ways in which the crisis has built up and where it is headed. I am also attempting to find some strategies for slowing the vortex. Can we imagine a different world?

Patriarchy is a critical element in this unfolding disaster. It is a system of social governance that has dominated the planet (though not universally) for around six thousand years. The root meaning of the word 'patriarchy' is the rule of fathers and while not all fathers rule and not all the rulers are fathers, the vast majority are men; they are men with wealth; they are men with physical strength; they are men who benefit from other men's advocacy and support; they are men who benefit from access to and exercise of more power and more kinds of power. Look around at the world's leaders. Just a few are women. And the women who do get to the top nearly always pay dearly for it. Look at the leaders of industry; look around your family. Patriarchy is a system of power that benefits men and men's interests (think football, prostitution and gambling). Patriarchy is not only bad for women; it is also racist and hierarchical in multiple ways; the origins of patriarchy suggest that slavery (often the result of war) and the oppression of women are both integral to patriarchal systems. Hierarchies of class, the oppression of people with disabilities, the separation of people according to differences in ethnicity, religion, sexuality or age are key elements.

Pre-patriarchal societies appear to have had no fortifications of cities, suggesting that wars were not yet a major part of those cultures. Think of the wars in place right now (I will not be able to list all of them): Syria, Yemen, Ukraine, Democratic Republic of Congo; as well as the war against the Uighurs in China, against the Rohingya in Burma/Myanmar or internally in Venezuela; the war on drugs; the war against women; the colonising wars of former empires; the war that creates resistance movements like #BlackLivesMatter and #MeToo. Before a war can end, another takes its place. Go back through history: wars are major events on every country's calendar. You will see from my chapter titles that wars are a central topic.

The oldest epics in the world concern themselves with wars. In India it is *The Mahabharata*; in Greek literature it is *The Iliad* and *The Odyssey*. From these two great Greek epics comes the story of the Trojan Horse and of Cassandra, the daughter of the Trojan King Priam and Queen Hecuba.

Cassandra was one of many children in the royal family of Troy. Her distinction was her ability to foresee the future. This is a god-given ability, but the god Apollo is said to have prohibited other people's belief in her prophecies because she refused his sexual advances. She was an ancient feminist with the same problem of being disbelieved that contemporary feminists face. Her prophecies included the destruction of Troy, the fate of many members of her family. She warned that the Greeks were planning to overthrow Troy using the trick of the Trojan horse. Instead of facing the Trojans on the battlefield, the trickster Odysseus built a huge wooden horse. It was presented as an offering to the city of Troy after ten years of war and the Greeks sailed away as if leaving and giving up. Inside the horse were their best soldiers and Odysseus. The Trojans, believing that the Greeks had given up, drew the wooden horse inside the gates. The citadel of Troy had huge high walls that could not be broken through but by means of this subterfuge the Greeks were able to enter the city. In the dead of night, the soldiers climbed out of the horse and rampaged through the city. The Greeks on ships returned and the city was routed.

In this book, I am using the term Trojan horse to signify ways in which neoliberal capitalist patriarchy creeps in undercover and before we know it, a new system is in place. Briefly here are some examples of neoliberal Trojan horses I refer to:

- Pre-natal screening offers pregnant women and their partners the hope of perfection; the promise is that more screening will mean that imperfections will be eliminated. Women are sold the idea but in reality there is no such ability to screen all imperfections and women's bodies are increasingly monitored and controlled by the medical industry. Eugenics in action.
- The use of the term 'sex work' promises freedom from discrimination for women in the sex trade, giving desperate women good 'jobs' and fulfilling men's sexual desires. In the real world, women in the sex trade are violated, made into 'products' and become the butt of racist and misogynous acts. All of these acts are justified on the ground of men's 'uncontrollable' sex drive.
- Capitalists claim that bioprospecting will usher in an era of prosperity for Indigenous and traditional peoples who can sell their knowledge to corporations and reap benefits for their communities; the promise of a Green New Deal and high-tech future for all. But the Green New Deal will commodify the natural world and just as likely be as destructive as the previous green co-option: the green revolution (Shiva 1991).
- In writing about deterritorialisation, I begin with the point of view of colonisers from several centuries ago: their movement across the world was seen as bringing European civilisation to the rest of the world. In the current era globalisation has made similar promises of prosperity through the market and promising to provide opportunities for westernisation; the promise is that this will save lives and lead to prosperity. In reality, poverty is increased, people are displaced or forced to migrate for badly paid work, sometimes in conditions of slavery.
- Same-sex marriage has been celebrated around the world for bringing gay and lesbian people into the marriage fold that also allows them to create 'normal' families; heterosexualising lesbian and gay lives is a way of normalising what were previously lives of resistance to heterosexual norms; weddings,

parties and celebrations are held because everyone knows that gay people have the best parties!

- In jurisdictions where same-sex marriage has been made legal, laws on behalf of transgender people have also been introduced; it promises diversity, and equality for all, but erases real-life girls, women and lesbians and creates a vortex for anyone speaking critically against 'gender'.

While patriarchy is in crisis, the patriarchs have many tricks up their sleeves. The Trojan horse is understood as a gift from the gods, but as I'll describe in the following chapters the offerings themselves are dangerous. Breaking the spirit is a key strategy because it makes people more amenable.

Is this what any of us wants, in these times of danger not only from trickery but widespread disaster caused by the ravages of war-mongering patriarchal leaders? Not satisfied with the immediate gains from war, capitalist patriarchs want more. They want the entire world. In the period when the Trojan War raged, the eyes of the leaders were on the Mediterranean, its lands, peoples and seas. The war against the planet has heated up and so many of the world's peoples are caught in a downward spiral — a vortex of destruction.

The coronavirus crisis has illuminated intensely the fractures that are integral to neoliberal capitalist patriarchy. Indeed, they reflect the crisis points I write about in this book. In Chapter One, I look at the way in which the global economic system structures power, determines who gets the opportunities and who doesn't. This connects to ideas explored throughout the book about money and the way money simultaneously creates poverty alongside a small number of multibillionaires who have excessive power to determine political, economic and social policies.

In Chapter Two, I discuss the ways in which disability is perceived at both the government level but also from my own experience and the personal experiences and analyses of others. The National Disability Insurance Scheme (NDIS) in Australia promised to provide financial, emotional and community support for people with disabilities. That support was already questionable, but Covid-19 has stretched the system yet further and there are insufficient support workers and carers to provide for the needs of people with disabilities.

In Chapter Three, I look at the many forms of violence against women. The Covid-19 crisis has highlighted the breakdown of services for women facing what is now commonly called 'domestic terrorism'. There are too few refuges still functioning and available to women in distress. Their funding has reduced over recent decades. Brothels are at the frontline and Angela Merkel was the first to close them down nationally. The pornography industry claims to be in shock because *Playboy* is no longer producing print copies.

In Chapters Four and Five the focus is on the interrelationship between the land, the environment and the bodies in which people live. To what extent is that relationship in the hands of those who live there? Or have they been dispossessed? Is the dispossession on the macro level of lands and what it grows or is it on the micro level of bodies themselves?

Chapters Six and Seven continue the focus on bodies and the ways in which the dignity of bodies is central to a life well-lived. In these chapters, I write about lesbians who are all too frequently left out of political analyses of this kind. Lesbian bodies are attacked by violence enacted by men in roles within state and non-state institutions, as well as Big Pharma and the medical industrial system with patriarchal agendas of silencing, assimilating and erasing lesbians.

In Chapter Eight, I take up the issue of climate catastrophe as experienced in Australia recently while in Chapter Nine I offer some perspectives on how across the globe people might act to ensure a liveable and sustainable future. Here I draw on notes taken during her Keynote Speech on 'Aboriginal Women and Feminism' at the Fourth Women and Labour Conference in 1984. Lilla Watson is a respected Murri elder, visual artist, philosopher and activist from Gangulu country in Central Queensland.

[She] pointed out that for Aboriginal people the future went as far forward as it went back. She argued that Aboriginal people had a 40,000-year plan.[4]

What I have in mind is a world something along the lines of Lilla Watson's 40,000-year plan. By envisioning a future of this length, it becomes essential to consider how resources — renewable and non-renewable — can be maintained, as if permanently (see also Hawthorne 2002, pp. 160–161).

I was profoundly affected by Lilla Watson's 1984 speech as it made me think how one might see the world differently. Life as a radical feminist is full of such epistemological epiphanies and I am grateful for all those who have challenged me so that I — in concert with others — might expand my understanding of the world. This book is part of that journey.

---

4   It is now widely accepted in Australia that the date has been pushed to a much earlier time: 65,000, 80,000, 120,000 years are commonly stated.

Patriarchal grammar

a way of knowing that all you know
is all there is to know

a way of speaking so that everyone
else knows to remain silent

a way of being that lets you walk through life
oblivious to the pain of others

a way of making asymmetric war
against the powerless

a way of using your body as a weapon
and then calling it love

—Susan Hawthorne,
The Sacking of the Muses
(2019, p. 77)

CHAPTER ONE

The Crisis of Economics: Patriarchal Wars against People and the Planet

When I first began to think about the issues covered in this book some 25 years ago, the world was quite a different place. There were many critiques of globalisation being developed by feminists internationally. I encountered some of these at a conference on 'People's Perspectives on Population' in Bangladesh in 1993. Feminists from 'developing countries' were critical of Structural Adjustment Policies (SAPs), others had a sophisticated critique of the international economic system and we activists felt that we were beginning to make inroads into these structural systems. In the late 1990s, there were protests and demonstrations around the world against the meetings of the World Economic Forum (WEF). When the protestors arrived in Seattle in November 1999, the media sat up and took notice, although there had been earlier campaigns against free trade agreements such as the MAI, TRIPs, and NAFTA[5] (among others).

---

5   TRIPs: Trade Related Intellectual Property rights; MAI: Multilateral Agreement on Investment; NAFTA: North American Free Trade Agreement.

In September 2000, I spent three days outside the World Economic Forum in Melbourne at what was dubbed S11 (September 11). In late September 2001, there were plans for a large anti-globalisation protest in Washington, but the protests lost momentum in the aftermath of 9/11. In spite of this — or perhaps because of it — the following year when the World Social Forum was held in Porto Alegre, Brazil, people arrived in their thousands and by the time it was held in Mumbai, India, in 2004, hundreds of thousands of people were attending.

Appropriation of politics

Over the last twenty years, the word 'globalisation' has shifted from a protest movement for the left to a voting handmaiden for the right. How could this have happened?

Globalisation is a universalised system of monetary and cultural trade that benefits the rich, mobile and male sectors of the world, including the transnational sector. It is built upon western knowledge and property systems, and assumes that these are regarded universally as good regimes.

Some examples:

- Walmart buys cheap products made in China and sells them cheaply to people on low incomes in the USA. The result for Americans is that manufacturing goes offshore, but the quid pro quo for the working class is cheap consumer goods and a throw-away culture that creates additional waste that clogs landfills and creates floating islands of plastic waste in the oceans.
- Industrial farmers, such as those growing GM crops, run factory farms in areas where land is plentiful. The result is that because so much of the work is industrialised there are no longer any jobs for farm hands and agricultural workers. The apparent reward is that food is said to be cheaper. But it contains pesticides, is over-processed with added sugar or hormones

and is possibly grown from GM seeds. The externalities are never made transparent and adverse effects on health take a generation to become apparent.

- In countries which depend on fishing, instead of the small-scale fisherpeople catching enough fish for their own use and for the local trade, their fishing areas are taken over by large international fishing trawlers who deplete the local stock. The local fishers can no longer live off their fishing, not only because of depletion, but because of increased pollution of the seas and the introduction of competing species. The price of fish drops for countries to which the fish is exported; the exporting country's product is depleted; fresh fish is no longer available locally.

- In countries with cheap labour forces — the fabrics industry in Bangladesh or the electronics industry in Mexico — where women work long hours in underpaid jobs and are discarded as they age — these industries set up factories and produce goods for export. There are numerous reports of building collapses in Bangladesh, of fires and of gross exploitation in these and similar industries. The promise is that women will gain financial independence. In Mexico, women are more likely to be murdered in the Export Processing Zones where maquiladoras[6] provide employment for young women (Cacho 2014).

- Globalisation has produced flourishing new industries such as the global sex industry and an immense increase in women exploited in prostitution. Laws have been changed to 'decriminalise' prostitution and the profits are returned to those who run the industry. The false promise is that women in 'sex work' will be so much freer under global marketing than they were under a local pimp.

---

6   Maquiladoras: Foreign-owned assembly plants of Northern Mexico, which emphasise transnational investment in export-oriented commodities. They are Mexico's version of the export processing zones found in many developing economies (Hawthorne 2002, p. 385).

- Sale of bodies and body parts has also become a flourishing industry. This can be seen in the contracts for surrogacy, where a poor woman, usually from a poor country has her body used by rich heterosexual couples and gay men (Klein 2017). The trafficking in organs goes on apace, with kidneys and other body parts being a lucrative trade. The promise is always that the poor women and men doing this will earn so much money that they will be able to send their children to school or buy a house or at least one of the latest flat screen televisions (Raymond 1995/2019).

In her book on prostitution and surrogacy, Kajsa Ekis Ekman writes about the split for women between reproduction and sex: "The whore may not become pregnant, the surrogate may not have sex; women all over the world are denied their complete humanity" (Ekman 2013, p. 191). Or, as she stated in a talk in 2014, "Prostitution is sex without babies; surrogacy is babies without sex" (Ekman 2014).

How has criticism of globalisation shifted sides?

In Australia, right-wing nationalist and racist politician, Pauline Hanson — first elected to Parliament in 1996 with her new party One Nation — was an early critic of globalisation because she wanted local jobs kept in Australia. As can be seen from the examples above, one of the key outcomes of globalisation is the loss of jobs in factories as they are exported to places where manufacturing and packaging can be done more cheaply. Among primary producers, foresters, and miners, much of the raw material is exported to be transformed into products and re-exported back to the original country.

Pauline Hanson, in her first speech after being re-elected to the Australian Parliament in 2016, refers back to One Nation's earlier policies. Criticising political leaders she says,

[T]hey have failed to discard old treaties and agreements that are not in our best interest and have signed new ones giving away our sovereignty, rights, jobs and democracy. Their push for globalisation, economic rationalism, free trade and ethnic diversity has seen our country's decline. This is due to foreign takeover of our land and assets, out-of-control debt, failing infrastructure, high unemployment or underemployment and the destruction of our farming sector. Indiscriminate immigration and aggressive multiculturalism have caused crime to escalate and trust and social cohesion to decline (Hanson 2016).

This sounds ominously like President Trump. In Hanson's and Trump's worlds, globalisation imperils nationalism and the prolongation of strong borders. The feminist critique of globalisation is very different. It is about the threat posed by male-dominated transnational capitalists buying up and controlling resources, whether of land or people, culture or production. And in contrast to Hanson, Trump and other right-wing nationalists, feminists welcome refugees, displaced persons and women fleeing violence.

In 2016, many of us were shocked to see Donald Trump elected as President of the USA. Not only because of his politics, but also because of his known history as a man who is a racist and sexually harasses women and, in social contexts, is a belligerent bully. One of Trump's key political messages in the lead up to the election was that globalisation and free trade threatened American jobs. This is a case of sheer hypocrisy. It is mega rich people like Donald Trump who have gained from the export of working-class American jobs so that their own companies can reap more profits.

What is behind this right-wing turnaround against globalisation and free trade? As a long-term critic of both, what I see here is an appropriative turn. Looking across a range of radical political movements over time, the reactionary forces — they are well named — trawl through the opposition's policies and find elements that they can co-opt. This is also how capitalism functions.

Capitalists find a product that is selling well on the street, an idea that appears to have a following. They pick up the product or idea, add money and marketing, shift it sideways a little — in other words remove from it the genuinely creative element — and sell it back to the same people, or better still the next generation.

Reactionary politicians can be seen doing this all around the world. Take ecology. Ecologist, Rachel Carson, in her book *Silent Spring* (1962) alerted us to the dangers of DDT and the impact it was having on birdlife and on human health. Four decades later, Bjørn Lomborg in *The Skeptical Environmentalist* (2001) attempts to counter all the claims of the ecological movement. In the process, he distorts the intentions of ecologists and proceeds to damn everything they have said. At the end he concludes that climate change is bunkum. Cherry-picking 'facts' and de-contextualisations of inequities are integral to the appropriative turn.

In the feminist movement, we have seen similar attempts to distort and water down feminist ideas by mainstreaming them (Hawthorne 2004a). In the 1990s, when postmodernism was on the rise, the author was declared dead just at the moment when women writers were beginning to be recognised (the process still continues with women authors receiving lower marketing budgets and fewer reviews than male authors). Mainstream liberal feminists would also have us believe that the most important thing for a woman is 'choice': choice to buy and consume the latest gadgets; choice to go into 'sex work' because it is such a rewarding profession; choice to use another woman's body to bring a child into the world; choice to join powerful men on the boards of transnational companies. These are all fake 'choices' and lie at the root of a neoliberal distortion of feminism as a marketing gimmick.

Appropriation is nothing new, but it has a new dangerous face connected in some ways to the postmodern view of the world. In a postmodern political world, the positions people hold are not clear. How do you tell if the person who is offering you shares in a company that protects rainforest is ethical? What if it turns out to be a bioprospecting company that wants to exploit the knowledge passed down through many generations by the local Indigenous people? What if it turns out to be a re-colonisation of country and knowledge? What if it is done by an Indigenous person? We see the same occurring within feminism, where those whom the media recognise as feminists are more likely to be apologists for 'gender equality' an idea that is a long way from radical feminism or Women's Liberation.

Postmodernism renders naming the enemy elusive and dangerous. When you do, chances are you will be called names, trolled on the internet and threatened with violence. Among theorists of ecology, the ecomodernists typify the approach taken by those who purport to sound radical, but in fact are adding to the disconnection of humanity from nature. Indeed, they reify the idea by calling it decoupling:

> … cities both drive and symbolize the decoupling of humanity from nature, performing far better than rural economies in providing efficiently for material needs while reducing environmental impacts (Asafu-Adjaye *et al.* 2015, p. 12).

The authors claim, for example, that "Violence in all its forms has declined significantly" (Asafu-Adjaye *et al.* 2015, p. 8). I ask, are they are not counting the epidemic of violence against Black men and women from all ethnicities, classes and countries? Are they not counting the destruction of the environment? In recent months, there has been a sudden appropriation of the word 'sovereignty' by libertarian Australians who claim that wearing a mask is an infringement on their living sovereign selves.

In this book, I call out the oppressors: I name the enemy; and I call on them to think again; to take responsibility for their behaviour and the impact it is having on the lives of people around the world and on the planet itself. By making their strategies visible, I am inviting the reader to reflect, to look, to contextualise, to connect their actions, rather than highlight isolated 'cherry-picked facts'.

The speeding vortex: every failure is a new business opportunity

Another element of the neoliberal capitalist push into every corner of the world is the view that every failure is a new business opportunity. Monocultural farming is seen as the norm in agriculture today, except by those who pursue traditional, subsistence, organic, biodynamic or regenerative farming practices. This is a huge shift globally where, until the industrial revolution, most food was produced by small holders and consumed locally, and indeed in many places it continued to do so until just a few decades ago and elsewhere it still is (GRAIN 2016). With the spread of monocultural industrial farming has come an increase in the spread of weeds. As industrial and digital farming produced weeds, the necessary product was a weed killer. Enter Bayer-Monsanto and other seed companies who specialise in killing plants. In recent years, this has been done using Round-up and other forms of glyphosate products. Because Round-up is a pesticide with adverse effects on plants, animals and humans, Monsanto has created Round-up Ready plants claiming reduced need for pesticides. Among them are Bt-potatoes, Bt-corn, Bt-brinjal (eggplant) and Round-up Ready soybeans. If the pesticide had not been dangerous, Monsanto would not have created plants using *Bacillus Thuringiensis* (Bt). The failure created the product. Increasing salinity is also an effect of monocultural farming. But it's not a problem for the proponents of GM farming who see it as a new business opportunity to develop salt-resistant crops. Not only is there a gap in the market, it is also a very good excuse to get GM crops into the farming industry through the back door.

Biotechnology creates an endless spiral of opportunities for research and development, and capital gain. An example of concern is the standard practice in genetic engineering of crops by inserting "an antibiotic resistance marker, which serves to facilitate detection of the altered gene" (Ferrara and Dorsey 2001, p. 59). Given the enormous problems of antibiotic resistance, this practice is likely to increase bacterial resistance to antibiotics in the general population,[7] with a particularly strong outcome in poor countries "unable to afford alternative drugs" (Garrett 1994, p. 414 and p. 438). But for the biotechnology companies it could be a boon, allowing them to justify genetic engineering of antibiotics to counteract new resistances. Recently, the CRISPR-Cas9 technique has been used in plants such as rice and wheat (Zhang, Zhang, Song *et al.* 2018).

Another growth area is aquaculture. In Canada, wild salmon is under threat from GM salmon produced with genetic material that promotes faster growth. Not only does the primary author, Garth Fletcher (1997), see himself as producing 'sustainable aquaculture', he also sees himself as solving the problem of fishery depletion, a problem caused by massive industrial levels of fishing. In 2019, Fletcher was still saying the same thing, this time because fish stock has come under threat and is down by one third. In 2020, AquaBounty[8] is selling fish with altered DNA that makes the fish grow faster. Once again a new business opportunity is flourishing because of previous transnational company mismanagement and failure (PBS 2019). How far will these companies go in their failures, and in their solutions, before they go too far?[9]

Toyota is also involved in investing in technologies that will help to counter their failure to reduce emissions, along with that of other car manufacturers. Toyota is investing in genetically modified forests with trees that grow at twice the rate of normal trees (Langelle 2001). By investing in GM forests, not only is

---

7   Laurie Garrett cites Mitchell Cohen, the Centers for Disease Control's director of bacterial research, as stating, "Unless currently effective microbial agents can be successfully preserved and the transmission of drug-resistant organisms curtailed, the post-antimicrobial era may be rapidly approaching in which infectious disease wards housing untreatable patients will again be seen" (1994, p. 414).

8   In 2020, AquaBounty Technologies, the Canadian company that owns [their words] the genetically modified fish that Fletcher developed, is boasting that it is the first genetically modified animal approved for food consumption.

9   Margaret Atwood's novel *Oryx and Crake* (2003) takes the biotechnologists' dreams to its ultimate conclusion.

Toyota looking to gain from increased profits through double harvests but, with the Kyoto Protocol and carbon trading on the international agenda in the early 2000s, they were also able to claim double credits, thereby profiting twice and avoiding the necessity of looking at the issue of emissions from the vehicles they produce (Hawthorne 2003c).

In short, the idea that an ever-increasing number of inventions, patents and land grabs can be an economic fix is not only misguided but it is whirling us ever deeper into the vortex.

Understanding neoliberalism

Neoliberalism is a broad-based philosophy that incorporates not only a dehumanised approach to economics; it is also an ideology that reifies productivity over sustainability, individual consumerism over collective social good. It is closely connected to libertarianism in which the state is reduced and the power of the individual increased. An inherent problem is that these are individualist and consumerist philosophies that ensure the rich get richer and get access to better quality lives, while the poor do not. The poor are told that they will have access to more consumer goods, but these are created as fake wants and needs. Neoliberalism is also connected to utilitarianism, a philosophy in which people are turned into 'utility' and what counts as utility will depend on the worldview. It frequently has negative results for women because 'utility' is almost always defined from an androcentric point of view.

Neoliberalists pretend that we live in a society that is free of racism and sexism; that has done away with class[10] and that

---

10   This view is not limited to neoliberalists. Thomas Picketty, widely praised for 'tracking inequality' does not appear to think outside the white male Marxist box. Listening to him speak at the Jaipur Writers Festival in 2016, I was shocked that he seemed to have no idea that women are the poorest group of people in the world. Bina Agarwal challenged him at the time, but in an article published in June 2018, he has simply learned to begin a speech with an example of women

everyone is free to pursue his own goals. I use the word *his* here deliberately because misogyny is deeply entrenched in neoliberalism, libertarianism and utilitarianism. As Hannah Arendt points out, a classless society depends on "an atomized and individualized mass" (1951/2017, p. 416). The atomisation has come through postmodernism, while individualisation is a necessity in a capitalist consumerist society.

A great deal of political damage has been done to the Women's Liberation Movement (WLM) over the last three decades as every aspect of the movement has been mainstreamed. Those who are known as feminist spokeswomen are very frequently delivering a message that is so watered down as to be meaningless. It has led to prostitution being seen as work; lesbians being co-opted and expected to call ourselves queer; it posits 'choice' as a key to liberation; and the ability to 'consent' to carry on practices that are harmful both physically and emotionally. Identity has become more important than collective action; and women are cautioned to be aware of their surroundings when walking in public spaces. Blaming the victim is alive and well; girls just need to lean in and all will be well (Sandberg 2013).[11]

Neoliberal ideologies are a key part of the so-called 'development' policies imposed upon countries that fall outside the 'West'. They include cultures inside the 'West' especially Indigenous societies in former colonies as well as within countries who gained independence in the late twentieth century but whose economies were never decolonised. Most of the countries of the global South fall into this as their former colonisers continue to try and reap as much from them through theft of land and of intellectual property, including that associated with the arts, medicine, orature and spiritual beliefs.

---

in poverty and then go on as usual (Leigh 2018). The summary of the *World Inequality Report* does not mention women, see Alvaredo *et al.* 2018.

11   Sheryl Sandberg, chief operating officer at Facebook, is a good example of a 'faux feminist', as bell hooks calls her. Sandberg ignores the realities of class, race, education and all the complications of life that hold women back (hooks 2013).

Neoliberal systems are isolated systems as per the chart below. In this book I will be arguing for integrated systems.

Isolated system	Integrated system
Selection from above	Dispersed selection
Management from the outside	Management by participation
External ownership	Involved ownership
Monocultural	Multicultural
Segregated	Integrated
Disengaged	Engaged
Belief in progress	Belief in renewability
Decontextualised	Context sensitive
Compartmentalisation	Connection
Displacement and deterritoriality	Located
Hierarchy	Complexity
Products	Relationships
Concentration	Decentralised or polycentric
Dependency	Interdependence
Scarcity	Abundance
External interventions	Local knowledge and traditions
Export orientation	Domestic and community driven
Single use	Multiple use
Short-term goals	Long-term goals
Privatised	Public or common ownership
Profit oriented	Biodiversity oriented
Utilitarianism	Connection between means and ends
Short term	Long term
Perfect information	Contextualised understanding
Immortality	Organic
Universal	Multiversity

Resistance

Resistance to the many varieties of colonisation and recolonisation has persisted among those who have a structural understanding of the politics of oppression, as analysed by Paulo Freire in 1971 and 1972. To resist, one needs to be clear about what is to be resisted and whose actions are to be resisted. The most interesting analyses of farming, development, and maintaining biodiversity come out of countries in the subcontinent: Bangladesh, India; in Latin America: Chile, Paraguay, Bolivia and Brazil; in Africa: Kenya, Uganda, South Africa and Zambia (see Akhter 2007; Shiva 2012; Galeano 1971; GRAIN 2016;); and the usually ignored island nations of the world (dé Ishtar 1994; Emberson-Bain 1994).

Seed saving projects in Bangladesh and India have been begun by small organisations that do not want their seeds taken by the big seed companies like Monsanto and Bayer.[12] These organisations exist within the context of local farmers making use of the seed and ensuring that local varieties survive over hybrid seeds sold by transnational corporations.

Indigenous communities in Australia have mostly carried on traditional ways; they have adapted to the intrusions of others, and sometimes created an interesting fusion of both.

Management strategies for fragile desert environments in central Australia, such as those of the Kaytej (see Bell 1983/2003), embody intimate knowledge of country made manifest in ceremonial, social and economic practices. This is an integrated worldview of responsibilities and obligations to kin and country rather than individually asserted rights. Western culture, if it is to move in the direction of long-term sustainability, will need to recast its relationship to land from one of dominance and control

---

12 On 7 June 2018, Bayer's acquisition of Monsanto was completed. It doubles the size of Bayer's agriculture business and the eventual loss of the name of Monsanto will probably help its public profile. It does not change the history of Monsanto's misdeeds (Robin 2010). Bayer has its own shocking history as a corporate ally of Hitler (see Shiva and Shiva 2018, pp. 55–56).

of a commodity to one of care for and abiding in country. As Diane Bell has shown, men and women have distinctive, complementary roles in caring for country, but these have been fundamentally disrupted by colonial and neo-colonial practices.

A culture inspired by biodiversity could begin to move in the direction of this level of responsibility for the environment. There are examples of Indigenous communities that have maintained their culture, including traditions that require women to have knowledge of ecology that is both broad and deep (Wadrill *et al.* 2019).

In proposing a different approach for economics, the emphasis has to shift from the decontextualised world of 'perfect information' represented by neoclassical economics and the widespread practice of further decontextualised data mining. Instead, relationship to land and to people are central, as is a sense of connectedness which takes account of real needs, rather than consumer needs generated by marketing. A decolonised economics would be grounded in a sense of place and community, and in the maintenance of the environment — including land, biodiversity, and non-renewable resources — to such an extent that it would not be difficult to imagine it remaining in a sustainable state for many thousands of years. The importance of culture cannot be underestimated as culture represents people's creative response to the world and the minds of a people (Hawthorne 2014).

Universalisation and disconnection come to the fore in western legal and economic systems. But Indigenous systems of land tenure challenge these notions by insisting upon relationship and responsibility as central to land tenure (Hawthorne 2002, pp. 162–205).

Markets, work and the Universal Basic Income

Neoliberalism marks every person as a consumer and secondly as an individual out of whom increased productivity should be squeezed. In a world where ecological sustainability is made compatible with the prevailing economic system, major changes need to be made. There are some interesting parallels between the creation of markets and the insertion of new groups into the workforce. For centuries, economic theory has ignored women for their productive capacity, as contributing nothing to the economy, and yet as Maria Mies (1999; 2012) and Marilyn Waring (1988) have argued, the economy relies on women's free labour, women's unpaid labour, women's uncounted labour. Neoclassical economics pretends to be 'value neutral' but its values lie centrally in a male dominated patriarchal world of profit making for the colonisers (or more recently decolonised elites). The *World Inequality Report* (Alvaredo *et al.* 2018) continues the invisibility of women's work and the ways in which women's work makes possible much of men's work. The report looks at inequality within countries and that is how it is framed. A different framework such as looking at inequality between men and women would provide starkly different data and make it necessary to draw vastly different conclusions. I do not have the resources of Facundo Alvaredo, Lucas Chancel, Thomas Picketty, Emmanuel Saez and Gabriel Zucman to produce such a report.[13] The authors would only have to read back issues of *Feminist Economics* to find more detailed data produced at lower cost. Or as Patricia Hynes writes:

---

13 I note that in 300 pages of the *World Inequality Report* there are 25 references to women. Twenty-one of these references appear from pp. 90–102, some as headings or sidebars in graphs. There are two references to women on pp. 10–12 and again on p. 278. Those multiple references between pp. 90–102 refer to the 'gender' pay gap in the US and France. It is clear to me that this report has severe failings. Furthermore, the misuse of the word 'gender' is very troublesome. It's the sex of women that has kept women's pay low.

> Women as a class are poorer than men worldwide: They eat less, own less, possess less, are invested in less, earn less, spend less. Income is a surrogate for consumption, and we can only conclude that women consume less, proportional to income, than men (Hynes 1999, p. 60).

During the Covid-19 crisis that pattern was replicated by

> women who received the Australian government's one-off stimulus package … [They] have spent up big on food, household bills and other essentials.
>
> But male recipients had other priorities — they spend more on video games, apps, music, car-related expenses, alcohol, taxis and insurance (Wade 2020).

Colonisers took large swathes of land for free (and let's not ignore the repercussions now in Zimbabwe, South Africa, the Democratic Republic of Congo, Myanmar, and all across the Middle East). Having appropriated the land and its resources (gold, diamonds, water, oil and agricultural land), the colonisers made a great deal of wealth for themselves and their descendants. Women's bodies have been similarly appropriated through wife capture and in the contemporary world the global sex industries of pornography and prostitution. The push around the world to decriminalise (or legalise) prostitution is not based on the welfare of women, but rather an intention to create new sources of wealth for pimps and for governments through taxes.

In the last 40 years, women have increasingly been drawn into the market. Again, this is not about women's welfare. Rather, when the economy needs women, new jobs will be created. Indigenous peoples and other groups living in traditional ways are probably the largest group who have not yet been fully incorporated into the market economy, but there are many companies attempting to do just that. Some are encouraging people in Indigenous and traditional societies to join the mining industry or the pharmaceutical industry, those of a more creative bent are invited into the arts. I am not suggesting that incorporation always occurs, but rather one must be wary of such intentions and make provision that it does not occur.

Naomi Klein in *No Logo* (2000) pinpointed the ways in which young people's ideas are appropriated and sold back to them. Similar efforts are being made in poor countries where the traditional crafts of women are in the sights of outsiders coming in to make a profit. Significant efforts have been made by Indigenous communities in Australia to protect the copyright of artists. And while copyright for individuals is clear under Australian law, community ownership and long-term rights over stories handed down over multiple generations or the use of particular visual symbols is not covered. In the meantime, outsiders come in for short periods of time and carry away the community property.

Micro-credit is another good example of appropriative method in which women are leveraged to pull the poor out of poverty. Farida Akhter writes:

> Now it's not the rich who should salvage the crisis of global capital, it is the poor and they must shoulder the burden to keep the system in order (2007, p. 112).

It is, as Akhter writes, "the feminisation of indebtedness" (2007, p. 112) and the idea that women should pay comes about because "women in the village are more easily traceable" and "are more reliable and more disciplined than men" (Gupta cited in Akhter 2007, p. 116). Furthermore, too frequently men in the family use the money but feel no responsibility to pay it back. Micro-credit has led to humiliation, domestic violence and divorce. As Patricia Hynes discovered in her research on men's and women's consumption, women and men consume very differently. Hynes expresses consumption as an element in an equation in which (A) refers to consumption:

> ... men [spend] more on luxury items for themselves, such as business junkets, golf courses, gambling, alcohol, tobacco and sex (^{A}LUXURY), and women more on necessities for their

families and households, such as food, clothing, and health care ([A]SURVIVAL) (1999a, p. 60; superscripts in the original).[14]

Work is a slippery subject if one wants to include the unpaid labour of women, of children, of the unemployed, rather than simply paid employment or earnings through business or investment. Wage labourers for global work, for which men and unmarried young women are well-suited according to the capitalist need for flexible workers, has moved from the manufacturing west to the so-called developing world and former Communist bloc countries. These are the workers who Trump appealed to in 2016, and the people that voters across the world have turned to in recent years including (but not limited to) Australia, Brazil, India, Austria, Hungary, Poland, Italy and the UK.

Global work is disconnected, dislocated and dehumanised. Some writers have argued that work is on the way out (Forrester 1999), that workers are expendable, irrelevant and eventually invisible (Rifkin 1995), disposable (Bales 2000) and deterritorialised, separated from place and any sense of belonging (Gorz 1999). And the future promises robots being used as substitutes for workers. In the case of sex dolls (sex robots), the diminishment of women and children is an obvious outcome, though the purveyors will claim otherwise (Roper 2017; Roper 2019). The promise of robots in other areas will have a similar negative effect on the understanding of what a worker is. Indeed, they become even more disposable.

While colonisation separated the state from sovereignty, it created an immaterial territoriality connected to dependence on a colonial power. Under globalisation, the dependence has shifted to a deterritorialised corporate power. Prostitution has become

---

14 The equation has become known as I = PAT. "The impact of humans on the environment (I) is a product of the number of people (P), the amount of goods consumed by a person (A), and the pollution generated by technology per good consumed (T)" Hynes 1999, p. 39). Hynes criticises the way in which this equation is structured and challenges its underlying assumptions, including identifying elements of the "universal P" which are "outside the scope of the formula" such as "the military trade imbalances and debt and female subordination" (1999, p. 39).

a significant part of feminised migration. Women are displaced from their communities and countries of origin, leaving them especially vulnerable to violence (Bindel 2017; Raymond 2015). Prostitution in such contexts cannot be framed as 'freedom of movement' nor an industry in which women's earnings are high. Rather, the chances of exploitation, violence, torture and murder are significantly higher than in other parts of the economy.

It strikes me as interesting that at this time of flexible, disposable and precarious work, the concept of a Universal Basic Income (UBI) is gaining some traction (Zeballos-Roig 2020).[15] I can't help worrying that there is something in it for big government and the mega corporations.

The world is changing at an extraordinary pace. Much of the work done today was unthinkable twenty years ago. What will it be like twenty years from now? What are we doing to take account of all the changes? Sustainable practices will not mean the end of work, but they could lead to very significant changes in prevailing ideas on what constitutes a job. Work, as women well know, goes on long after the job has finished. The likelihood of governments introducing the Universal Basic Income (UBI) has increased in 2020, though until now it has been regarded as a fringe idea (Gorz 1999; Hyman 1999a). The UBI would give many people — the young, the old, the carers, those who work at home or in the community, those studying or retraining, those living subsistence or semi-subsistence lifestyles, artists and independent public intellectuals — many more options. And now, the huge number of unemployed around the world made redundant by the coronavirus. The armies of people currently engaged in policing social security fraud could be disbanded. Because of the drastic reduction in administrative costs, the UBI would cost little more than current pension and benefit schemes for a comparable number of people

---

15   On 7 April 2020, Spain announced that it is considering implementing the UBI in response to Covid-19.

(Hyman 1999). Its introduction would reduce unemployment by reducing the need for what is currently regarded as full-time work (the underemployed — mostly women — are ignored). But this idea has received little discussion outside futurist think tanks. Finland ran an experiment from January 2017 to January 2019 with the UBI with apparently mixed results (Martinelli 2019) and in the 1970s, Ronald Henderson in Australia proposed that everyone receive a universal basic income and the rich would be taxed proportionally (Howe 2018).

Feminists noticed decades ago that caring for children does not fit into the market economy. Children get sick at 3 a.m., their needs are unpredictable and the times of laughter and play are not captured by notions of quality time. Parents now working from home with children home-schooling are noticing the needs and contradictions on a scale not seen before in western countries.

Work which centres on life involves relationships with others, in communities, families or with nature. And work/life relationships can be unpredictable, slow or simply need to reflect the body's rhythms (Forrester 1999, p. 19).

Or, as Ana Isla writes, "… the market economy is a small island surrounded by an ocean of unpaid, caring, domestic work and free environmental services" (2019, p. 190).

Let us assume for a moment that this is not so. What sort of system would we want so as to avoid deterritorialised global work?

For starters it should be meaningful, local and sustainable. Some of it is necessary work, such as private housework as well as the public housework of maintaining services and maintenance in community spaces. We have all read the news articles about men and housework and many have experienced the ways in which men not only avoid housework, but when they do it, they create more work.

A Universal Basic Income simply slipped into the neoliberal capitalist system will not work. Only structural change informed by radical feminism can shift social dynamics. If not, women will be expected to continue to carry out the work that men and the wealthy don't want to do.

The language in my body and in my tongue
is the language they spoke in Delphi.
The language of the seizure that dispels time,
that defies death, that returns the orator
to the world of light, that single point that
draws me back from the inertia, the gravity
field of a hole so black, nothing exists
and nothing matters

—Susan Hawthorne,
Four New Poets
(1993, p. 160)

CHAPTER TWO

Less Than Perfect: Medical Wars against People with Disabilities

Sometime during my adolescence, around age sixteen, I had a conversation with my mother about having children. My menarche was very late and the thought crossed my mind that I might be sterile (that was the word I used). Around my 14th birthday, my mother for the first time had used the word 'epilepsy' and suggested I read an article in *Life Magazine*. There were men in white coats and photos of EEG machines that I recognised from my annual trips to the doctor.

Adolescence is such a weird period in anyone's life and the coming together of these two new bits of knowledge suggested to me that perhaps it would be good if I were sterile, since I was now being informed that sometimes pregnancy and epilepsy do not go together well. The subtle eugenics of these conversations was lost on me at the time. Ten years later, after the epiphany of feminism, consciousness-raising[16] groups, political action and an

---

16 Consciousness raising (CR) and collective political action were the cornerstones of the Women's Liberation Movement. In the early anthology, *Radical Feminism* edited by Anne Koedt, Ellen Levine and Anita Rapone (1973) there is a how-to on

understanding of what had occurred in Germany under Nazi rule, I was no longer so naïve. I understood that had anyone had the capability to scan and test my mother while I was in her womb or before, I might never have been born.

This is a shocking thought the first time you have it and the knowledge of this has had a profound effect on the way I see the world. Since people with epilepsy were among those killed in the concentration camps, I saw that my own experience was not unique. I potentially shared being marked in the same way as Jews, Gypsies, political activists, 'asocials' such as lesbians and other 'enemies' of the Führer.

Feminism

In the intervening years since coming to feminism nearly 50 years ago, the bodies of women have been poked and prodded by the medical and scientific (mostly) fraternity; bodies have been theorised almost to extinction by postmodernists; and in resistance to both of these standpoints, bodies have been reclaimed by radical feminists, women of colour, old women, fat women and disability activists.

Disability is one of a number of oppressions that make up a matrix of interlocking oppressions. As a radical feminist and a lesbian with a (mostly) invisible disability, it is sometimes a difficult juggling act to speak about oppression. There are no hierarchies in real life; there are experiences which one has according to sex, race, class, language, region, age and disability — whether visible or not. One thing is clear: the oppressed know their own worlds as well as the world of their oppressors. The reverse is not true. This epistemic advantage can be seen in the puzzled looks and comments by men following the #MeToo social media campaign beginning in 2017,

---

consciousness raising (pp. 280–281) as well as Joreen's (Jo Freeman) important essay 'The Tyranny of Structurelessness' (pp. 285–299), a useful essay to read as a counter to the way in which some CR groups foundered.

many of whom are grossly unaware of what women put up with repeatedly over years, too often on a daily basis.[17]

An understanding of the politics of knowledge is important if we are to change the ways in which disability is perceived and how the tropes of disability affect policy in relation to medical practice.

The processes of incorporation of disability into the mainstream follow the same routes as other oppressions; they simply occur in different time frames and most people speaking about disability are caught in the all-inclusive net of normality. Below, I spell out some of the common ways in which people with disabilities are treated and the ways in which theoretical discussion is tainted by the strictures of oppression.

Ruling classes

The ruling class in charge of the welfare of people with disabilities consists overwhelmingly of people who do not have a disability. Given the difficulties people with disabilities have getting a job, let alone one that would allow for progress up the ladder of promotion to a position of decision-making, people with disabilities are in the main left outside those decision-making positions. This applies to government, as well as to research, medicine and a range of employment positions for which a person with a disability might aim. Of course, there are always exceptions and in addition, some will follow the path of non-disclosure if that is possible. These are political decisions and like race, sexual orientation, class accents, passing is an option only for some; others will decide to disclose even if they could pass. An example of this is that I could and probably do pass as someone without a disability, but when a seizure occurs in public, it is obvious to everyone that I carry this disability even when it is invisible (Hawthorne 1996).

---

17 After Covid-19, some men are beginning to realise how stressful it can be taking a walk in the park and needing to be constantly aware of others who are or are not practising social distancing.

Poverty is the outcome many people who are disabled can expect because a patriarchal society deems them incapable of working or contributing to the common good. It goes along with a certain attitude of expediency inherent in capitalism. Capitalists are endlessly appropriative and if more workers are needed inside the system, they will find ways to get people with disabilities into work through specific programs. And when the need has passed, they will drop them. This is familiar to anyone who has watched as migrants, women and retirees are drawn into the workforce and thrown out again. In countries where the medical system is pay-as-you-go instead of a subsidised system to enable people to live with as much health as possible, poverty literally kills people with disabilities and chronic illnesses.[18]

Infantilisation

Disability can increase ... emotional friction unendurably. Whenever we come in contact with an institution around our disabilities, those institutions demand our immediate submission to their paternalism (Dykewomon 1989, p. 71).

Infantilisation of the disabled is a regular occurrence. It is not restricted to people with disabilities because those of a different skin colour, so-called lower classes or castes and women also suffer infantilisation, namely the assumption that those outside the ruling class are lacking in intelligence. In fact, the epistemic advantage of

---

18 Indigenous people have a significant chance of a shorter life span, particularly in the USA. Two anecdotal examples are Latina, Gloria Anzaldúa and Native American, Paula Gunn Allen, writers, whose untimely deaths occurred because of their lack of access to medical treatment. The figures in Australia show an average of 8 to 9 years difference in life expectancy for Aboriginal and Torres Strait Islanders. See Australian Bureau of Statistics (ABS) 2020. Depending on remoteness for women the difference between non-Indigenous life expectancy and that of Aboriginal or Torres Strait Islanders can be up to 14 years; in major cities it is 7.2 years. For men the range in difference is 13.8 years in remote areas and 8.6 years in major cities.

the oppressed might suggest that the opposite is the case. A sense of entitlement can lead to what I have called elsewhere 'Dominant Culture Stupidities'.

> The syndrome is widespread among people who belong to several dominant cultures: white, male, able-bodied, heterosexual, rich and mobile are some of the groups most prone to the syndrome (Hawthorne 2002, p. 47 ff).

Among those who exhibit Dominant Culture Stupidity are those who do not consider the step that obstructs the wheelchair or the person living with severe arthritis; those who think that a strobe light is such a lot of fun when it might trigger a seizure in people who have photo-sensitive epilepsy; even something like the use of hairspray, perfumes and strong smelling bathroom cleaning products which might badly affect a person sensitive to perfume (Grenville 2017); bathroom taps, screw top bottles and a range of packaged goods can similarly be obstructive for people with hand injuries or pain. There are many other insensitivities that I could mention.

Lesbian activist, Caryatis Cardea, responds to the ways in which people with disabilities are treated with disdain.

> And I don't want your pity. Much of the silence of the disabled springs from the near-impossibility of being treated with dignity once able-bodied others know of the indignities imposed upon us by or because of our disabilities (Cardea 1989–90, p. 127).

Debra Keenahan is an artist and in her essay 'The Female Dwarf, Disability and Beauty' she writes:

> For myself, I often say that my dwarfism does not disable me, rather, what disables me most is people's attitudes to it. Because it is negative attitudes that result in unnecessary limitations being placed upon me (Keenahan 2017).

And, writing about her sculptural work, she has this to say:

> [It] represents a style of interaction all too often experienced
> by people of extreme short stature. That is being spoken to like
> a child rather than an adult and an equal. The white marble
> finish of my sculpture 'Little Big Woman: Condescension' is
> reminiscent of Greek statues — often considered the epitome
> of classical beauty (Keenahan 2017).

Colonisation

Colonisation is an experience that is had by people from various
oppressed groups; it is not restricted to colonisation of one state by
another. Colonisation is the process of stealing, appropriating and
reinventing the insights and cultures of the oppressed and taking
the credit for them. In the arts and sciences of human culture,
this has been standard practice by men over women. Nobel prizes
awarded to men, when women made the discoveries and did the
work.[19]

We are currently in a time of recolonising people with
disabilities through the industrial medical system. The use of
prenatal diagnosis in order to prevent the birth of people with
disabilities who have genetic markers is a process of colonisation
with the intention of the theft of a life because that life is considered
by the medical industry to be not worth living because of 'costs' to
the taxpayer.

Part of this arises from the dualist philosophy put forward by
utilitarian and libertarian philosophers such as Peter Singer who in
weighing up the benefits has decided that in terms of social good,
people who do not fit the norm should not live. This is an ideology

---

19   To mention just five women: Jocelyn Bell Burnell who detected the first radio
     pulsar; Vera Rubin who discovered Dark Matter; biophysicist, Rosalind Franklin
     whose X-ray crystallography made possible findings about DNA and RNA; Emily
     Noether, mathematician who worked in the area of abstract algebra; Mileva
     Marič Einstein, mathematician and wife of Einstein both of whom worked on the
     theory of relativity (Troemel-Ploetz 1990; Gagnon 2016).

of eugenics with roots in nationalist imperialism, colonialist and fascist regimes. As Victoria Brownworth writes:

> Theories of eugenics have always been predicated on the concept that disability, physical or mental, is a scourge, weakening the very structure of society (Brownworth 1999, p. 141).

The propaganda around prenatal diagnosis has become more sophisticated. It is no longer presented as keeping out undesirables, but rather cloaking the philosophy in medical jargon, terms like 'benefit', 'quality of life', 'minimising harm', reducing medical costs and a host of others. While not everyone is duped by such jargon and hyperbole, a considerable percentage of people take it at face value. The language used is instead enveloped in the psychology of fear, and even so-called feminist arguments focus on the burden to mothers, and costs to the community and public health systems. These are arguments founded on eugenics and utilitarian economic theory.

Harm minimisation

As mentioned above, the concept of harm minimisation is central to the philosophy of eugenics and the practice of prenatal diagnosis. This was strongly refuted by the participants at an international conference on reproductive technologies and genetic engineering in Bangladesh in *The Declaration of Comilla* in 1989. They stated in Clause 26:

> We are against any kind of bias and discrimination against disabled people including that of genetic screening, and counselling. We particularly oppose the human genome project within this context. Prenatal diagnosis, genetic screening and genetic counselling do not offer the solution for disability (Akhter 1989, p. x).

One of the delegates at the conference was Theresia Degener, born with severe physical disabilities due to Thalidomide, who said:

> ... technology has not offered a solution to prevent disability. The right approach is that disability is another way of life and society needs to create enough scope and facilities for a life to be lived well (Degener in Akhter 1989, p. 165).

One of the most insightful collections of writings about the selection — or more rightly, the deselection — of people with disabilities is *Defiant Birth: Women Who Resist Medical Eugenics* (Tankard Reist (ed.) 2006). Nineteen women from around the world speak about their decision to resist the results of prenatal diagnosis. In some cases it was because the women fell into a perceived risk category of 'passing on' their own disability, or because an amniocentesis or other early intervention showed risks of disability in the foetus.

The medical profession is trained to minimise suffering and that is a reasonable action in the case of pain or other kinds of suffering. Disability arising *in utero* represents only a small percentage of those in the overall population with disabilities. Some appear early in life, other disabilities are acquired through accident or illness across all of life's age spectra.

The term 'harm minimisation' is dragged out whenever politicians and social commentators have to talk about a subject they consider 'grubby' in some way. The push to decriminalise prostitution, for example, is frequently cloaked in 'harm minimisation' language. Similarly, the rights of people with disabilities who might act in ways considered antisocial (twitching, having an epileptic seizure, speaking in ways that are difficult to understand, acting 'crazy' or showing some kind of 'deformity' or 'handicap' in public). Those with disabilities often reclaim the derogatory language used against them whether it be 'mad', 'unpredictable', 'crippled', or 'fat'.[20] Theorists of disability are not immune to ignoring interlocking oppressions. Leonard J. Davies in his book *Enforcing*

---

20   Jeffs 1993; Jeffs 2015; Hawthorne 1996; Mairs 1992; Dunsford 1994.

Normalcy: Disability, Deafness and the Body, while aware of class and race, is less attuned to the ways in which sex and sexuality affect the lives of people with disabilities (Davies 1995, p. 11).[21] The harm minimisation ideology is directed at the able-bodied person who has to 'tolerate' the behaviour of the disabled person.[22] It is, in other words, a push toward the so-called 'normal'.

Normalisation

What is normal? This is a question asked by many in the community of people affected by disability, either their own or someone they are close to. Australian poet, Andy Jackson writes about his first experience of reading his poem about Marfan Syndrome.

> 'I have a hunch / that curvature / can be an aperture / given that light, like water / does not travel in a straight line ...' and something in me had, painfully and beautifully, broken open. I had not only reclaimed a word that had been used against me, but I had suggested that 'deformity', rather than being a curse or a problem, is in fact the pre-eminent source of insight (Jackson 2017, pp. 32–33).

And Anne M. Carson writes in her poem 'Axiology':

> If I was a ceramic, I'd be *kintsukuroi*,
> pottery which has been knocked,
> dropped broken into shards then
> mended with gold or silver lacquer
> flowing into the breach (Carson 2017, p. 20).[23]

---

21 For a more inclusive analysis see Brownworth 1999.

22 When a disabled person displays behaviour that is not regarded as 'normal' e.g. involuntary shaking or vocalising, a psychotic episode, an epileptic seizure, the discomfort of the non-disabled person can never match the 'shame' of the person with the disability.

23 *Kintsukuroi* is a Japanese ceramic technique used when an item is broken or fractured. Carson writes: "The gold restores to the vessel its capacity to hold once again, not in denial of it having been fractured but even made more beautiful because of it" (Carson 2017, p.19).

Part of the push for normalisation is the assumption that a person with a disability cannot be happy and healthy. That the disabled person should aspire to be able-bodied as Naomi Chainey (2017) argues in an article in *The Sydney Morning Herald* newspaper. Nancy Mairs writes of multiple sclerosis:

> I may be frustrated, maddened, depressed by the incurability of my disease, but I am not diminished by it, and they [doctors] are … I'm not sorry to be a cripple … It has opened and enriched my life enormously (Mairs 1992, p. 20).

Fyodor Dostoyevsky, in the 19th century, had a similar insight.

> If in that second — that is to say, at the last conscious moment before the fit — he had time to say to himself, consciously and clearly, "Yes, I could give my whole life for this moment," then this moment by itself was, of course, worth the whole of life (Dostoyevsky 1955, p. 244).

Fiona Kumari Campbell also rails against the notion that only normality can bring happiness and when a person with a disability appears to be happy it creates antipathy in the able-bodied. She writes:

> Because so-called 'wrong people' can be happy, this may in fact induce a politics of not only resentment but a claim to return to that which is not deserved. For how could a disabled person be fundamentally happy? Surely not! (2017, p. 284).

Erasure

> If memory has for a moment   (or for several unquantifiable moments)   been erased scrubbed clean by the fall through time through space   what proof has she that she exists (Hawthorne 1999, p. 88, spacing in the original).

The ultimate in any political oppression is erasure of an entire class, sex, caste, religion, or ethnic group. It has been called ethnic cleansing, genocidal rape, mass murder and almost to a person — a decent person — it is regarded negatively. But when it comes to the erasure of people with disabilities before birth such negative connotation rarely manifests itself. Instead, erasure is embraced by the medical profession, by the reproductive technology industry and by many ordinary people who do not carry a developed politics that recognises systemic acts of oppression.

Fiona Place, writing about her decision not to undergo an amniocentesis even though her age meant she fell into a high risk category, points out that unlike children born with illnesses or disabilities that cannot be detected *in utero*, the birth of a child with Down syndrome "is singled out as *preventable*" (Place 2008, p. 126). And therefore, children with Down syndrome should be eradicated. Place continues: "… the presence of genetic screening programmes is not conducive to creating an inclusive society" (Place 2008, p. 126).

Recalling the birth of her son, Fraser, she writes:

> On Saturday 17 February 1996 at 2.45 pm in a busy maternity hospital, I gave birth to a live, crying newborn with almost perfect Apgar scores. But instead of elation and joy, instead of sparkling sentiments and congratulatory words spilling into every nook and cranny of the room, the delivery space collapsed into an uneasy silence, into whispers of palpable disquiet. A stillness no mother would find pleasing.
>
> Or manageable.
>
> I knew something was amiss … (Place 2019, p. 1).

Fiona Place in her book, *Portrait of the Artist's Mother*, goes on to describe both the joys and challenges of a son with Down syndrome. Her story, and that of her son, Fraser, exposes the eugenic ideas underlying prenatal screening and society's treatment of people with disabilities.

So-called abled people	People with disabilities
Belong to the entitled ruling class of so-called normal people.	Are endlessly classified into different groups and subgroups according to severity of disability, a little like the half-caste, mulatto, quadroon system under slavery in the USA.
Belong roughly to their own age group as children and are treated as adults after reaching legal adulthood age.	Through the process of infantilisation children are treated as lacking intelligence and as adults assumed to also be lacking in education. Re-infantilisation happens to ageing people.
Comparing the treatment of people with disabilities with the colonised, there are many similarities. The colonists want to make decisions about whether those with disabilities should live and what kind of life they should lead.	People with disabilities are eliminated from living through early medical intervention and pre-natal screening. This is regarded as a positive move from within the medical and technological industries.
Having eliminated those with disabilities, anyone found to have not taken the test potentially faces the prospect of not receiving social support, after all the child's birth could have been avoided. This is called 'harm minimisation'.	What can be said by those whose existence has been 'deselected'?
Normal people are considered happy and healthy (most of the time).	People with disabilities are considered to be unhappy and unhealthy (most of the time).
A measure of one's existence is recognition by others.	Erasure and the prospect of invisibility and erasure is what so many people with disabilities experience on a daily basis.
The state of normality, while not common among the so-called normal, is assumed.	The state of abnormality is assumed for those who have disabilities.

The technology of bodies

Women are at the forefront of being used and abused by technological incursions on the body. Women's bodies have been treated for millennia as if they were for the free taking: an act of colonisation and domination. Within these parameters, women's bodies have been mined and appropriated in numerous ways and this has been particularly evident in the logic that demands the elimination of girls and people with disabilities. Vibhuti Patel writes:

> We need to counter those who believe that it is better to kill a female foetus than to give birth to an unwanted female child. Their logic eliminates the victim of male chauvinism, does not empower her (Patel 2003, p. 19).

This same logic is used to argue for the elimination of people with disabilities before birth, and similarly collecting the DNA of Indigenous peoples that is justified on the grounds that certain groups might become extinct. The logic puts future profits ahead of providing resources to the oppressed so they can live with dignity now (Hawthorne 2007a, pp. 314–323).

Western society privileges youth, physical fitness and beauty (Jeffreys 2005) and these are the images used in advertising. In this context, it is very easy to discriminate against people with disabilities. They are separated out on the basis of a perceived physical, mental or psychological disability that may encompass a very wide variety of 'conditions', some of which are inherited while others are acquired, or both. Ableness is privileged, even though it may not be the most advantageous state for some human activities. Some disabilities come with heightened abilities in other areas. Rebecca Maxwell, who lost her sight at three years of age, responds in this way in a radio conversation about architecture:

> Well, if one had to connect it to the five senses, one might say it's the sense of touch, but it's touch without a conventional physical contact. But I believe that there are a lot more senses. We haven't identified them and we don't use them. I think by identifying them we would begin to turn them on, as it were. You see, I think there is a sense of pressure, a sense of balance, a sense of rhythm, a sense of movement, a sense of life, a sense of warmth, even a sense of self, which psychology is beginning to recognise (Maxwell 2004).

Accessing these different abilities takes time and mental perseverance. There is hardly a person who has not at some stage of their lives experienced immobilisation and illness. It is part of being human.

Just as gender rigidifies sex and race institutionalises skin colour, the 'normal' body is distanced from bodily changeability and variability. Disability theorists are constantly questioning what counts as disability. Is it biological, cultural or socially constructed or is possible that disability is the norm?

There is, however, a major cultural and scientific push against this view. Instead, as Jennifer Fitzgerald (1998) writes:

> Through the geneticizing of self, the lives of those with imperfect genes become delegitimized. The imperfect thus become the primitive; become the undesirable; become the avoidable; become the unconscionable; become the illegal, and therefore, become the punishable.

The cultural logic of separating out disability ensures that these practices will continue. Here are some of the sentences we find:

- the elimination of differences that are feared (Wendell 1996, p. 156).
- the separation between the 'fit' and the 'unfit' through the ideology of eugenics (the unfit includes the "feeble-minded, insane, epileptic, diseased, blind, deaf [and] deformed" (Bajema cited in Finger 1985, p. 294).
- the so-called 'designer baby', the basis of which is the word 'undesirable' (Tankard Reist 2006; Goggin and Newel 2005; Brownworth 1999).
- living in the shadow of Mönchberg (a Nazi 'killing center' in Germany where people with disabilities were "systematically starved to death or gassed and cremated" (Schiltz 2006, p. 184).

The evidence from over-screening and testing is that both those who will potentially be either female or disabled are over-represented in the resulting terminations. This suggests that both these features are regarded as imperfections (Bal 2007; Ghai 2007).

Melinda Tankard Reist in her book, *Defiant Birth* notes that screening has become routine. We all have to ask what — or who — is being screened out? If it is human imperfection, what exactly is this, what defines it and who gets to define it? For the ruling classes and the colonisers the answer is simple: it does not include them. Where does perfection lie? Could it be that male, white and able-bodied is not the place to find perfection? It would be easy to argue that the traits of masculinity are aligned with destruction (see Chapter Three; Barry 2010).

Most societies in the world have stories about the origins of the earth, the universe and natural landscapes. The oldest of them feature female figures, ancestors and goddesses and the power of giving birth plays a critical part in these stories. Later, the goddesses are turned into demons, witches and sorceresses, all of which are given negative connotations.[24] Just as women are erased in these stories so too are Indigenous peoples erased from the tales of discovery that the imperial cultures call history (see Chapter Five). These ruling-class histories are now being transformed once again. Giving birth is no longer considered terribly important,[25] even the conquest of lands has slipped down the chart. The biggest race on is the privatisation of knowledge through owning of patents.

Taking its place is the conquest of the immaterial, the minds, and digital economies. In such a world, the presence of people with disabilities is, for the immaterially minded, an unpleasant reminder that we *are* material, we *can be* vulnerable and we *can die*. In saying this, I am not suggesting that those with disabilities

---

24 Max Dashu's the Suppressed Histories Archives has lots of material and visual resources and can be found at <https://www.suppressedhistories.net/>; also see Sjöö and Mor 1987; Lerner 1986; Gimbutas 1989; 1991; Dexter 1990; Foster 2013; Beavis and Hwang 2018.

25 Unless a woman wants to take birth into her own hands with homebirthing or freebirthing. See Fraser 2020.

are the only ones to whom this applies, rather that the pretence of immortality, invulnerability and youth cannot be sustained.

DNA, genes, chromosomes, marks on screens, measurements indicating this disorder or that condition are regarded as far more important than the contexts of people's lives. Little regard is paid to emotions like love and attachment to the loved person. Carrying a child to term when you are told that the child will have a disability is an act of courage and resistance to the ideologies of detachment and dissociation. It is a political stance that many women take against social criticism. Like other courageous political stances it can have negative effects on those in and around the woman and such decisions might only be possible if a person has some other privilege such as class or social position.

Money

Disability is an area that is creating new opportunities for previous failures in the system. The opportunities are there for technological companies and those who are part of the medical industrial complex (Bilek 2020c). Radical feminists have long critiqued the reproductive technology industries (Arditti, Klein and Minden 1984; Corea 1985; Scutt 1989; Rowland 1993; Raymond 1995). Likewise, medical abuses have been documented, both historical and contemporary.[26] The latest moves are towards creating lifelong dependence on drugs and predictive medical interventions that involve genetic testing and early interventions. What this does within our cultural forms is to distrust the body, to separate us from ourselves more and more and thereby introduce opportunities for more widespread and continuous intervention in the whole of human life.

---

26 Robert Jay Lifton's *The Nazi Doctors* (1988; revised 2017) details the horrors of that period. On menopause, see Coney 1993 and Greer 1993; on euthanasia see George 2007.

In this book, you will read of the many different ways in which disconnection and separation from self are pursued by large corporates, by billionaires who are changing cultural narratives and affecting the ways in which we see ourselves. It stretches from microcolonialism to colonialism and deterritoriality on a massive scale; it includes the many varieties of ways in which women are colonised from testing for Down syndrome to being convinced that their bodies are not good enough; from a sense of homelessness in the body that pervades women who have been prostituted, to refugees incarcerated for escaping violence in their countries; to being made homeless and landless in one's own country or seeing the destruction of land, water and air on which we all depend.

The personal is political

In my own life, I have variously succumbed to the prescriptions of disability, followed by anger, researching and finally resisting the medicalised system into which my body was being pushed. In my twenties I read up on the medications prescribed to me and discovered there were side effects that I wanted to avoid. I decided to disobey the doctors and instead take charge. I began to manage my own treatment. In retrospect, I am grateful to my younger self who took me on that path. Without her, I would, by now, be experiencing serious drug-induced adverse effects. In my forties, I joined a circus — first one, then another — and shockingly, as a person with epilepsy, my chosen skill was aerials. The upshot was that I became much stronger and fitter and it was clear to me that engaging in such an activity was good for me, as it ensured that I remained thoroughly engaged and in the present (Hawthorne 2007b).

In the intervening years, a form of technological funda- mentalism has come into being and is influencing how medicine is practised. As Robert Jensen writes:

Technological fundamentalism promotes the view that life is an engineering project, whether we are focused on the planet's ecosystems or the systems that make up the human organism. At the core of a more ecological and life-centred approach to humans' place on the planet is respect for the integrity of the body and an awareness that our bodies are governed by the same laws of physics and chemistry as the ecosphere (Jensen 2016, p. 143).

I would not wish away from my life my experience of living with epilepsy. I cannot say that it is fun, however, I have learnt a great deal because of it. It has helped me frame a politics in keeping with my epistemic advantage in this area. It has given me insights and lessons in wariness and improved my patience (a goal that shifts). It has increased my empathy for others. I am happy not to embrace the ideal of 'normal'.

Genuine care entails context sensitivity. Each person deserves to be treated with utmost respect and dignity for their wellbeing. There is a great deal of talk today of an appropriated version of this under the guise of personalised medicine, much of which involves feeding data into a computer that spits out the medicines or treatment regimes for various disorders and illnesses. I am yet to be convinced that the programmers of systems like IBM Watson®[27] have gone beyond the male Caucasian model as their starting point. Even if the system were more sophisticated, pharmaceutical companies will be pressing researchers to include their patented drugs on the schedule of recommended remedies. I do not trust this kind of 'personalised medicine' any more than the mainstream medical model currently used to determine medical action. Screening that personalises the data of a patient will be no more trustworthy than the pre-natal screening that highlights a person's potential for a child with a disability. As Fiona Place puts it:

---

27 IBM Watson® is a natural language data analysis system that is being used in personalised medicine.

I can see how much the presence of the test [for Down syndrome] complicates things. How much of a double-edged sword it has become. I also realise many other women may come to experience a similar pain and a similar sense of loneliness as more and more disabilities come to be perceived as *preventable*. As the drive towards detecting the less than best gains momentum.

It is easy to see how the list could grow. How conditions such as autism, ADHD, childhood leukaemia, schizophrenia, breast cancer and heart disease could be added (Place 2008, p. 126).

What will we lose if we eliminate people with disabilities? For a start, it is simply not possible. In spite of all the talk of genetic counselling and using techniques such as CRISPR that will allow scientists to remove a single gene at a time, no one knows the consequences.[28] We could achieve a much more liveable society if we gave support to parents whose children are born with disabilities; if we were to support those children as they grow into adulthood and provide them with ways and means for a meaningful life throughout their adulthood; if we did this, then those who acquire an injury or illness during their life would probably be far less debilitated when that occurred. We will lose different ways of understanding the world. Multiple perspectives, multiple senses — in the way used by Rebecca Maxwell — and multiple ways of experiencing life and turning that experience into creative, intellectual or practical forms that can enrich all of us.

This raises many questions. Was the injury caused by a car crash (the major cause of spinal cord injury)? Is this another case of every technological failure is another business opportunity?

Jennifer Bilek (2020i) raises the issue of how far we should take technology in order to improve the lives of those with disabilities. She uses the example of Elon Musk's Neurolink which Musk intends to use to create links between computers and brains. After

---

28   For more on CRISPR see Klein 2017, p. 169–175.

experimenting with monkeys in 2019 he claims that he will be using it for humans with spinal cord injuries.

Is the slippery slope towards transhumanism one we as a species want to traverse? Are huge amounts of money and capitalist profit the most important thing to do for those with spinal cord injuries?

Bilek sums up her objections to this kind of technological fix as follows:

> I think we should ask the monkey what it thinks. Let's ask the monkey Musk minions tried this on shall we? — or the several hundred which he probably used who didn't have spinal cord injuries, who were taken from their home in the wild, stuck in a laboratory in some cage, away from their land base and family so Musk could experiment — all for us amazing, superior humans who get to use and abuse anything or anyone in our path as long as we're doing it for "progress" (Bilek 2020i, p. 2).

The resisters in the disability community are many and varied. Each draws on her or his own experience and takes it into the world. What is missing is not analysis, understanding and creativity by people with disabilities, it is the push for normalisation from the mainstream some of which comes through technological fixes. Disability activists are well aware of the Trojan horse of the forever-young-and-beautiful mantra, of a perfect life without hurdles and obstacles. But as medical technology speeds up and sweeps so many into its vortex of perfection, who will have time to stop and think?

I screamed
but no one in that godforsaken hole could care less
they've seen it too many times
I tried to leave but they barred my way
said since I'd eaten that damned red pomegranate
I had to stay

—Susan Hawthorne,
Cow (2011, p. 28)

Not the crime but its heralding turns men pale
and furious. I know that from my own example.
I know that we would rather punish the one
who names the deed than the one who commits it.

—Christa Wolf,
Cassandra (1984, p. 14)

CHAPTER THREE

Feminist Cassandras: Men's Patriotic Wars against Women's Intimate Lives

N
aming deeds. That is precisely what feminists are best known for. And, as Christa Wolf notes, we are punished for speaking up about violence, about hatred, about exploitation and oppression. And when we name the violators, when we name men and patriarchal institutions, the punishment is severe. Feminists have and do name the perpetrators and their abuses. As many have long recognised that only by doing so, can change come. In 1976, Diana Russell began using the word 'femicide' to describe the systematic "killing of women by men *because* they are women" (Radford and Russell, eds. 1992, p. xiv, emphasis in the original). This word has continued to be used by feminists working in the field of violence against women, especially the murder of women.

War and the institution of heterosexuality intersect

I am at an exhibition of Diane Arbus' works at the Victoria and Albert Museum in London. I look ahead and see an image I immediately want to turn away from. It is an image of a young man. He is holding an American flag. His eyes are slightly glazed, looking up. His tongue is protruding just a little between his teeth, appearing to have witnessed a victory. The look on his face is starkly sexual, as if he has just finished masturbating. Is he gloating? The photo is entitled *Patriotic young man with a flag*. It is emblematic of the ways in which patriotism and sexual conquest are connected. I had to make myself look at this young man's face. My turning away was an instance of recognition of something I did not wish to see. His face reminded me of another face, another look.

I am twenty. It is a hot day. A friend comes to visit and asks me if I'd like to come over to his house. He is a friend of a man I share a house with. We have socialised on many occasions. Half an hour later, I am desperately wanting to get away from him. I don't recall the way the conversation built, but I remember fear. And I remember that look. A look filled with possessiveness, with a lust for conquest. Somehow, I talked him down. I never saw him again.

In Iraq, a woman writes about her daily life and the effect that the war is having on her son.

> From the first day of the conflict, in March 2003, Ahmed [her son, aged 10] and his friends started playing war, asking for little soldiers, machine guns, tanks, and planes. Ahmed often imitates the Americans. Weapon in hand, he kicks open the doors shouting "Go! Go! Go!" He always chooses the GIs' side, their technology fascinates him. He's glad when Iraqis are killed. His cousins talk the same way, and use the same logic: that of whoever's stronger. It doesn't matter how much I explain to them that they're occupiers and that it's necessary to defend one's country against occupiers, or point out how much damage the war is doing, it doesn't matter, they're so

traumatized that it seems impossible for me to cure them of it in such a short time. Violence is turning them into agitated, perturbed, anxious children, obsessed by the fear of being killed or kidnapped, which happens often enough to others (Ahmed 2005).

This boy who sides with the soldiers with the best weapons is not unusual. How many boys have you seen wielding guns? How many fathers and mothers have you seen reward boys for aggression? How many politicians have you seen returned to office when they display 'strength' and masculinity in their responses to international aggression? These are ordinary, everyday events, hardly remarked upon.

The logic of war and the logic of violence against women have many common strategies. One aspect of the common logic is the control of territory of the Other by means of fear and violence. The Other is a country of the 'enemy' or the body of a woman (Mladjenovic and Matijasevic 1996, p. 127).

The practice of masculinity as a force of social control is no more self-evident than in the use of systems of masculine 'honour' and 'shame'. There are many such systems. Honour killing is one (Hossain and Welchmann 2005), but there are many others including the legal defence of provocation, so frequently used by men who kill their wives, partners, and ex-partners. It includes abuse of girls, more accurately called, as Elizabet Ward does, *Father Daughter Rape* (1984). It includes the act of raping virgins which is said to cure HIV-AIDS (Motsei 2007). It includes the violations of lesbians in forced marriage, rape, and torture as a punishment for stepping out of line. It includes the killing of women and children for fear that they might be raped by the enemy. It includes the outlawing of freedoms for women that would ensure reproductive health, including safe abortion and safe contraceptives, given that the responsible use of condoms is not considered necessary to a man's honour. It includes the requirement that women dress to please men, to speak and move in ways that men find sexual, to satisfy the urges of the male gaze.[29] It includes the mutilation of young girls and women in order to control women's sexuality (Rioja and Manresa 1999). It includes punishing women who leave a violent relationship (McLellan 2000; Hill 2019). Indeed, men's definitions of 'appropriate' behaviour for women are all about controlling sexuality.

It includes the excessive punishment of girls and women such as the sentence of execution (later commuted) of Noura Hossain in Sudan who killed her husband as he raped her; or the 51-year jail sentence imposed on Cyntoia Brown in USA who killed a man who had bought her for sex after years of rape and because she believed he was going to kill her.[30] In July 2019, a 19-year-old British woman holidaying in Cyprus was found guilty of 'public mischief'. Instead of the twelve men who allegedly raped her, the allegations were turned against her for apparently fabricating the accusations of gang rape (Bindel 2020).

By contrast, extreme violence against women by men can go unpunished or unnoticed. The former includes what is routinely called 'domestic violence' but which can include torture even though occurring in the domestic sphere. Jeanne Sarson and Linda MacDonald write about the case of Lynn who was "… held captive, tortured and sexually trafficked by her husband and three male friends" (2019, p. 108). Sarson and MacDonald go on to write about the legal loophole that in Canada does not recognise such violation as non-state torture, but rather as domestic violence. Lynn was considered to be 'difficult' by social services, but when she tried to talk about what had happened to her, she was disbelieved or dismissed. Christine Stark's research reveals that trafficking and

---

29 In the early 1970s, before feminism came into my life, I spent some months as a photographic model for men. While I was not beaten, I was violated by their objectification of my body.

30 Cyntoia Brown was released from jail on 7 August 2019. She has written a memoir of her experience called *Free Cyntoia: My Search for Redemption in the American Prison System* (2019).

prostituting of Native women in the USA has gone unnoticed for hundreds of years (Stark 2019).

Judith Herman, in her book, *Trauma and Recovery* writes:

Rape and combat might ... be considered complementary social rites of initiation into the coercive violence at the centre of adult society. They are the paradigmatic forms of trauma from women and men respectively (Herman 2015, p. 61).

This is an indictment of our contemporary society, one that needs to be thoroughly undone. Herman also notes that in the mid-1980s, a group of male psychiatrists in the American Psychiatric Association (APA) attempted to add 'masochistic personality disorder' for anyone who stayed in an abusive relationship. They were challenged by outraged women's groups, and Herman notes that, "What struck me most at the time was how little rational argument seemed to matter" [to the APA men] (Herman 2015, p. 117).

Men's concern for honour and masculinity peaks among fundamentalists who across the board agree on only one thing: the repression of women's sexuality and punishment of breaches of the heterosexual code. I include among fundamentalists incels (involuntary celibates) who consider they have a right to use women's bodies whether women want them to or not. I include market fundamentalists who want to count prostitution as a job, taxable by the state and for their own profit making. I include right-wing Christians who want to control the bodies of women in multiple ways. I include the members of Daesh (Islamic State) and governments for whom human rights abuses are standard practice. Fundamentalists of every stripe act on a sense of entitlement entwined with misogyny, racism and violence.

Only on the question of women and sexuality do the fundamentalists of either side begin to converge. Homosexuals and loose women are held responsible for God's turning away from the US, just as they are sometimes blamed for the woes of Islam (Brennan 2003, p. xvi).

The strongest form of this results in murder and violence against women; other forms can be seen as easy access to women's bodies through varying degrees of sexual harassment as 'part of the job', advertising, prostitution and pornography; in its soft form it comprises daily social pressure to conform, and appropriate behaviour according to sex stereotyping. Colette Guillaumin (1995, p. 185) proposes that women are "held in common by men," other than those women who are clearly the property of a man — father, brother, uncle, husband, even son.[31] Any woman not claimed in this way is considered common property that is for the free or forced taking.[32]

It is at this intersection of common property as held by men and autonomy or independence as held by women, that the danger of violence to women erupts. It occurs when the property of one man is trespassed on by another; it occurs in war when the property of the enemy changes hands, and is taken over by the victors. Those men stake their claim, as if staking a claim to common land or enemy land, take the women, by force if they deem necessary. These acts of violence are often not perceived as violence by men, but as their right, an appeal to the male sex right (Moschetti 2006). Also at this intersection are lesbians and unhusbanded heterosexual women. Since they 'belong' to no man, they too can be punished or taken. Violence perpetrated against these women is often excessive in times of war or conflict, as lesbians and unhusbanded women pose a threat to the male property right and male sex right and, therefore, to men's defences of war. Rape, torture, beatings, humiliation and degradation are meted out along with taunts

---

31 In the Greek classic, *The Odyssey*, Telemachus, the son of Penelope and Odysseus, assumes that he has power over his mother while Odysseus is absent. He chides her saying:
Go in and do your work.
Stick to the loom and distaff. Tell your slaves
to do their chores as well. It is for men
to talk, especially me. I am the master (Wilson 2018 p. 116, lines 256–260).

32 The free and forced taking of women is a model for the free and forced taking of land in colonisation, and of colonised peoples.

that such acts are being carried out for the woman's own good (see Chapter Six).

War and masculinity, torture and heterosexuality

Elaine Scarry, writing of the ways in which torture and war are connected, points out that war is perpetrated against an enemy 'out there', whereas torture is a more internal matter. In thinking of 'the logic of war and of the logic of violence against women' the two intertwine. Both are based on the use of coercive power. War is institutional and based on the legitimate power of the state or community; violence against women is also institutional but is made out to be personal.[33] It is not clear which precedes the other except that the violence of one man must have preceded the violence of many. The woman is tortured, raped, beaten as a warning to other women. 'Enemy women' are raped to punish and pollute enemy men. Men 'own' war. They are proud of it. It proves their masculinity like nothing else. Except, sometimes, raping a woman, especially when raping her in the presence of other men. For a man to step back and to refuse is not read as a challenge to men's humanity but rather as a challenge to his masculinity.[34] He is labelled unmanly. Men own war and in the midst of war, men's ownership of women is not questioned.

The institution of heterosexuality[35] thrives on the stereotypes of women as traded goods and men as the trader and perpetrator of violence. If a man is tortured by another man, he is emasculated. Treated as a victim, as a woman. He too, might be raped. He is the property of the torturer. He is penetrated. Just like a woman. It is a parody of intimacy. But this intimacy, based on heterosexual

---

33 See Hawthorne 2019 for an extended discussion of power and institutions.
34 See Robert Jensen's *The End of Patriarchy* (2017) for ways in which men can challenge their own role within patriarchy.
35 For an analysis of heterosexuality see Hawthorne (2019).

gratification (of the man) is torture when played out on individual women's or men's or children's bodies. It is war when it is played out on entire peoples. Including the people of women.

Scarry also refers to the destruction of culture. The culture of a people; the culture — the mind and body — of a person. Women too possess culture. Women's cultures are visible to women. Among Indigenous Australians, it is called 'women's business'. The destruction of women's cultures is profound, including in western European-derived countries.[36] Across the 16th and 17th centuries in Europe, two centuries of attacks on women as witches had a massive impact particularly on peasant women who made up the majority and who constituted the proletariat within European societies at that time.[37] The destruction of women's cultures in Europe became a model for the enslavement and massacre of peoples across Latin America, North America, Africa, Asia and the Pacific nations including Australia.[38] It has been a long and slow process. There are whole mythologies around war and nationalism from which literature, social rituals, songs and poetic traditions have sprung: *The Bible, The Iliad, The Mahabharata* and a host of others.

"[T]he structure of torture resides in, takes shape in, the physical and verbal interactions between two persons" (Scarry 1985, p. 62). Likewise, heterosexuality defines a relationship between

---

36 Ask men what they know of women's culture, art, literature, social practice, few even recognise it; ask women the same question about men, and they'll be well informed. Look around and see the ways in which women's cultures are destroyed. When did you last see a well-funded women's sporting or performing group? Compare the funding with the local army reservist force, or sporting stadium or brothel. Even the language is different. For a sustained celebration of lesbian culture — one aspect of women's culture, see Hawthorne (2005).

37 Silvia Federici argues this point of view in her book *Caliban and the Witch: The Body and Primitive Accumulation* (2004).

38 For two examples of the process of colonisation in Australia, see Cassandra Pybus' book *Truganini: Journey through the Apocalypse* (2020) in which she details the invasion of Tasmania and how that was resisted; and Diane Bell's *Ngarrindjeri Wurruwarrin: A World that Is, Was and Will Be* (1998/2014) in which she examines the continuing colonisation and resistance in the settled southeast of Australia.

people. Once rigidified into an institution, it resembles more the interaction between the torturer and the prisoner, the hero and his treasure, his prisoner, his property, the heroine. Masculinity, on the other hand, describes a state of being, an approach to the world. It can resemble war; it could also resemble other roles men play including as mentor or uncle or even benign protector; sadly, the latter is less often the case (Jensen 2017).

Masculinity and heterosexuality applied to Empire highlight the features of conquest. Conquest of the land as the Other, the culture, the body of the Other. Women's bodies are used as resources; as an analogy to land. Women's bodies are battlefields for men's wars.

Intimacy and war

In *An Intimate History of Killing*, Joanna Bourke notes that soldiers say that their instructors have told them "that 'we could rape the women' and they were taught how to strip women prisoners, 'spread them open', and 'drive pointed sticks or bayonets into their vaginas' afterwards" (Bourke 2000, p. 190). Jane Caputi (2004, p. 100), in her analysis of popular culture shows how advertising images of women create acceptance of violence against women in so-called times of peace. During war, the hatred of women becomes more overt. This 'pornography of everyday life' as Jane Caputi (1987, 2004) describes it, has become a cultural given, a harmful cultural practice that contributes to the level of violence in contemporary societies touched by global capitalism. Like the songs and poetry, the ancient pride of civilisations, American advertising builds and sustains a masculine culture of violence.

But even among men in the midst of combat, there can be a kind of closeness. Robyn Rowland captures this in her book about the battle between the Turks and the Australians at Gallipoli in 1915. She writes:

he knows death is here for us, no other way.
line after line of us both sides, one defending the place
he loves, the other knowing it. they don't want us killed.
we'd all be lonely here. we have no boundaries anymore.
we are killing ourselves in this intimate war (2018, p. 40).

War is a public event. It is a national event. It is an international event. So how did intimacy get mixed up with war? Wars among men are symbolic of wars by men on women. The practice for warfare is the rape of women. The practice for demeaning the enemy, turning the enemy into a non-human is the dehumanising of women.

As Annie McCombs points out: "when a man is tortured to death anywhere, people see political persecution; when the same thing happens to a woman the same people see sex" (1985, p. 86). Furthermore, Jane Caputi argues that the acceptance of pornography as a part of normal everyday life allows people to "see the torture of women and think sex" (Caputi 1988, p. 164). Pornography and torture exist simply as variants of one another and although torture in international law is prohibited, the spread of pornography is now allowing the argument for legalisation of torture to develop momentum.[39] Not only that, but since September 11, 2001, the escalation of all kinds of terrorism has become part of our daily news fodder. The exception has been the terrorism wreaked on women's lives. Catharine MacKinnon (2002) writes about this in an essay on September 11 and points out that in the USA roughly the same number of deaths had occurred in the year leading up to the Twin Towers attack, but no one was counting them in the same way. Is it because the victims of the bombing are seen as innocent and women who are killed might have deserved it?

More recently, women in different countries have been counting the annual murders of women by husbands, ex-partners

---

39 A fine feminist analysis of this argument can be found in D.A. Clarke (2004); among the apologists for torture are Mirko Bagaric and Julie Clarke (2005).

and immediate family members, and the figures are gruelling (Easteal 1996).[40] This is not new. Jane Caputi (1987) noticed it, and Robin Morgan commented on this in her book *The Demon Lover* in 1989.[41] In the same year, on 6 December 1989, fourteen women were shot and killed at the University of Montreal. They were feminists, and even those who might not have claimed the name of feminist, the very fact that they were studying engineering was enough to condemn them (Mallette and Chalouh 1991; Blaise 2014).[42] Inappropriate behaviour. And, as Nicole Brossard writes, the press was not keen to show solidarity with feminists even though feminists were expressly the murderer's target because, "To show solidarity with feminists would mean admitting that feminists have not exaggerated the magnitude of men's contempt toward women" (Brossard 1989 in Mallette and Chalouh 1991, p. 32).

D.A. Clarke (2004) takes the media shudder further. She argues that the use of 'girl/girl porno' (2004, p. 198) as a profitable commercial enterprise is based on the belief that the shift from private acts to public fantasies — otherwise inaccessible to men — is sexually thrilling because in the process lesbians have been humiliated. As lesbians, they are humiliated when the intimate is made public; or if they are heterosexual women posing as lesbians, the sexual acts are perceived to be humiliating. Further, she argues that lesbians, along with the Arab men depicted in the Abu Ghraib torture images, represent the threatening figure of the 'Uppity Other' (2004, p. 198). The eroticised 'suggestively homosexual tableaux' are humiliating to the Abu Ghraib prisoners. They are the feminised bodies of the enemy.

---

40 BBC World News (2018) 'The women killed on one day around the world' estimates that 87,000 women were killed in 2017, of them 30,000 were killed by an intimate partner and 20,000 by a relative.
41 *The Demon Lover: The Roots of Terrorism* was reprinted in 2001.
42 I do not name the perpetrator of this crime. He has far too much fame already.

To counter war is to counter the militarism embedded in daily life

At the core of fundamentalism there is masculinist fundamentalism. As Dubravka Ugresic writes: "In this male mindset woman has the fixed, unchanging status of an inferior being" (2003, p. 143). She writes of how men getting together at a bar to drink reflects the misogyny and 'patriarchalism' of the adventure of war which is presented as a highly sexualised event in which "War is shooting and shagging, screwing and killing" (2003, p. 145).

The 'war on terrorism' has been no different. As Jane Caputi (1988), Cynthia Enloe (1983), Robin Morgan (2001) and Kathleen Barry (2010) have all documented, the training of military recruits, the level of prostitution around army bases, and the ideology of terrorists share many common elements. Those elements include emotional disconnection combined with hatred of women, the portrayal of women as subjected to pornography and prostitution, and the widespread rape of women in war.

I decided to check whether I could make a similar thought experiment comparing the military and the sex industry with market and religious fundamentalism.

Militarism	Capitalism	Fundamentalism	Sex industry
New recruit — move him away from family and community.	Take in an overly-protected young man who has a sense of entitlement or traumatised young man who wants to make up for trauma.	Take in an already traumatised young man — orphaned, displaced, abused, refugee etc.	Take in already traumatised young women and men — displaced, drug addicted, abused, victims of war or violence.
Provide basics for him — food, shelter.	Provide him with a dream.	Provide basics for him.	Provide basics for her or him or promises of freedom and wealth.

Militarism	Capitalism	Fundamentalism	Sex industry
Add porn, make alcohol and drugs forbidden — but allow them to be available underground.	Add promises of material reward.	Add promises of heavenly reward.	Add promises of earthly reward — money, escape, fame.
Instil high level of patriotism — revere president; obey all military with higher ranks.	Instil high level of market fervour — revere venture capitalists.	Instil high level of religious fervour — revere priests, rabbis, mullahs.	Instil high level of fervour for the rewards offered — revere money and material goods.
Instil high levels of belief in masculinity and the naturalness of heterosexuality. Punish all instances of homosexuality.	Instil the idea that everything can be made profitable. Appropriate homosexuality and create the pink market.	Instil hatred of homosexuality; raise it to the level of blasphemy and punish all instances of homosexuality.	Instil hatred of women and the self; encourage the belief that the penis is necessary for fulfilling sex.
Pound with rote learning of drills (Swofford 2003, p. 105).	Pound the profit mantra and put the economy ahead of everything else.	Pound with rote learning of religious texts.	Pound with images of women's naked bodies.
Punish severely any misdemeanours — especially any kind of insubordination.	Punish the unemployed, the homeless, the poor and anyone engaged in unprofitable work.	Punish severely any blasphemous behaviour.	Punish severely any lapses of behaviour that might suggest sex is overrated or that prostitution is violence.
Make examples of those punished.	Make examples of those punished.	Make examples of those punished.	Make examples of those who have moved out of the sex industry.
Move them around so that links to former lives are reduced/broken.	Move around so links to former lives are broken. Give up everything for the job.	Play on the insecurity caused by broken links to former lives.	Play on the insecurity caused by broken links to former lives.
Make them form strong horizontal bonds to their platoon.	Make them form strong horizontal bonds with their closed community of financiers and investors	Make them form strong horizontal bonds with their closed community.	Keep them in a closed community — brothel, military base, red light district.

Militarism	Capitalism	Fundamentalism	Sex industry
Make them fear their superiors.	Make them fear market losses and the god of materialism.	Make them fear their superiors — especially god.	Make them fear pimps, traffickers and punters.
Make them despise their inferiors.	Make them despise the poor or unproductive.	Make them despise non-believers.	Make them despise as prudes those outside their community.
Create an uncertain future which might contain a fantasy future as hero.	Create an uncertain future which might contain a fantasy future as a famous billionaire.	Create an uncertain future which might contain a fantasy future as a martyr.	Create an uncertain future — which might contain a fantasy future as rich and famous.
Hand out medals to dead heroes.	Give publicity to the super rich through Forbes 500 and rich lists.	Give publicity to the martyrs.	Make them believe that one day they can become immortalised — even snuff movie actors — a famous model for pornography or fashion.

In the above chart, the military encourages masculinity and domination. The military ideology is to despise the enemy and demean them so that they become monsters, animals or beasts, or sub-human. In the sex industry, masculinity is reified, and simultaneously women are demeaned (this is the case with homosexual men and 'transwomen' in the sex industry who are associated with playing the female role, of being penetrated by a penis). Fundamentalism creates a similar kind of hatred of non-believers while among capitalist fundamentalists, non-believers in market forces are similarly despised. Entitled capitalists separate the moneymakers from ordinary mortals. In the sex industry there is a double play at work, because it is at once carried out on behalf of men and men's apparent sex drives (uncontrollable), and at the same time the industry needs to recruit women — and a few boys and young men — into it. Women in the sex industry play a role that is similar to the role of women in fundamentalist religions, among the very rich or as fervent nationalists in times of war. Keeping women in a closed place such as a brothel is akin to keeping women in captivity. These are the conditions of "prolonged and repeated trauma" (Herman 2015, p. 75). I have seen (and protested) a passenger heading for first class groping a woman flight attendant as he boarded the plane. His sense of entitlement was very visible when I yelled at him to stop.

The case of the images of torture from Abu Ghraib exemplifies this intersection of violence, dehumanisation, feminisation and the rewards (or punishments) offered by the masculinist discourses of heterosexuality, patriarchy and patriotism. The complexity is further amplified by the postmodern theoreticians, for whom anything goes, including valorising torture as sexual play (Hawthorne 2011; Weiss 2009). The postmodernist, instead of seeing sadomasochism and the distribution of photographs of victims of torture as an appropriation of the act of torture in which the victim does not have the luxury to say no, sees it as 'performative'. The thing about torture is that you do not know if you will be alive at the end of the day. You do not know when it will end. It is more than just 'powerlessness'. It is subjugation, degradation, abandonment and dehumanisation. To defend such acts as 'performative' is an instance of moral neglect (Hawthorne 2006a; Hawthorne 2011, pp. 107–117). Reading the experiences of women who have been tortured makes the idea of performativity insulting and offensive to any woman who has withstood such treatment (Rivera-Fuentes and Birke 2001; Pavaz 2018; see Chapter Six).

Dee Graham *et al.* (1994) argue that women's social relationship with men suggests a form of Societal Stockholm Syndrome, that is, that the institution of heterosexuality and the individuals who patrol it — men and apologists of men's power — act as though women are hostages to men. The captive perceives the behaviour of the captors ranging from extreme violence to kindness. Kindness creates a belief in safety in the midst of violence and abuse. As

Lara Fergus (2005) has suggested, women are given 'temporary protection visas' in men's households.[43]

To create a wish for peace is to set in motion a process that resists violence in all areas of society.

The institution of heterosexuality is central to propping up systemic violence. When heterosexuality is associated with rape, it is embedded in violence. Germaine Greer, in her book *On Rape*, refers to the 'normalisation' of persistent rape that occurs in marriage (2018). As many feminists have argued, rape is sexualised violence. In war, it is structured into the conflicts between men. If war is to cease, then structural violence must be brought to an end.

But how? Lepa Mladjenovic in a thoughtful essay asks the question: "To shoot or not to shoot?" For a feminist, this is an important question. She follows it up with the collective question: "Military intervention: Yes or No?" Both questions raise important issues around the justifiability of violence. Whether in the individual case the person should defend her own life or that of, say, her child or mother. Under what circumstances is defence better than compliance and possible death? Does short-term or controlled violence have a place in resisting war? On the collective level, when is military intervention justifiable to bring war to an end? This is the world of high theory, of legal argument, it is the age-old question, is war ever justifiable? Mladjenovic concludes:

> It pains me that patriarchy as manifested in a military system has placed us in positions in which our free desire has no expression that can be recognized by the patriarchal reality.

---

43 Complicity is the product of fear. It is how fascism digs in its roots. It reminds me of other debates among feminists. We have, on the one hand, postmodern 'feminist' theorists arguing for the healing power and the performative value of torture; while on the other hand we have legal theorists — including women — arguing for the legalisation of torture because it will be safer. This is very reminiscent of the alliances made over prostitution (Sullivan 2004; 2007; Farley 2007; Bindel, 2017). Both are libertarian stances and dangerous to women. For an extended discussion of these issues, see Hawthorne 2006a.

Patriarchy damages the free choice that we make (2003, p. 166).

Patriarchy, masculinity, and the institution of heterosexuality combine to distort reality. The senselessness of war is deemed sensible. By contrast, the world of lesbians is deemed a non-sense within heterosexual discourse (Hawthorne 2003b). In war, lesbians become a target for repression. And, why not? Lesbians symbolise a kind of release from the wheel of life. Is that why Achilles was so vehement in his killing of Penthesileia, Queen of the Amazons? Is that why the Greeks portrayed their battles with Amazons on the great frieze of the Parthenon, the Amazonomachy? Back then, were women a clear enemy? (See Mayor 2014.)

Postmodern war

Women have been subjected to a postmodern war for the last 6000 years (or thereabouts). In the 21st century, this postmodern war is extending its tentacles around the world. What do I mean by a postmodern war? Like the theory of postmodernism, a thoroughly conservative theory, it is dispersed; there are no clear boundaries between 'us and them'; it is borderless; it transgresses all the established rules of war and combat; it disconnects from reality and suggests that the real is immaterial (heroism, martyrdom); it pretends flatness of structure thereby confusing the combatants (the poor who remain cannon fodder, including poor women); it is life hating; it makes claims for complexity and then annihilates all. At its centre is a great emptiness, the emptiness of the vortex (see Brodribb 1992).[44]

These are the conditions of many women's lives under patriarchy. And since the invention of patriarchy some 6000 years ago

---

44   Somer Brodribb's chapter titles in her book, *Nothing Mat(t)ers: A Feminist Critique of Postmodernism* (1992), are wonderfully instructive regarding the emptiness of the patriarchal vortex. They contain words like nothingness, de/generation, death, de/meaning, ethical lack and oblivion.

(Foster 2013) — a transitory human period in the long history of humanity — women have been dodging violence from the more powerful human beings: men. The war against women has been dispersed. In almost every household lives a man. Not only that, but for him, the women and children provide. Many of these households are minor despotic kingdoms. But the ideology of family proclaims them as a unit. "Who is us and who is them?" ask the women. The transgressions come in the form of random rape, of gang rape, of persistent rape in marriage, of violence against women in their own homes, of violence against women on the streets, of violence against any individual or group of women who resist the patriarchal rules, of violence against women to protect men's honour (Easteal 1995; Hossain and Welchman 2005; Hattingh 2017). How can a woman escape? To which country can she migrate and be safe? Is her body the commons of men? Because she is stateless, is the whole world her country? As a foreign woman in a strange country, can she ever be safe?

The disconnection from reality comes in the form of religious beliefs, laws, economic structures and medical procedures which suggest that women are irrational; women are hysterical; women are mad and bad and the source of all evil. And any woman who fights back is by definition all these things. She is also a ball breaker, a lesbian, an unnatural woman, a woman with ambition, a threat to men and must therefore be eliminated (at the very least a social death). This will be done either randomly or by the man she has taken in to protect her, the man she loves most. For his position in male society will come under threat if he doesn't keep 'his woman' in line (Bray 2013).

Men pretend that the structure of society is flat. They love women; women love them; and everyone is equal. Rarely so. The women who are loved so much, are captives of patriarchy (Hawthorne 2012). In their love for men, they make themselves vulnerable in just the same way that the hostage is vulnerable to her captor (Graham *et al.* 1994). Any small kind thing done on her behalf is rewarded with gratitude and ever-greater sacrifice by the woman. It is confusing to be beaten by the one you have expressed love for. Just as it is confusing to be killed in a war because your side knowingly gives the wrong order, pursues a strategy that they know will result in many deaths.

In a cartoon by Australian artist, Judy Horacek, the social worker says to the woman sprawled and injured in the background of the cartoon, "Tell us about your husband's troubled childhood." Meanwhile, the husband is supported in the foreground (Horacek 1992, p. 27; Hawthorne 2003a).[45] He creates false complexities. He makes her feel sorry for him. He says, "Come, make love with me." And when she says, "No, I'm too tired" (from looking after you; from looking after the children; from looking after my parents and yours; from looking after the community; from looking after the earth, the sky, the universe) he rapes her. Perhaps he is jealous. He imagines that if she doesn't want sex with him then she must be getting it from somewhere else. After all, she's just like him and wants sex all the time. He kills her because she laughs at him.[46] He kills her slowly by raping her daily, by belittling her. He kills her by setting the children against her. He kills her by ignoring her, by assuming she has no independent thoughts or ideas. He kills her socially, politically, imaginatively and in real life. He annihilates her.[47]

And when she is safely dead, he falls in love with her. Just as Achilles did after killing Penthesileia, Queen of the Amazons. The only good woman is a dead woman (Moorhead 2000).

---

45 In the arena of international relations, misuse of past suffering is used as an excuse for going to war. Think of the Thousand Year Reich; think of Israel after World War II; think of Greater Serbia; think of the USA after September 11. These are just like the excuses men make for perpetuating violence in revenge for their violation. Why is that response so rare (it does happen) among women?

46 "Margaret Atwood writes that when she asked a male friend why men felt threatened by women, he replied that, 'They are afraid women will laugh at them.' When she asked a group of women why women felt threatened by men, they said, 'We're afraid of being killed'" (Moulton 1982, p. 5).

47 See Chapter Two in Hill (2018) for a detailed description of coercive control.

Money

Vast amounts of money are tied up keeping prostitution and pornography going. After the military and the drug trade, the sex trade is the next largest industry in the world. And as can be seen from this chapter, it is intimately connected with the military industrial complex. Soldiers are disconnected from their humanity (Barry 2010) and prostitution thrives around military bases (Enloe 1988; Raymond 2015). But the problem is far broader; there are a significant number of multibillionaires funding the prostitution industry. They include the Open Society Foundations (OSF) founded by George Soros who through his foundations has gone on to fund "legal recognition of sex work and gender identity" (Raphael 2018). A sampling of just some of the organisations funded includes Global Network for Sex Work Projects $15,000; Human Rights Watch $10,080,225; Amnesty International $2,018,206; American Civil Liberties Union (ACLU) $336,167: all figures in USD (Raphael 2018). These are just four of 28 named pro-sex work organisations funded in 2017. Of those, thirteen smaller organisations received approximately $325,000 between 2006 and 2009. One received a grant of $104,000. That was the Hungarian-based organisation Sex Workers' Rights Advocate Network (SWAN). The funding goes towards doing research that supports the views of the funders. As Jody Raphael says:

> With a relatively small amount of funds OSF has thus shored up a network of grassroots groups promoting full decriminalisation of prostitution throughout the world, readily available … to advise official bodies (Raphael 2018).

The recipients of these funds go on to sit on government advisory boards, on municipal and regional councils. They represent themselves as reflecting the women in the sex trade industry. But as is clear from the women who are active in the movement to abolish prostitution, especially those who are survivors, this is not the case (Moran 2013; Norma and Tankard Reist 2016; Mara 2020).

It also bears out the work of other researchers in this area such as Sheila Jeffreys who writes about the way in which prostitution is being universalised (Jeffreys 1997, pp. 343–348).[48] Kajsa Ekis Ekman documents the ways in which so called prostitute unions are in fact run by pimps and brothel owners and she too notes the connection between money for HIV/AIDS prevention and an increase in funding for 'sex worker' unions (Ekman 2013, pp. 59–64). Julie Bindel notes that since the late 1980s, AIDS funding from the Bill and Melinda Gates Foundation and George Soros' OSF have funded the decriminalisation of prostitution, often alongside other misogynist funding. Connected to HIV/AIDS prevention, in Australia the Bobby Goldsmith Foundation (BGF) has an annual 'bake off' fundraiser in which the cakes objectify and humiliate women (Bindel 2017, pp. 182–188). Retired Justice Michael Kirby is the patron of BGF.

In New Zealand, where prostitution has been decriminalised, Michelle Mara, who co-founded Wahine Toa Rising, writes about the way in which Covid-19 support is not reaching those most in need. She says that women who need access to 'sensitive claims' services that could be similar to those that women fleeing domestic violence can access, find that none are available. Her next point is that women in prostitution "need to know that their information won't be passed on, publicized or shared with an organisation like NZPC" (Mara 2020). The New Zealand Prostitutes Collective, Mara argues, acts as though it represents women in the sex trade, but Mara maintains that they are not a union. Instead, NZPC acts more like the so-called unions that Ekman describes in *Being and Being Bought* (2013).

When so-called human rights organisations and people known in the media for being advocates of superficially progressive forces

---

48   See also Kate Millett's early book, *The Prostitution Papers* (1973); Lydia Cacho (2012) on prostitution as slavery; and Andrea Dworkin's essay on grooming 'The Pedophilic Teacher' in her book *Heartbreak* (2002, pp. 13–19) and Andrea Dworkin's novel *Mercy* (1993) for a gruelling first-hand account of a prostituted woman's life.

endorse such views it makes you doubt the world in front of your eyes. Astroturfing is a practice in which an organisation masks the origins of a message, especially one that purports to be from a grassroots organisation, but is in fact sponsored by funding from billionaires or companies that make a profit, for example owners of brothels and pornographers.[49] So-called sex worker unions fit this definition with individuals like Douglas Fox pretending to be a male escort when in fact he is co-owner of Christony Companions, one of the largest escort agencies in England (Ekman 2013, p. 63). As Ekman concludes,

> A trade union that not only is led by a known pimp but also fights measures intended to prevent exploitation should cause most people to raise an eyebrow but seems to have gone unnoticed (Ekman 2013, p. 64).

Astroturfing, pimps as members of trade unions all funded by billionaires, ought to do more than just have us be surprised, it should make us angry and motivated to change the world. At the very least it is likely to make us lose faith in the methods of social cohesion being used.

Governments too become pimps as they become reliant on taxes paid by brothels and prostituted women (Sullivan 2007; Farley 2007). But even while this remains a reason for governments to be attracted to the idea of prostitutes as workers and brothels as workplaces, the increase in organised crime, tax evasion and violence, illicit drugs and other underhand activities makes it an expensive way to gain revenue. It is also an activity that destroys community.

---

49   See Chapter Seven for more on 'astroturfing'.

What would it take for a woman to be free of injury and to live without fear for her safety?

- It would take a wholesale shift in men's attitudes towards women.
- It would take men disavowing their loyalty to patriarchy and to the institutions that support it including racism, heterosexism, and discrimination based on marginalising people for reasons of bodily formation, mobility, age, ethnicity, religious beliefs and culture — without supporting cultural or sexual relativism.[50]
- It would take men recognising their accountability for their own and other men's actions.
- It would take shutting down the military industrial complex beginning with a ban on small arms.
- It would take respecting women and fostering the space for women to live in our bodies freely.
- It would take ending the assumption that women's bodies are for men's use — whether for sex, labour, domestic service, 'breeding services' or emotional support.
- It would take respecting children and their growth into adults not burdened by childhood violation and violence.
- It would take the development of a social and political ethic that resists privileging power.
- It would take unthinking the possibility of patriotism and the use of women's bodies as property.
- It would take the development of a politics that respects and honours the lives of the living beings among whom we live.

---

50 Carole Moschetti has coined the term 'sexual relativism' as an analogue of the term 'cultural relativism'. Cultural relativism is used to excuse men's violence on the grounds of custom, tradition, religious or cultural beliefs. Cultural relativism is used as if it were gender neutral. Sexual relativism "enables the identification of practices that specifically operate to subordinate women" (Moschetti 2006, p. 24).

- It would take respecting the earth as a bio/diverse eco/social system in which profiteering at the expense of life — plants, animals, the soil, rocks, the seas, the atmosphere and their inhabitants — is socially sanctioned and subject to international inspections with penalties.
- It would take the introduction of systems set up to eliminate violence against women: introducing the Nordic Model in which the buyers — the users of women — are prosecuted, named and jailed if they are found to be involved in other crimes against women (Tyler 2016; Nordic Model Now 2020); the establishment of women's police stations where women can go to report intimate terrorism / domestic abuse / coercive control (Hill 2019, pp. 254–257); Jess Hill also suggests 'focused deterrence' a policing system which shares a number of features with the Nordic Model including calling out perpetrators, enabling previously siloed services to work together and share information (Hill 2019, pp. 348–366).
- It would take the formalising of documents such as the *Declaration on Women's Sex-Based Rights* (2019) and implementing it.

I make these suggestions because the injury to women and threats to their safety emerge out of a context of socialised violence that is not only supported by the social, political and religious policies of governments of almost every nation, but it extends through to the living rooms and bedrooms of our homes.

We need a world in which women are free of the threat of death because of some mistaken sense men have of their 'honour'. We need a world in which men do not rape virgins whether they are babies, children, adolescents or adult women because men believe that their compromised health is more important than the life or well-being of children and women and that raping a virgin will free them of HIV (Motsei 2007; Morgan 2003). We need a world in which women are not ghettoised as wives or prostitutes and as the common property of men or as commodities for men's sexual pleasure in pornography. We need a world in which it is unthinkable to kill children in ritual murder because men value their lives ahead of everyone else's (Dow 2002). We need a world in which women do not fear the sound of men's footsteps behind them. We need a world in which women can say no, can walk their own chosen path and not be punished. We need a world in which we begin again at zero, a world with a new beginning.[51]

---

51 This is a variation on Monique Wittig (1970). See also Hawthorne (2005, pp. 231–233).

Post-graduate awards.
Graduate awards.
It doesn't matter
What you call it.

But did I hear you say
Awards?
Awards?
Awards?

What
Dainty name to describe
This
Most merciless
Most formalised

Open,
Thorough,
Spy system of all time:

For a few pennies now and a
Doctoral degree later,
Tell us about
Your people
Your history
Your mind.
Your mind.
Your mind

—Ama Ata Aidoo,
*Our Sister Killjoy or Reflections from
a Black-eyed Squint* (1977, pp. 86–87)

CHAPTER FOUR

Biocolonialism and Bioprospecting: Wars against Indigenous Peoples and Women

grew up on the southwest slopes of New South Wales. It was dry farmland and the traditional owners of the land are the Wiradjuri people. At the small school I attended in the 1950s, this Aboriginal nation's name was never mentioned. The only stories I recall were of the type "Why does the kangaroo have a tail?" It was no better at the secondary school I attended in Melbourne. We learnt none of the names for the Indigenous nations. In the 1970s, I began to hear more and meet Aboriginal women at feminist events. In 1982, I studied Warlpiri at Monash University. Being introduced to words of an Australian Indigenous language had a profound effect on me. I began working with Aboriginal students in high schools through a home-tutoring program and in 1986, I taught in the first year of the Koori Teacher Education Program (KTEP) at Deakin University. But the years 1984 and 1985 were also important. In 1984, I wrote an abstract for a presentation on 'Aboriginal Women's Traditional Stories: A White Perspective' for the Brisbane Women and Labour Conference. Jackie Huggins from Bidjara Central Queensland and Birri-Gubba Juru North Queensland peoples said I should not present the paper. After some discussion, I agreed and said that instead I would change the focus of the session to discuss protocol on who can speak; how one goes about getting permission and other subjects raised by the attendees. At the beginning of the talk, I apologised that I would not be giving my paper because of the demands made by Jackie Huggins. A few rows from the front an Aboriginal elder put her hand up and said, "There are no men in the room, go ahead, speak your paper." I had met her ahead of the session and knew that her name was Nganyintja, a highly respected Pitjantjatjara woman from central Australia. I had read her contribution in the book *We Are Bosses Ourselves* (Gale 1983). Because she requested that I give my paper, I proceeded. Halfway through, Jackie Huggins entered and assumed I had not followed her orders. She did not ask me after the session. Accounts of the session were hugely over-blown at the conference, in the media and in academic essays written later. What was the most informative aspect of the experience was the rapport extended to me by the traditional women. Sitting in a lecture theatre later that day, Nganyintja and four other women sat next to me while everyone else kept a wide berth. This action seemed to be a matter of supporting the weakest person in the group. They knew what I had agreed to and why I presented the paper when they asked me to. They then invited me to sit with them for a while so they could talk to me about protocol more specifically.

Since that time, I have worked with Indigenous authors from different parts of Australia and internationally. Whenever possible, I have increased the profile of Aboriginal women in various art forms. I have organised state, national and international festivals in which Indigenous writers and publishers have had prominence. I hope that the work I have done in the years following my encounter with the women from central Australia would make up for my first awkward, but respectful, steps.

What is bioprospecting?

In the worlds of exploration and mining, *prospectors* make claims on parcels of land looking to making a profit in the future; *bioprospectors* are making claims on biological resources with a view to making a profit (Hawthorne 2002a, p. 266). There are several ways to understand resources. *Resources* in an unadorned way can mean the plants, animals, and products of the land. However, this does not adequately cover what bioprospectors are claiming, since the claim is made as if these things have no deeper meaning for people, let alone that there is equal and open access to resources.

The claims on biological resources come from two sources:

- land that is inhabited by Indigenous and Traditional peoples, as well as the resources of rivers and seas;
- the bodies of colonised and isolated peoples, of women and lesbians, as well as people with disabilities and chronic illnesses.

I want to look at these sources separately, although the issues involved are analogous. In the same way, it can be argued that the bodies of the poor, people of colour, and women have been colonised in the preceding centuries along with the colonisation of land, so too the methods employed in bioprospecting are colonising. The difference is that this latest permutation of colonisation is occurring in a knowledge-based economy. Privatisation is achieved through patents, through the exploitation of women's bodies, of body parts such as women's eggs or the cell lines of isolated populations, and through appropriation of knowledge that has been handed down over generations, very frequently among women. The important issue here is the recognition of the connection between women's bodies and the land as expressed by Indigenous women across the world: from Siberia to South America, North America to Australia, Africa to Asia, the Pacific Islands to the Indian Ocean Islands. Both the land and women's bodies have suffered colonialist intrusions, and both colonialist and imperial agendas have capitalised on exploiting women's bodies and land (Hawthorne 2002a, p. 162–205).

Land as resource	Colonised* bodies as resource	Women's bodies as resource	Disabled bodies as resource	Lesbian and Gay bodies as resource
Declaration of *terra nullius* (empty land) or uselessness of the land.	Declaration of barbarism or inferiority of those living on the land.	Declaration of inferiority of women to men and accusations of uncontrollable sexuality (e.g. witches).	Declaration of inferiority and abnormality of people with disabilities.	Declaration of unnaturalness of sexual orientations such as lesbian, gay and bisexual.
Declaration provides 'need' to conquer the land.	Declaration provides 'need' to kill, subdue and govern the 'natives'.	Declaration provides 'need' to marry or prostitute unruly women.	Declaration provides 'need' to institutionalise people with disabilities.	Declaration provides 'need' to do anything to 'normalise' lesbian and gay people.
Separation of connection to land by invasion, war, colonialism.	Separation of peoples from lands, seas and the natural and cultural environments.	Separation of women from one another through patriarchal systems of violence and domestication.	Separation of people with disabilities through shame and fear and endless classification.	Separation of lesbians and gays through hatred, shame and the need to hide.
Poisoning and pollution of land to make it uninhabitable.	Criminalising traditional practices and languages to strip meaning from cultures.	Creation of the 'good' and 'bad' woman and the untruth that every woman needs a man to protect her.	Highlighting of illness, abnormality, unhappiness resulting in fear of disability.	Creation of shame thereby increasing the likelihood of exile and suicide.
Mining land as resource and depleting its living value (cf. sterilisation).	Mining the bodies of subordinated peoples through slave labour, organ trafficking, trafficking in the sex industry and surrogacy.	Mining women's bodies as resource, using their bodies for parts, sex trafficking, prostitution and surrogacy.	Experimenting with unnecessary medical procedures, and sterilisation.	Promoting 'fixes' for lesbian and gay people by declaring them mad and in need of drugs, through gay conversion therapy and/or the promise that all will be well if you transition.

Land as resource	Colonised* bodies as resource	Women's bodies as resource	Disabled bodies as resource	Lesbian and Gay bodies as resource
Profiteering through exploitation of resources and land and endless regulation in gaining Native Title.	Profiteering through the Human Genome Project (HGP) and Human Genome Diversity Project (HGDP) for the unregulated benefit of Big Pharma.	Profiteering from women's bodies by pimps in prostitution, producers of pornography, lawyers and middlemen in surrogacy and endless regulation.	Profiteering by the creation of tests which instil fear into prospective parents, creating yet another business opportunity in medical technology.	Profiteering through provision of drugs to those declared mad, medical services for those wanting to be converted or to transition; or in the case of intersex people reversing early unnecessary surgery.
Acting rapaciously towards resources in and on the land such as precious metals, rainforests, rivers, and seas.	Stripping colonised, enslaved and displaced peoples of their humanity and their culture through racism, imprisonment and high rates of violence #BlackLives Matter.	Stripping women of a sense of power through sexist and demeaning comments, misogyny, harassment, rape and murder #MeToo.	Ensuring that those with disabilities are dominated by those considered 'normal', infantilised and subjected to normalisation.	Appropriating the stories of lesbian and gay people in order to exoticise and eroticise but never according recognition. Hate speech is considered normal.
Corporate monopoly of mind creates monoculture in the form of poisoned aridity, monocultures of agriculture, aquaculture and forestry.	Corporate monopoly of mind creates cultural monocultures. Corporates appropriate Indigenous cultures by exoticisation through fashion, arts industries and through biopiracy (Hawthorne 1989).	Corporate monopoly of mind creates monoculture; creates stereotypes of the acceptable thin, white, blonde woman.	Corporate monopoly of mind creates a 'normal' body in a world where there is no such thing, instead people with disabilities are considered imperfect.	Corporate monopoly of mind creates compulsory heterosexuality (Rich 1980).
Elimination of relationship with land through contamination of land for a very long period.	Elimination of language and culture through cultural decimation, cultural domestication, imprisoning and killing.	Elimination of women through murder or domestication.	Elimination of people with disabilities through screening, testing or complete domestication.	Elimination of lesbian and gay people or by domestication into hetero-normative practices or conversion or transition.

*(Indigenous, enslaved, displaced)

What is biopiracy?

Corporations argue that bioprospecting is a beneficial event for Indigenous communities since it can generate money for social and other services in poverty-stricken communities. It is, however, a two-edged sword because it involves making public an earned system of knowledge and entering into the contested knowledge systems of colonialist corporations whose main concern is to privatise knowledge as patents on life forms. Although there are many who claim that benefits accrue to Indigenous communities in the form of royalties, I argue that communities are much more likely to lose not only access to their traditional knowledge but also control over how that knowledge is used, just as when the industrial revolution occurred, the value of labour was alienated and the profits passed into the hands of the owners. It was precisely that alienation and loss that prompted Vandana Shiva and others to challenge W. R. Grace's patent on the neem tree, *Azadirichta indica* (Shiva 2000).

The neem tree, *Azadirichta indica*, grows in Asia and Africa. In India it has been used for millennia as an insect repellent, spermicide, and medicine for skin diseases, sores, and rheumatism. It is found as an ingredient in toothpastes and soaps and can be used to prevent fungal growth such as rust and mildew. Long called the blessed tree or the free tree, it was not perceived as particularly important in the eyes of those from the west until the 1970s, when some of its traditional uses began to be taken seriously. W. R. Grace, a US company, isolated the active ingredient and took out a patent on the neem, claiming that patent on the basis of novelty. In 2001, this patent was revoked on the grounds that it constituted, as Indian antiglobalisation activist Shiva (2000, p. 42) points out, "piracy of existing knowledge systems and lacked novelty and inventiveness." This is a positive move with regard to the recognition of traditional knowledge. There are a number of key examples of biopiracy in the literature. The case against W. R. Grace's patent on the neem tree is one of the most cited. But, unlike many other traditional medicines, the neem was backed by written Sanskrit sources.

Biopiracy of earth-based resources

Earth-based resources used by Indigenous and Traditional peoples include medicinal uses for plants, fish, animals, trees, plants, rocks for building, tool making and production of art and other resources located on lands, rivers, and seas. This knowledge comes from long attachment to the environment and from a history of maintaining that environment over millennia — in Australia, for more than 65,000 years. The identification, collection and use of medicinal plants is mostly carried out by women (Gott 2018).

Most Indigenous communities rely on oral, not written, histories and it is the oral sources that are the key to Indigenous knowledge in Australia. As one of the megadiverse regions of the world, Australia is home to numerous flora and fauna that corporate scientists are exploring. One example is the Western Australia smokebush, which has been used for medicinal purposes by Aboriginal people and whose active ingredient, concurvane, has been examined for use against HIV (Christie 2001). This may appear to be a benign, indeed very positive, development. But as Henrietta Fourmile (1996) from the Gimoy Clan of the Yidindyi Nation in Australia points out, Indigenous people were not consulted and their knowledge is being stolen. The peoples of Africa are facing similar challenges. The San people of the Kalahari challenged British and US drug companies that took out a patent on an ingredient of the hoodia plant which was marketed as an appetite suppressant.[52] As a result of the court challenge, the San will now receive royalties in a benefit-sharing agreement. A later paragraph in the news item suggests something more sinister. "The San are likely to be involved in farming and cultivating hoodia, and to be *offered scholarships to study so that their ancient botanical knowledge may lead to other products*" (Barnett 2002, p. 3; emphasis added). In 1977, Ghanaian novelist Ama Ata Aidoo warned that scholarships are a 'merciless' way of finding out about the mind of the colonised (1977, p. 86). What better way in a knowledge economy is there to mine for information that can later be privatised and patented? Furthermore, because royalties are distributed unevenly in communities, conflicts arise when some groups and families receive more than others. The commodification of community knowledge disrupts the whole society.

A similar story is told about the Guinea Hen Weed, *Petiveria alliacea,* a plant used by traditional healers in Jamaica, Guatemala, Dominica, Grenada and other Caribbean islands. Systems are reduced to data and properties, while knowledge is turned into profitable information. It is women's knowledge that is appropriated to maximise profit and cultural significance is minimised (O'Donnell 2019, pp. 215–218).

Biopiracy and value

The concept of value with regard to knowledge resembles much of the debate that has centred on the value of women's work. Michael Dove, in his study of rainforest management in Kalimantan, Indonesia, argues that whatever of value is found or developed by Indigenous forest peoples — particular tree species, mineral deposits, butterflies, and medicines — will never earn for the forest people what it would earn in the open market. Instead, centralised power appropriates the resource, sometimes for allegedly public

---

52 Over several weeks during 2007, I received a large number of junk emails advertising hoodia.

interest, and then pockets the profits (1993, p. 20). A disjunction also occurs between what is known to be valued by Indigenous forest peoples and what governments and corporate interests value. Dove argues that UN-sponsored development projects define what they will "allow the forest peoples to keep ... butterfly farms, crocodile farms, fish farms and [the activity of] medicinal plant collection" (1993, p. 21).[53] This list, he suggests, is not for the peoples' empowerment "but for their *impoverishment*" (1993, p. 21; emphasis in original). For, if empowerment were the goal, the list would include trees for timber, hardwoods, gems, and the biodiverse resources that the rainforest holds, and the forest people would be in charge of forest management. His concern is not just for what has been taken away from forests but what has been "taken away from forest peoples" (1993, p. 22).[54] He notes that, "In a perverse irony, the instrument of forest peoples' impoverishment, deforestation, is blamed on them" (1993, p. 22).

Women are familiar with these reversals of blame and Dove's observation applies to resources developed by women, often developed because there is a domestic or local need for the product or for ways of spreading knowledge. Jane Mogina (1996) speaks of the ways in which older women in Papua New Guinea use the forest not only as a way of passing on knowledge about medicinal contraceptive plants but also as a safe place to pass on to young women information about sex. The plundering of forest resources results in plundering women's knowledge systems and bodies.

---

53 The medicinal plant collection will remain in the hands of forest peoples only so long as no cure for cancer, AIDS, or menopause is found in their region. On June 7, 2001, I visited the World Bank in Washington, DC. In the lobby was a huge display titled "Biodiversity in the World Bank's Work." The World Bank is funding Indigenous peoples, such as those in Kalimantan, to preserve their heritage because it is worth billions of dollars. It is clear, however, that the forest peoples, the desert peoples, and the fisher peoples are very unlikely to end up billions of dollars richer.

54 The example of the neem tree bears out Dove's argument that, until the 1970s, the neem tree was not perceived by the west as anything other than a lowly tree. This is analogous to the ways in which women's knowledge is treated, that is, it is irrelevant until someone decides there's a buck to be made.

This is in stark contrast to western industrialised systems of forestry which, for more than two centuries, have been militarised.

The most telling quotation I have read about how forests were conceptually militarised and turned into a site for war against nature comes from Julius von Brinken, a forester who visited Lithuania in 1820.

> What was needed ... was a methodical forestry that would, over time ... bring it into some kind of proper hierarchy. Varieties would be massed together so that those suitable for one purpose, like shipbuilding, could be efficiently harvested at the allotted time, while timber more suitable for building materials would be cultivated elsewhere. In this ideal regime, the trees would be graduated in age, so that foresters would not need to wander all through the woods looking for trees of maximum maturity or whatever the designated age might be for the job. Specimens of a like variety and maturity would present themselves *in tidy battalions ready for their marching orders* (Schama 1996, p. 50; my emphasis).

Biopiracy of body-based resources

> σῶμα [soma] *the body*: in Homer *the dead body ... a corpse, carcase. whereas the living body is* δέμας [demas] ... 2. *body* as opp. to *soul* (ψυχή) [psyche] ... II. *any material body.* III. *person, a human being*; esp. of slaves as opp. to other goods (Liddell and Scott 1986, p. 688; italics in original).

Separation, the dissociation of mind and body, creates acceptability for abuses of women in reproductive, biotechnology and sex industries. As Maria Mies, Veronika Bennholdt-Thomsen and Claudia von Werlhof (1988) put it, women are the 'last colony'. The global growth of somatic services — biotechnology,[55] prostitution[56] and torture[57] — necessitate dissociation of mind and body.

I have three premises:

1. The process of biotechnology is one of separation and fragmentation (Klein 1996; 1999). Biotechnology reifies the soma — the dead body, the body parts and this separation is an alienation of the self and a philosophy rooted in death, not life, as indicated in the translation and definition given above.

2. Biotechnology is racist, sexist, ableist and classist and these ideologies are central to the biotech industry. Firstly, the biotechnology industry promotes the elimination of people on the basis of their 'genetic pool' especially people from Indigenous and 'isolated' groups. Secondly, the biotechnology industry promotes the elimination of people on the basis of sexual orientation, specifically the elimination of lesbians and gay men. The latest move is to eliminate lesbians and gay men through hormonal and surgical transition (see Chapters Six and Seven). All these features make it clear that biotechnology is *ideological* science based on a fundamentalist view of the body which selects out those bodies deemed 'imperfect'. The consequence is to put at risk the lives and the health of the poor (the vast majority of whom are women), those marginalised by race, culture, religion or ethnicity, people with disabilities as well as lesbians and gay men.

3. I conclude that the profits made by those with a stake in the biotechnology industry are unconscionable. The profits of

---

55 Among them feminists such as Farida Akhter, Rita Arditti, Gena Corea, Jalna Hanmer, Renate Klein, Maria Mies, Janice Raymond, Robyn Rowland, Vandana Shiva — to mention just a few prominent names — have documented the failures, the misrepresentations and the dangers of biotechnology to women internationally. See also Hawthorne, 2007a.

56 See Jeffreys 1997; Stark and Whisnant 2004; Sullivan 2007; Farley 2007; Jeffreys 2009; Moran 2013; Ekman 2013; Raymond 2015; Norma and Tankard Reist 2016; Bindel 2017.

57 See Rivera-Fuentes and Birke 2001; Clarke 2004; Hawthorne 2006a.

biotechnology go to investors and are intended for use on the behalf of the well off, the healthy and the powerful. The quest for perfection is an ideology of disengagement with violence against the body at its heart. It is a form of weaponising corporate power through technology against people.

Separation

Central to my theoretical stance is the concept of separation. I could also use words like fragmentation, abstraction, disconnection, disengagement, objectivity, dissociation, segregation or tear asunder. All represent different degrees and styles of separation.

I distinguish separation, segregation, and disconnection from separatism. The former is 'a manifestation of domination' (Hawthorne 2019, p. 67), whereas separatism is withdrawal of support for the dominant group. Separatism is voluntary; segregation is involuntary (Hawthorne 2019, p. 68). This distinction is important because segregation is used to perpetuate oppressive social systems, while separatism is a political strategy used by the dispossessed to counter the oppressive social system.

The 'corporate monopoly of mind' has disengaged from reality and targeted particular groups for bodily amendment, all in the guise of promising to produce perfect babies, disease-free future generations and a social fabric free of the disruptive presence of misfits such as those who reject heterosexuality, and those who fall outside the current definition of able.

Microcolonialism of Indigenous bodies

Body-based resources include the results of research carried out under the auspices of the Human Genome Diversity Project (HGDP), a project in which the bodies of Indigenous peoples — among them women — have been used to colonise DNA from human bodies and make a profit. The much-touted Human Genome

Project (HGP) and its sister the Human Genome Diversity Project (HGDP) which Indigenous activists call the Vampire Project, have come under severe criticism from feminists, from Indigenous peoples, and from people with disabilities. Both projects aim to collect genetic samples from populations, in much the same way that early colonial prospectors collected botanical, animal, and human samples for scientific cataloguing. Such prospecting would not have been possible without a particular worldview that allowed easy transfer of property into colonial hands and the development of patents (Hawthorne 2002a, 314–322). The HGP and HDGP have created a new kind of colonialism: biocolonialism. No longer is the integrity of the human body assured, and the products of botanical and zoological colonisation are also transferred into private hands.[58]

Separation is central to acts of microcolonialism. Victoria Tauli-Corpus (2007) from the Philippines writes:

> … we link the theft of our human genetic materials to the theft of our biodiversity and knowledge. We look at biopiracy and the patenting of life as the invasion, colonization, privatization and commercialization of nature and the human body and the appropriation of indigenous knowledge for profit seeking (Tauli-Corpuz 2007, p. 336).

And from Latin America, Ana Isla notes that for Indigenous peoples "selling biodiversity is comparable to selling their culture and, more deeply, their souls — a kind of suicide" (Isla, 2007, p. 328). The literature is filled with examples of people tricked into giving samples of cheek scrapings to scientists. A Hagahai man from New Guinea; similar cases from the Solomon Islands; a 26-year-old Guaymi Indian woman from Panama (Hawthorne 2002a, pp. 352–359).

At issue, among other things, are two competing worldviews. The Guaymi of Panama consider such commodification as violating

---

58   See Horvitz 1996, Awang 2000, Tauli-Corpuz 2001, Hawthorne 2002a.

"the integrity of life itself, and our deepest sense of morality" (Shand 1994, p. 11). The biotechnologists see the lure of cure, rising share prices and profits. They claim that the Guaymi carry a virus which, because it stimulates the production of antibodies, *might* prove commercially profitable in treating leukaemia and HIV. The obvious next move for the biopirates is to appropriate and privatise the Guaymi woman's *somata* for the benefit of their corporation. An application for a patent was made. The appropriation was followed by privatisation of the woman's body parts for the benefit of a large corporation. The profit generated was not returned to those who had provided the original resources but instead went to foreign-owned companies. The Guaymi see themselves as connected to the whole, not separable into parts, cells, or genes. There is no remedy for the degree of violation they experienced through these western techniques. On the other hand, the US patent laws specify precisely how life can be owned, patented, and 'invented' by scientists and corporations (Hawthorne 2002a, p. 352–359).

This is reminiscent of how the prisoners on Manus Island — which is part of New Guinea and the location of an Australian-run detention centre for refugees seeking asylum in Australia — become so socially fragmented, complicit, dependent on other prisoners, fighting among themselves for food or cigarettes or access to phones or toilets that they begin to hate one another. Kurdish Iranian journalist, Behrouz Boochani writes "The prison is designed to breed hostility, animosity" and that "hatred makes the prisoners more insular" (Boochani 2018, p. 165).[59]

---

59 Behrouz Boochani is a Kurdish-Iranian journalist. The author of the prize-winning *No Friend but the Mountains* (2018) which was written in Farsi on a mobile phone. A refugee, he was held in the detention centre on Manus Island run by the Australian government from 2013 to 2017 and in 2019 transferred to the capital of Papua New Guinea, Port Moresby. In November 2019 he was invited to a writers festival in Christchurch on a one-month visa. He was granted refugee status in New Zealand in July 2020.

Sandra Awang (2000) also points out (like Shiva 1993) that Intellectual Property Rights (IPRs) are promoted as new ways of looking at knowledge, when in fact they represent the "institutionalisation of *Western orientation toward information as a world system of thinking*" (Awang 2000, p. 125; emphasis in original). The pretence that enclosing knowledge systems through patents is going to benefit Indigenous and Traditional peoples is as morally corrupt as the pretence that colonisation makes underdeveloped countries rich through catch-up development (Mies 1999; 1994).

Colonial theft was extended to human anatomy. When Australia was colonised, the body parts and skulls of Aboriginal people were collected by 'eminent' 19th-century scientists who saw nothing wrong with the practice.[60] In the 20th century we have seen the growth of a number of organ industries, among them kidneys, pituitary glands, foetal tissue and more (Raymond 1995, pp. 165–173). Today the practice continues, albeit on a level that cannot be perceived by unassisted human sight. Molecular colonisation continues the practice of colonising human bodies. The process of appropriating, patenting, privatising and profiting is not dissimilar from the concept of *terra nullius* enshrined in Australian law until 1992. The knowledge system and the body are considered vacant and therefore open to exploitation by business.[61] The vacancy of the body and the land represent the emptiness at the centre of the vortex.

---

60 The result was that the bodies were removed to the mother country, England, from which they now need to be repatriated. Indigenous people call it bringing the old people home. They are not considered skeletal remains but rather are considered part of the community that needs to be properly looked after and returned to the land.

61 Billions of dollars are spent for such research on people who are considered under threat of extinction. It does not seem to occur to the scientists that they themselves are part of the problem in preferring to gather samples rather than respect the dignity and culture of these people. But to withdraw and not impose their agenda would mean no potential profits. The same cascading effects apply here as with climate change (see Chapter Eight).

Terra nullius (Latin) means literally empty land. In the minds of the colonisers, because they could see no formal structure for ownership and improvement of the land, they could not see the land as inhabited. People in Africa and Australia were epistemologically disappeared. *Terra nullius* represents a legal and ontological perspective which sees earth as empty, as unused, as a wasteland, and as a resource to be plundered and made profitable.

Gynocolonialism

Her womb from her body. Separation.   Her clitoris from her vulva.   Cleaving.   Desire from her body.
We were told that bodies rising to heaven lose their vulvas, their ovaries, wombs, that her body in resurrection becomes a male body (Griffin 1978, p. 95; spacing and italics in the original).

Patriarchy has provided the means for dominant institutions of science and politics to appropriate women's body parts — *somata* and women's bodies — *soma* — as if they were dead. In the case of body parts, poor or desperate women are expected to give up time and parts of their bodies. They are pressured to donate, or sell their body parts, the genetic cell lines or their organs — not for their benefit, nor the benefit of someone close to them — but for profit, for access by companies. Women from poor communities are particularly vulnerable to exploitation. Women from poor countries or lower socioeconomic classes are encouraged to sell nine months (and more) of their lives as 'surrogates' for rich heterosexual and gay couples in well-off countries (Ekman 2013; Klein 2017; Saravanan, 2018). These are problems not only inside single countries, but also globally, with women in poverty-stricken parts of Africa,[62] Asia or Latin America and countries from the former USSR: Russia, Georgia, Ukraine (Lahl, Tankard Reist and Klein eds. 2019) and Serbia[63] vulnerable to trade in their body parts, their *somata*.[64] Middle class women tend to be pressured to donate their body parts to family or friends. In South Africa, it is illegal to sell body parts, however,

> ... vulnerable, young poor women are lured into donating their eggs in return for cash payments for the 'distress and disruption' to their lives. In South Africa payments of up to R20,000 (US$3000) have been made for such donations (Loots 2006, p. 154).

Removing the living, sparking[65] element so that the body is reduced to *soma* and *somatic* parts is the underlying purpose of separating the body from itself. Such separation allows for body parts — especially eggs — to be reduced to a commodity. Such a reduction turns women into the new slaves of the biotech industry without any concern for the living bodies, the souls and psyches.

Colette Guillaumin (1995), in an essay first published in 1978, writes about the way in which women are regarded by men as common property. The treatment of women in biotechnology and in war exemplifies the way in which women's bodies are

---

62 Africa is the latest frontier for burgeoning surrogacy industry with clinics in Nigeria, Tanzania and Kenya.

63 The laws on surrogacy were changed in 2019 with the incoming lesbian Prime Minister, Ana Brnabić who made it legal for women to become 'birth givers'. Not all lesbians are radical, but nor are all gay men and lesbians in favour of surrogacy (Solis 2017; Bindel and Powell 2018; Hawthorne 2019c).

64 Others have written about the trade in organs (Raymond 1995, p. 138 ff), in brides (Akhter 1995), in the selling of women's bodies through an entire pregnancy in surrogacy (Klein 2017; Ekman 2013; Lahl, Tankard Reist and Klein, eds. 2019); in women's bodies for 'sex' (Radford and Russell, eds. 1992; Barry 1995; Jeffreys 1997; Stark and Whisnant, eds. 2004; Sullivan 2007; Farley 2007; Raymond 2013; Moran 2013; Tankard Reist and Norma, eds. 2016; Bindel 2017; Stark 2019), in foetal tissue (Raymond 1995/2019 172ff), as well as in eggs and somatic cell nuclei (FINRRAGE 2006; Tankard Reist 2004).

65 This is a reference to Mary Daly's notion of 'sparking' as an indication of feminist vitality and fire (Daly 1978, pp. 354–384).

appropriated for men's use. And, I would add, *biotechnology is tantamount to a declaration of war on women's bodies.*

Guillaumin's contention that women are held in common by men, means that they are for the free or forced taking. Indeed, the 'free and forced taking of women', that is, prostitution and trafficking, is a model for the free and forced taking of land in colonisation, and of colonised peoples, peoples used by the forced trade of free trade.[66] In spite of all the campaigns for autonomy around reproduction and sexuality since the 1960s, in 2020 we find that the call for such change has attracted a sinister response: the development of the biotechnology industry which keeps women's bodies in men's hands. Christine Stark makes this point clearly when she writes:

> Columbus and his men were the first known sex traffickers of the Americas, making the sex trafficking of Indigenous girls and women a central component of the colonization of the America (Stark 2019, p. 3).

Stark refers to the violence perpetrated on Native women as 'gynemutilation' (2019, p. 5), a word intended to reflect the extreme violence "against Indigenous women, other women of color, and prostituted and trafficked women" (2019, p. 5).

An echo of these concerns can be heard from Korea, where experiments have been carried out using women's eggs in a now discredited series of studies. Researcher Hwang Woo-suk claimed in February 2004 he had created the first human stem cell line.[67] Korean feminist Joo-hyun Cho (2005) has argued women's bodies are being used as a resource for Korea's economic development. In the move to produce customised stem cell lines, scientists require cell lines from countless women to make enough embryos for

---

66   Christine Stark writes about the historical trafficking in women by Christopher Columbus and others as an inherent part of colonising. She states that this practice continues with the ongoing massive disappearance of Native American women (Stark 2019).

67   On 23 December 2005 he resigned his professorial post at Seoul National University. *The Guardian* (2005).

their experiments. Furthermore, she argues, nationalism and science are entwined as a dual justification for the use of women as a resource. The so-called benefits to Indigenous and Traditional communities are rather like the so-called benefits to women of entering prostitution: apparent economic independence, but in both cases those groups must enter the worldview, the paradigm for the dominant culture and adhere to its rules. This is not freedom, but a new form of social abjection. They are being introduced as Trojan horses, promising much and delivering destruction.

A key example of the colonisation of the entire female body is surrogacy. In her book *Surrogacy: A Human Rights Violation* (2017) Renate Klein argues that surrogacy not only treats the woman as a dead object: a 'vessel', a 'suitcase', a 'gestational carrier', she also rightly points to the theft of the child from the birth mother. It is a replay of the Stolen Generations in which Aboriginal children were removed from their families, the forced adoptions of children from single mothers in the mid-20th century and the abduction of children in war (Arditti 1999; Çetin 2010; Atkinson 2002; Haebich 2000; Stark 2019). She asks how can surrogacy be any better when theft is inherent in the process of surrogacy? It violates the birth mother, the child and the egg donor so that heterosexual couples and gay men can buy children. Klein writes:

> It is the global advertising campaigns that groom infertile couples and gay men that have led to the establishment of multibillion cross-border industries: money made literally from women's flesh (Klein 2017, p. 65).

Kajsa Ekis Ekman in *Being and Being Bought: Prostitution, Surrogacy and the Split Self* (2013) points out how similar the sex industry and the surrogacy industries are in reducing the whole body of women to parts that are used by men.

The sex industry, as Gail Dines (2010), Julie Bindel (2017) and Janice Raymond (2013) point out, is an industry worth many billions of dollars. According to Havocscope, Global Black Market Information in 2018, it is worth at least $186 billion (Havocscope,

2018). Given the impossibility of gaining accurate figures, chances are that it is much higher. As noted in Chapter Three, it is the third biggest industry in the world after the military and drugs. How is it possible that there is not a total uproar about this? Just as grooming is part of the softening up process to make surrogacy acceptable in the mainstream, so too grooming of women starts at a young age with girls being groomed to see nothing unusual about sexual harassment, assault and rape (Tankard Reist 2009). While #MeToo is having some impact on how these violations are viewed, as the contributors to *Prostitution Narratives* (2016) and *Broken Bonds* (2019) show, grooming is an essential part of introducing mostly young women into both the sex and surrogacy industries.

Laura Gallagher in a review of Julie Bindel's book, *The Pimping of Prostitution*, states:

> The sex trade is rape culture ... It involves people (mostly men) having sex with other people (mostly women) who do not want to have sex with them. To legalise it is to sanction and normalise men desiring sex with women who do not desire them.
>
> Normalising, or indeed eroticising sex with people who don't want sex: that's rape culture" (Gallagher 2018).

It is hard to imagine why so-called progressives, who assert the priority of women's 'free choice' in western cultures steeped in the ideology and practice of rape, could argue that prostitution is empowering. Instead, women's bodies have become 'things' or commodities to be used.

Women's bodies are resources and major sites of colonisation and profit making. Like the land of Indigenous peoples under *terra nullius*, women's bodies are conceptualised as inert, passive, and empty, that is, ripe for exploitation and appropriation. In advertisements, it is not unusual to see fully clothed men and almost naked women. While the sexualisation of women in ads for cars and clothing is not unusual, they hardly rate against ads like Tom Ford's Menswear (Roper 2014). In these advertisements, the lives of women are assumed to revolve around men's sexual needs and constant readiness for sex. Women's lives are represented as empty, but in reality it is the emptiness of the vortex that is showing here.

Women's traditional knowledge and their collections of seeds — from that of Russian peasants to Bangladeshi farmers — are vulnerable to the demands of biocolonialism. In India and South Africa, traditional healers are being criminalised for their continuing use of healing methods that women have passed down through the generations (Hawthorne 2005a). In South Africa, the *muti* industry is a sector in which "80 per cent of the *muti* sellers in Durban and Johannesburg are women who collect plants within a five to ten km radius of their rural homes" (Rangan 2001, p. 19). There are moves to commercialise the industry through large-scale growing of plants, including endangered species. This, as Michael Dove argues, immediately removes the knowledge and the control from women's hands, and out of the hands of local men as well. A further issue of concern to Haripriya Rangan is that women *muti* collectors and sellers are threatened by their decreasing access to common lands. In a move that resembles the impact of the Enclosure Acts in Britain, in South Africa today "the rapid expansion of homesteads and fencing on common lands ... was the most urgent threat to rural women and their livelihoods" (Rangan 2001, p. 24). Just as the Enclosure Acts criminalised poor people in Britain, as Vandana Shiva points out in an article about the Covid-19 pandemic, "Indigenous systems of health care have been criminalised by colonisation and the pharmaceutical industry" (Shiva 2020). Furthermore, there is more than one kind of *muti*. The *muti* practised by 'big men' involves ritual child murder (see Dow 2002), whereas the *muti* industry described above concerns women's traditional practice. The conflation and resulting confusion means that women are being wrongly vilified and their practices made illegal.

The term *muti* is used in southern Africa (including South Africa, Namibia, Botswana, Zimbabwe, Mozambique, Swaziland, and Lesotho) for Indigenous medicinal plants. The benefits of the misrepresentation of *muti* are to bioprospectors and pharmaceutical companies. Parts of animals are also used in *muti*, and the ecological damage resulting from this also tends to get more media exposure. Certainly *muti* is complex, but it is critical that we separate out the strands and not be induced into supporting the demands of bioprospectors.

Bodies with disabilities

Research on the bodies of people with disabilities challenges disabled people's legitimacy as worthwhile human beings, calling attention to big science, raising questions such as the following: if a disability is genetically detectable, should the person bearing that disability be eliminated? Are people with disabilities made up only of their genes? If we were to agree that people are their genes, what of those people injured later in life or suffering from an illness such as motor neurone disease or multiple sclerosis that often appears later in life? Indigenous peoples have resisted being reduced to their genes; people with disabilities are also resisting. The delegitimisation of people with disabilities through a focus on genetics, as Jennifer Fitzgerald (1998) has argued, becomes a state of being that is punishable. The mainstream view — deeply saturated with eugenic ideology — is that to bring a child with a disability into the world is irresponsible. As Fiona Place discovered, liberal feminists will run that line (2019, pp. 293–294). Radical feminists and disability activists are among the few who see through ever-present eugenics (see Chapter Two).

Heterocolonialism

As attempts to biologise sexual orientation pick up pace, lesbians and gay men will be subjected to the same pressures as people with disabilities are now. Within a paradigmatic heterosexual discourse, as in a dominant ableness discourse, parents do not want their children to suffer physical, psychological, or social prejudice. Under the guise of 'choice', the reduction of people to their genetic make-up threatens all sorts of attempts to maximise social justice.[68]

In a move that benefited IVF clinics, in 2000 an IVF doctor mounted a federal court challenge to a Victorian State law that specifically excluded lesbians and single women from accessing IVF.

Renate Klein points out that:

> ... the media — gay and straight — were totally incapable of separating the issues of equal access, homophobia and the inherent dangers and manifold problems of reproductive technologies — especially in the wake of new stem cell research and cloning which has brought the IVF industry closer to their always intended long-term goal: the control of reproduction (2004, p. 3).

Lesbians themselves are being used by the technodocs to further the interests of biotechnology research and thus are being heterosexualised.

Now that the reproductive technology industry has access to the eggs of lesbians, even with all the safeguards in place, what experiments are being considered? Will they be used for research into whether there are certain biological differences, therefore bringing forward the 'knowledge' that could be used to eliminate lesbians? Or will lesbians become the fall guy for a new kind of

---

68 The odd thing that has occurred is that the genetic make-up is not targeted but the perceived gender make-up is and people diagnosed with gender dysphoria (correctly or otherwise) have been undergoing expensive and very dangerous surgery. Some of these are outlined in Nandini Krishnan's book, *Invisible Men* (2019, pp. 105–130). See also Brunskell-Evans (2020).

heterosexualisation of radical lesbian and feminist analysis? This is the 'I-want-just-the-same-as-the-oppressor' model: marriage, children, family — the normalisation project. For 'transmen' undergoing surgery, Nandini Krishnan (2019, p. 442 ff) finds this to be a regular trope in her interviews with 'transmen' across India. Heather Brunskell-Evans in *Transgender Body Politics* (2020, pp. 41–81) examines the ways in which young women are encouraged to transition and the responses of detransitioners who refute the politics of transgenderism.

Victoria Brownworth asks, "How do lesbians protect themselves from a society that would, given the option, practice genocide against them through genetic testing and eugenic abortion?" (1999, p. 150).

The other area of the biotechnology industry that has a profound effect on lesbians and gay men is the research into the 'gay gene'. The 'gay gene' has been used by (primarily) gay men and those who identify as queer as a political tool to indicate that same-sex attracted people should not be discriminated against or punished because 'they can't help themselves'. To me, this is a naïve and unhelpful political road to take, since it plays straight into the hands of the genetic engineers and venture capitalists who are only too happy to oblige in looking for a genetic cause for homosexuality. Assuming there is a gay gene, it raises the spectre of genetic elimination after testing of pregnant women or embryos, even if it is never shown to be a true or plausible explanation.[69] The 'heterosexualising' of lesbians or gay men is ultimately a social engineering project with heavy-handed political intentions.

---

69 In her incisive review of the literature, Lesley Rogers (1994) has concluded that the hypothesis that lesbian and homosexual behaviour is caused by hormones or genes is deeply flawed. See also Tauli-Corpuz (2001, p. 265).

Intergenerational sustainability and cultural integrity

In order to get out of this vicious cycle of failed technology followed by new business opportunity, followed by yet more failed technology, we need to begin to look at the world in other ways. Elsewhere I have argued that there is an alternative to the drive for profit at the cost of everything else. That alternative is based not on being inspired by money and profit but instead being inspired by biodiversity (Hawthorne 2002a). To be inspired by biodiversity and sensitivity to the cultural norms of those outside your own culture (without kowtowing to oppressive cultural practices) fosters the creation of knowledge systems and ecosocial systems that maximise the chances of planetary wellbeing.

Globalisation through appropriation and privatisation introduces new layers of criminalisation into our societies. The poor and the political have long been criminalised, and Australia has been built on that basis. Globalisation criminalises traditional health practitioners, who without a licence to practice their traditions are in conflict with transnational pharmaceutical companies. Just as people with disabilities were criminalised under Nazism, as Jennifer Fitzgerald notes (1998), those with genetic disabilities — and those women harbouring them by taking their pregnancies to term — will also be criminalised (Hawthorne 2005a; Place 2019).

Bioprospecting leads to biopiracy, which in turn leads to biocolonialism. The continuing appropriation and privatisation of the poor, especially of women's and Indigenous peoples' knowledge, is a major issue of concern for feminist activists in areas as diverse as law, agriculture, science, politics, and international trade. Here is where conflicts pertaining to globalisation and social integrity intersect; where the interests of the poor conflict with the interests of privatised profitmaking; and where it is so easy for the poorest and most powerless to be drawn into the empty vortex of promises made by representatives of the transnational corporate sector. It is not easy to say no to royalty programs, and I am not suggesting that the poor maintain their poverty for the political gratification of people in industrialised nations. But raising the issues of appropriation, of research ethics, and of long-term social justice may help keep the knowledge and the control of these resources in the hands of those who have developed, used and maintained it for so many millennia.

No feminist should be under the illusion that any forms of bioprospecting will benefit women by giving women more money. Rather, it is an aggressive instrument of corporate globalisers in the rush to make even greater profits. Instead of bioprospecting opening a door to economic sustainability, it closes the door on intergenerational sustainability and on cultural integrity. It is also a call for the destruction of autonomous women's cultures in which women determine treatments for ailments and illnesses. As Ama Ata Aidoo (1977) has said, scholarships are a very fine way of getting the colonised to spill the beans on their cultural knowledge, in this instance knowledge that will make billions of dollars in profits for transnational corporations. Do not be fooled by calls for freedom or calls for 'empowerment'. They are liberal rhetoric and will not deliver.

Biotechnology is a declaration of war against bodies — foremost among them women's bodies, but also the bodies of those who challenge the white, heterosexual, able-bodied mould. In 1989, Renate Klein noted that

> ... whatever loopholes in the legislation, the scientists will find them and use them. This is why no *regulatory* legislation will ever guarantee that the fiddling around with women's bodies will end. *Nothing less than legislation to stop IVF and to end the availability of embryos for genetic screening and 'therapy' experimentation will do* (Klein 1989, p. 285, italics in the original).

She restates this in the context of surrogacy.

> … regulations only wait to be scratched at the surface so that weak spots can be found and exploited. Welcome to a black surrogacy market enabled by regulation (2017 p. 97).

Biotechnology relies on philosophies of cultural relativism and sexual relativism (Moschetti 2006, p. 24). In the scientific context, relativism excuses violence against women and marginalised peoples on the grounds of utilitarian benefit to all of humanity, but it is never made clear that, as usual, the bodies of the powerless are used for the benefit of the powerful. The phrase 'all of humanity' is false because it does not include those whose bodies are used and abused for science and biotechnology.

Critiques of colonisation and globalisation, although resisted by the powerful, do meet with acceptance by many ordinary people. But a radical feminist critique of the biotech industry as an example of oppressive behaviour and policies, faces the same resistance as do critiques of prostitution and pornography. What they share is that it is women's bodies that are most at risk. It is women who are pressured to 'donate' on behalf of others. It is women who are asked to sell their bodies. This is not to downplay pressures on men who fall into the other groups I have mentioned in this chapter, but it is to say that in every group it is women who are most at risk. As with every other form of violence, it cannot be regulated: it must end.

In my experience, these issues are well understood among activist groups in South Asia and in some other places. In Australia, there has been considerable activism around copyright and moral right issues of Indigenous artists and discussion of biopiracy in Indigenous communities. Outside of this, including in feminist circles, the political understanding of how bioprospecting and biopiracy affect our lives, is limited. The links between Indigenous and Traditional peoples' intellectual property rights and those I have discussed here affecting women, lesbians, and people with disabilities have, to my knowledge, not been discussed anywhere. Challenging biopiracy provides an interesting starting point for further radical feminist theorising, connecting and synthesising economic, political, cultural, religious, and ethical issues.

Money

The money trail is clear in the areas discussed in this chapter. Profit is at the core of colonisation, of slavery — whether of women or colonised peoples, or those escaping war or some other person regarded as 'less than' — by the dominators. Biotechnology and reproductive technologies are systems of profit by the military industrial complex and the 'medical industrial complex' (Bilek 2020c): Big Pharma is another beneficiary, freely taking what is not theirs and reaping the profits without acknowledgement of where their profits come from. Vandana and Kartikey Shiva document the intersection of IT and Bt.[70] They write:

> Information technology and biotechnology are integrating in a new 'green' gold rush, with Bill Gates and Monsanto in the lead. IT is being used to 'mine' genetic data and claim patents on plants that neither Gates nor Monsanto created and about which they have no knowledge — they only have data (Shiva and Shiva 2018, p. 63).

This is theft.

The Bill Gates digital empire is not about communication but about patents.[71] He grew Microsoft by acquiring patents and he is now privatising knowledge that has been developed over millennia by enclosing it in patents. Biopiracy is the chosen method. When climate change seriously impacts the planet, Bill Gates, Monsanto (now Bayer) and others will own the climate resilient seeds that

---

70 Bt is a reference to Bt brinjal (aubergine or eggplant) which contains *Bacillus thuringiensis* (in North America, Bt cotton, Bt potato, Bt corn are grown commercially). These are genetically modified crops about which Vandana Shiva and others have been very critical.

71 For my critique on patents see Hawthorne 2002, pp. 314–322.

farmers have developed over millennia (Shiva and Shiva 2018, pp. 94–100).

What practices and laws can be implemented to prevent knowledge theft and biocolonialism?

- Recognise the sovereignty of Aboriginal and Torres Strait Islander Peoples and establish "a Makarata Commission to supervise a process of government-making between governments and First Nations and truth-telling about our history" (Uluru Statement from the Heart 2017). Similar treaties should be passed in all countries where Indigenous Peoples live.
- Implement Traditional Resource Rights (TRRs) and Community Intellectual Rights (CIRs) and enforce those who steal property governed by these agreements. It applies, but is not limited, to cultural research, creativity, development projects.
- Enable educational resources for groups identified here. That could include properly funded bilingual education especially in Indigenous communities; in Uganda Paul Wangoola (2000) proposed an Mpambo multiversity, the guiding principle of which is education being rooted in peoples' own knowledge bases; on the basis of this the re-establishment of radical Women's Studies and other disciplines as required.
- Abolition of biocolonialism and bioprospecting.
- The recognition that people have many needs and that both respect and responsibility lie at the base of a society in which people are treated with dignity and not used to manufacture profit.
- An end to experimenting on women's bodies for profiteering and the diminishment of women.

- An end to turning all people into *soma* and *somata* thereby alienating people from their bodies.
- An end to the propaganda around dysphoria and the idea that anyone can be 'born in the wrong body' (see Chapter Seven).

1980s

I live under plastic
between lines of trauma
my lungs fill with mud
grief corrodes my heart

He stalks me
hunts me like an animal
takes me in a place
where only the birds can hear me scream

Day after day the birds wait
and listen for my cries

—Susan Hawthorne,
The Butterfly Effect
(2005, p. 238)

CHAPTER FIVE

Deterritoriality and Breaking the Spirit: Land, Refugees and Trauma

Along with molecular colonisation there is colonisation on the macro scale: the dispossession of peoples through displacing them from their land, separating them from their culture and ruining their lives. While this is patently more obvious than what is occurring on the bodies of people, there are many ways in which the operations of dominance go unseen.

Valerie Kuletz describes deterritoriality as the ultimate in "separation between self and nature" (1998, p. 7). Implicit in the notion of separation is dividing the world from the person. There is the 'European' and the 'other'; there is 'man' and 'nature' (read as woman). Division and dislocation lend themselves to the systematic negation of 'the other' which is then redefined as having the sole purpose of serving the needs and desire of 'man' (European man). At the centre of this worldview is the logic of domination and disconnection "which is critical for a system based on profit"

(Hawthorne 2002a, p. xiii).[72] Vandana and Kartikey Shiva (2018) highlight this kind of separation and label it 'violence'. They go on to list three separations:

> ... the separation of humans from nature; the separation of humans from each other through divisions of class, religion, race and gender; and the separation of the Self from our integral interconnected being (Shiva and Shiva 2018, p. 16).[73]

Deterritoriality goes along with dissociation — a disengagement from feeling or from an immediate environment that causes distress. Susan Griffin's *Woman and Nature*, Book Two, is called 'Separation'. Griffin writes:

> The errant from the city. The ghetto. The ghetto of Jews. The ghetto of Moors. The quarter of prostitutes. The ghetto of blacks. The neighborhood of lesbians. The prison. The witch house. The underworld. The underground. The sewer. Space Divided (Griffin 1978, p. 96).

Robin Morgan writes, "If I had to name one quality as the genius of patriarchy, it would be ... the capacity for institutionalizing disconnection" (Morgan 1990, p. 51). Vandana Shiva states that "Compassion arises naturally, from connectedness and the consciousness of being interconnected" (Shiva and Shiva 2018, p. 3). These tropes of separation and connectedness appear over the decades in feminist writings. Banishment, exile and displacement feature in many critiques of capitalist patriarchy (Mies 1999; Said 1995; Hawthorne 2002a; Federici 2004, 2018; Salleh 2009).

Deterritoriality arises out of the insult of homogenisation and stereotyping of the sort that results in sentences like "They are all the same," where 'they' is any group considered other. From the ancient world, we can see it in words referring to foreigners. Greeks called foreigners 'barbarians', a xenophobic term that suggests

---

72 See also my essay on fundamentalism, violence and disconnection, Hawthorne 2002b.

73 On the separation of self in prostitution and surrogacy, see Ekman 2013.

those speaking another language sound as though they are saying bar-bar or perhaps baa-baa. There is a similar story in Sanskrit in which the Mleccha are people who sound as though they are gagging or vomiting when they speak.[74] As Betty McLellan argues in *Unspeakable: A Feminist Ethic of Speech* (2010), there are plenty of jokes about women's speech that don't need repeating which sink to the same low level.

Colonisation and deterritoriality go hand in hand and make it possible for the coloniser not to give a damn about the people he is dispossessing of land, language and culture. The imposition of sameness (homogeneity) is applied to everyone else (false universalism) and ignores location and local conditions (decontextualisation). These ideas have been structured into western approaches to economics and ecology; to land and natural resources; and to the bodies of the 'other'. Or as Nicole Brossard writes, "Making an effort to be normal, that's what it is to be colonized"(2020, p. 17). Cassandra Pybus notes the treatment of Tasmanian Aboriginal woman, Truganini by George Augustus Robinson. In an interview she says of Robinson that, "He understands he has to break that connection with country in order to break their spirit basically, in order to turn them into people that they are not" (Cassandra Pybus quoted in O'Brien 2020).

Within colonialist practice, assimilation is used as a weapon to separate colonised people from language, from history, from healing practices, from methods of farming and food preparation, all of which are linked to the maintenance of knowledge systems by the colonised. The same process is used against women: women are told they must fit into men's systems of work, speak men's language and service men sexually according to their wants. Such ideas have generated a liberal feminist ideology in which it becomes axiomatic that the more often women act, speak and have sex just

74 The Mlecchas are all peoples who do not speak Sanskrit. Ironically it includes Yavanas: Greeks; and Scythians: also known as Amazons (Mayor 2014).

like men, the better off women will be. Unsurprisingly, the media and other institutions of culture consider liberal feminists as the sole spokeswomen for feminism and radical feminists are silenced, ignored and erased.

Being homeless in the body

As noted in Chapter One, appropriation is a tool used against the oppressed and dispossessed as a means by which the powerful gain access to the hitherto 'private culture' of the colonised. Then that access is used to gain market advantage. The process of homogenisation by the powerful takes place through appropriation of the knowledge and practices of the colonised. The process involves the following sequence of events: separation, incorporation, commodification, distortion, homogenisation and de-differentiation.

Dispossession continues apace in the space of *terra nullius*, in the not-seen world of the other through the imposition of new knowledge systems, replacement of food stuffs and crops and introduction of animals and pests not native to the country. The people become homeless in their own lands, making it difficult to continue their ways of living. In the same way that the abused and traumatised woman is "homeless in her own body" (Mladjenovic cited in Copelan 1994, p. 202), separated from her self and her own needs. In her book *Paid For: My Journey through Prostitution*, Rachel Moran writes of homelessness that "… you are not invisible to people, but rather not worth looking at" (2013, p. 44).

> When a person is homeless, their sense of social significance is reduced to zero. It doesn't exist. Their sense of themselves is of being worthless and unwanted; a social pariah, an exile, an outsider whose very body is an unwanted intrusion they must carry with them wherever they go (Moran 2013, p. 40).

Jean Améry, a survivor of Auschwitz, in his book, *At the Mind's Limits*, writes about torture. Torture, he says, possesses an "indelible character", since "whoever was tortured, stays tortured" (Améry 1980, p, 34). As social animals, humans are socialised to believe others will assist them. The deliberate infliction of pain shatters that expectation, since, "whoever has succumbed to torture *can no longer feel at home* in the world" (Améry 1980, p. 40, my emphasis). He makes the connection between shame and torture. The destruction of the soul, of the self, creates shame. How many prostituted and raped women have kept silent because of shame? Kurdish-Iranian refugee Behrouz Boochani makes the point that starvation in prison "has two objectives: to implement a variety of control mechanisms on the minds of prisoners, and to make the prisoners enmeshed and complicit in the system" (2018, p. 209). To be complicit in one's own oppression is to feel shame.

Naomi Klein in *The Shock Doctrine* (2007) writes about the psychological process of 'depatterning' in order to turn the mind to a blank slate and to 'repattern' it later with new input. She documents experiments carried out during the 1950s at McGill University, Canada, on Gail Kastner. The experiments, funded by the CIA, went under the guise of treatment. They included electro-shock 'therapy' (ECT), large doses of insulin and a plethora of uppers and downers (Klein 2007, p. 30). In later chapters, Naomi Klein sets out how entire nations were given economic electro-shock: nations like Brazil, Indonesia and Chile were early economic experiments. Torture and neoliberal economic theory have worked hand-in-hand and recovery from both is long and arduous.[75]

Political exiles suffer from the trauma of displacement and the rebuilding that is necessary to create a new life in a new country. Judith Herman compares this process of rebuilding with what happens to battered women or survivors of childhood abuse.

> … the psychological experience can only be compared to immigration. They must build a new life within a radically different culture from the one they have left behind. Emerging

---

75 Other nations which were subjected to 'shock doctrine' include, but are not limited to: Argentina, Russia, Poland, China, Sri Lanka.

from an environment of total control, they feel simultaneously the wonder and uncertainty of freedom (Herman 2015, p. 197).

The Greeks called it *aidos*, Sappho knew its meaning. She said, it's when you want to speak but *aidos* stops you. Young black women the world over know its meaning, Aboriginal people call it shame job. I want to tell you what happened that day, she says to herself, but how to put it into words. How can I say it?

I know it too. The first day I spoke of my affliction, the falling sickness. Everything I knew was bad. Everything. Was my body the crime? The body, the body wrapped in culture lets so many down. I am reading the novel *An Atlas of Impossible Longing* (Roy 2011, p. 152–153). I open it and on the tenth line I encounter the word 'shame'. The character, Meera is ashamed of expressing her desire to eat everything once. Her desire for the beloved transformed into an appetite for food. Children too feel shame when caught out doing something forbidden. Shame is an emotion of the powerless because they cannot change the rules. Or, as Judith Herman writes, "Shame is a response to helplessness" (Herman 2015, p. 53).

Abigail Bray sums it up nicely in the first two sentences of *Misogyny Re-loaded*,

They made it clear from the start that the slightest deviation from the norm would be punished. They turned everything into prisons, even our own bodies (Bray 2013, p. 1).

If bodies can be turned into prisons, as Rachel Moran writes of prostitution (2013, p. 70), so too can the places where people live or have lived. Deterritorialised, depopulated and diminished in multiple ways.

There are other ways of thinking about shame. In the Ngarrindjeri culture of South Australia shame is connected to disrespect especially of elders.

Violating the respect system brings shame. In this way 'shame' reinforces the respect system. Shame is an aspect of your *miwi* [inner spirit] telling you things, letting you know what's right and wrong (Bell 2007, p. 2; different font used in texts for quotes from the Ngarrindjeri women telling their stories).

Shame here is caused by behaviour that is negative for the community. In our society, particularly for women, *shame is connected to who they are rather than what they have done*. More frequently, shame is connected to how men have violated them. The victim, not the perpetrator, is expected to feel shame. Dissociation, or what Kajsa Ekis Ekman calls 'the split self', is a common reaction among women who have been captured by patriarchy because of rape, prostitution or a level of oppression that infantilises them so they have no strong sense of self. That is they are rendered selfless.

Dispossession

Ownership of land, in the European tradition, has shifted from one of collective ownership (in pre-agricultural Europe) to one of royal ownership where the King owns the land and all that he can see is royal, real: real estate (Frye 1983, p. 155). It then shifts to private ownership by rich individuals of the aristocratic class and later the merchant classes. Silvia Federici argues that witch-hunting from the 15th to the 18th centuries specifically targeted women — especially older impoverished women. She writes, "… women were charged with witchcraft because the restructuring of rural Europe at the dawn of capitalism destroyed their means of livelihood and the basis of their social power" (2018, p. 25).

Federici goes on to argue that the rise of accusations of witchcraft in the 21st century parallel the same events 500 years ago. Structural Adjustment Programs and neoliberal economic restructuring are the catalyst for the new wave of witch-hunting (Federici 2018, pp. 60–86).[76] In the late 20th century the shift is to corporate

---

76   The term 'witch-hunting' is itself instructive and I am reminded of the epidemic of Corrective Rapes in South Africa also occurring in the same period. For more on this see Chapter Six.

ownership in which the transnational sector owns and controls large tracts of urban and rural land. Property as ownership[77] arises from 18th-century liberal views of property rights as preserving the liberty of the ruling classes. It is clear that the liberty of masculine and wealthy individuals is preserved under this regime; the system of power that supports corporate ownership has changed little. It holds sway in spite of challenges to property rights through the waves of anti-capitalist movements, Native Title and other claims. With a slogan reminiscent of feminist protest, the Wangan and Jagalingou's 'No means no' has formed the centre of their struggle against the Adani mine on the grounds that it encroaches on their sovereignty.[78] The imposition of the Queensland mine follows a history of dispossession, murder and incarceration of people within the community. In 2018, three books were published within a few months of one another detailing the dispossession (Beresford 2018, pp. 233–255; Ritter 2018, pp. vii–xii; Simpson 2018, p. 218–222). By August 2019, Adrian Burragubba had been bankrupted by Adani in his fight for Indigenous sovereignty instead of corporate vandalism. The Indian-owned Adani company want him to pay AUD$600,000 in legal costs (Bunch 2019). This is a fight against the Adani coal mine, and others, with plans to drain the Galilee Basin of its underground aquifers, destroy farmland and environmentally sensitive areas. Adani seeks to impose on Indigenous peoples a flawed system of Native Title that fails to recognise the rights of the Wangan and Jagalingou people.

In a similar vein, Federici has found that in Zambia the number of witchcraft accusations has risen "in areas earmarked for game

---

77 For a brief and incisive critique of western property laws versus traditional African approaches to 'property' and their impact on women see Majeke (2001).

78 The Adani Carmichael Mine in the Galilee Basin, western Queensland, is owned by Indian billionaire Gautam Adani. The Adani company's track record in India in business and environmental practices has been poor. Adani has been the focus of widespread protest in Australia, comparable to the protests against Canada's oil sands industry and in the US, the protests against the Dakota Access Pipeline (see Beresford 2019; Simpson 2019; Ritter 2019).

management, game ranching for tourism and for occupation by big landowners" (Federici 2018, p. 67).

The European ownership of the world began with colonisation where land was either claimed for the Crown (or the Pope) or declared 'unowned', 'empty' (the system of *terra nullius* in Australia and parts of Africa) and was thereby appropriated. Land was then put to use in ways deemed best for the European economy. As Ursula Rakova says, in a highly understated way, through the appropriation of land in Papua New Guinea, "We know that where land was forcefully passed away to companies, consequences have happened" (2000, p. 9).

The consequences of a worldview driven by the idea of land as possession can be seen throughout the world in a range of industrialised and disconnected uses of land and the people as the following examples demonstrate. Each shows how the concept of empty space, of deterritoriality, is based on that same emptiness that lies at the heart of the patriarchal vortex.

- *Plantations*: The development of plantations went hand in hand with the spread of slavery. This is emblematic of the way in which slavery functioned in ante-bellum America as described by Orlando Patterson (1982). And in Latin America and the Caribbean, the numbers of slaves traded is unknown. Eduardo Galeano notes that from the 16th to the 19th centuries in Brazil alone at least five to six million people arrived from Africa (Galeano 1973/1987, p. 80). Australia did not escape this blight: indeed, as slavery was winding down in other parts of the world, the Kanak people of Vanuatu were being captured and sold as slaves to the owners of cotton, and later, sugar plantations in Queensland (Bandler 1984; Bandler 1994, pp. 11–12). The establishment of plantations has created places for wildfire in Indonesia and Borneo, and across the Amazon Basin, West Africa and Australia.

- *The milling of timber on a grand scale*: Merv Wilkinson (Loomis 1995, p. 9) provides figures for the forestry industry in British Columbia, Canada.

The Department of Forestry claims that in 1988 the forests grew 74 million board feet during the year. The cut during that year was 90 million. I have heard that the more correct figure is 108 million. Is there any worse 'deficit financing' than that?

Levels of deforestation globally are causing enormous long-term destruction to biodiverse regions of the world. In Brazil, it is estimated that during the 1980s, the number of hectares deforested ranged from 1,013,000 to 3,000,000 (see Kolk 1996, p. 68, Table 2.2). In 2019, in the Brazilian Amazon, 976,200 square hectares were deforested; this was an increase of 30% over the previous year (Butler 2019). In the years 2015-2016, the Australian state of Queensland was rated alongside Borneo and the Congo Basin as one of the worst places for deforestation in the world. In Queensland, bulldozers were "mowing down trees twice as fast as Brazil" (*The Economist* 2018). Brazil, where far-right President Jair Bolsonaro is currently in power, is seeing vast areas of the Amazon on fire following intense logging, and extensive clearing for sugar and cattle farming and other kinds of industrial plunder (BBC 2019).[79] In 2019, almost a million hectares of land is estimated to have been lost in the fires across the Amazon Basin. Most of these have occurred in Brazil, but Peru, Bolivia and Paraguay are also affected. At the time of writing, March 2020, under the right-wing Morrison government, Australia is faced with destructive fires across the nation resulting in the burning of an estimated 18.6 million hectares (see Chapter Eight).[80]

---

79 In a speech to the UN in September 2019 and in a move that resembles the rhetoric of Trump, Bolsonaro labelled critics as speaking "in a disrespectful manner and with a colonialist spirit" (BBC 2019).

80 This is a constantly changing figure and as of 4 March 2020 this summary is from Wikipedia: 18.6 million hectares (46 million acres; 186,000 square km; 72,000 square miles), destroyed over 5,900 buildings (including 2,779 homes) and killed

- *The mining of gold and diamonds*: Examples include the use of Black workers in gold mines under Apartheid in South Africa (Richardson and Van-Helten 1982); the war in Angola has been fuelled by diamonds (Global Witness Report 1998); the use of children as slaves in mines in Niger (Jennings 1999). In 2018, Human Rights Watch published a report on compliance by major jewellery retailers and concluded that not one company could be classed as fulfilling all the requirements for a responsible supply chain. Instead, they found many cases of poor children working in unsafe and badly paid conditions (Human Rights Watch 2018).

- *The mining of phosphates*: Nauru, once the "richest nation per capita in the world" (Niesche 2001, p. 28), is a small island nation in the Pacific Ocean (area 20 square kilometres; population in 2018, 11,000) whose entire ecosystem has been destroyed by the mining of phosphates by the British Phosphate Commission for farmers in Australia and elsewhere in the western world. Nauru is now paying the price with a barren landscape that resembles a war zone and extreme poverty due to the single-minded profiteering from exporting phosphates. Australian farms are also paying a price with increased soil acidity and inland waterways with blue-green algae blooms (Vanclay and Lawrence 1996). In 2001, Nauru — for a price — entered the market for 'processing refugees' for the Australian government. Refugees are being commodified, and used to earn desperately needed foreign currency for a bankrupt Nauruan government. In the case of Nauru, the phrase 'homeless' applies doubly: no refugees can ever settle on Nauru and the Australian government has declared that no person arriving by boat, claiming asylum and detained on Nauru will ever be settled in Australia. This in spite of the fact that the vast majority of refugees on Nauru and Manus Island in Papua New Guinea who have been assessed

---

at least 34 people. An estimated one billion animals have been killed and some endangered species may be driven to extinction. See Chapter Eight.

have been found to be genuine refugees and have a genuine fear of persecution. These refugees are homeless and have now been rendered stateless by Australian government policy (Doherty 2016; Green and Dao 2017; see also Boochani 2018).

- *The mining of copper*: The BHP-owned mine at Ok Tedi in Papua New Guinea has been the subject of protest and lawsuits due to its ecological destruction of the Fly River. Wep Kanawi, the PNG Country Director of Nature Conservancy said that it has "destroyed over 1000 square kilometres of wetland and virgin forest" (Green 2000, p. 13), and that the destruction of "all life in the river, and all the arable land close to the river [has affected] … about 100,000 people" (Green 2000, p. 13). Because Europeans divided West Papua and Papua New Guinea down the middle in 1828, the Dani people, who live in West Papua just across the border from the Ok Tedi mine, are governed from Jakarta, some 3500 kilometres away. This inappropriate border separates them, and their kin in Papua New Guinea. This is yet another way of displacing people through colonisation. The area, largely inaccessible, is regarded by the Indonesian government as a new 'uninhabited' area, a new *terra nullius* for the taking by corporations (Gilberthorpe 2017). A new site of patriarchal vortex. In 2001, BHP Billiton announced that the mine would close. The devastation of the Fly River ecology has been enormous, but the mine contributes 11% to PNG's gross domestic product. By 2013, this was insufficient and the PNG government took over the mine. In terms of sustainability, this may not benefit the local people any more than the previous mine operation.

- *The building of factories where dangerous substances are manu-factured*: The 1984 gas spill at Bhopal, India, resulted in the poisoning of at least 10,000 people living around the pesticide plant (Butalia 2002, p. 53–55). Owned by US company Union Carbide, the spill brought to the attention of the public the systematic manufacture of toxic substances in poor countries and the dangers it poses to poor people (See Reich 1991, pp. 98–139). But the lives of poor people around the world are never seen to be as important as the lives of the well-off (Butalia 2002, p. 53). The same can be said of violence against women. Terana Burke in an interview with ABC Radio National noted that in reporting #MeToo, the media has picked up on 'white Hollywood actresses' rather than the numerous black women raped and abused (ABC Radio National 15 November 2019).

- *The creation of wastelands through dumping of wastes*: The people of Saipan Island in the Northern Marianas protested locating military installations in their forest where there are birds "that you only find on Saipan and Rota" (Chailang Palacios cited by dé Ishtar 1994, p. 92). In Hawai'i, the local people complain about the intensity of military activity including "nuclear waste from submarine reactors in Pearl Harbor, which was once a very rich fishing area" (dé Ishtar 1994, p. 113).

- *The imposition of military sites in which sacred landforms are blown up and the ecology polluted*: The Kanaka Maoli, the people of Hawai'i, have protested the establishment of Kaneohe Marine Corps Base on the "sacred peninsula of Mokapu where, we believe, the first Kanaka Maoli was created" (dé Ishtar 1998, p. 10). This is akin to locating a military base in the Vatican.

- *Military sites making people targets for the wars of others*: In August 2017, Guam found itself in the line of fire for nuclear annihilation by North Korea after President Donald Trump said he would react with "fire and fury" if North Korea threatened the USA. Most telling was a statement by the Governor of Guam, Eddie Calvo, that "Guam is American soil ... We are not just a military installation" (cited in McCurry 2017). The erasure of the Chamorro people's history is separated by almost 13,000 kilometres from Washington DC.[81]

- *The mining of cobalt and lithium to power batteries for renewable electricity*: The war-torn Democratic Republic of Congo is

---

81 This list could be endlessly expanded from places around the globe. This is just the tip of the iceberg.

where most of the world's cobalt deposits are found. Lithium carbonate is mined near the borders of Bolivia, Chile and Argentina, one of the driest places on the planet. Enormous amounts of water are required and leakage into watercourses is polluting what water streams there are (Cox 2020, p. 68). The flourishing of renewable energy sources should not be at the expense of people in Africa, Latin America or Australia.[82]

Deterritoriality allows increasingly large tracts of land to be sacrificed in order to maintain the global system of power. Not surprisingly, many of the areas chosen for sacrifice are lands that have been lived on by Indigenous peoples for millennia. As these lands do not represent a sovereign nation under the terms of western definition, they are vulnerable, in a legal sense, to misappropriation. Comparable to *terra nullius*, and as Valerie Kuletz points out, representative of the play of nuclear politics, it is native lands that are most likely to be subjected to deterritoriality. Valerie Kuletz is writing of the American southwest, but in Australia, in the Pacific Island nations, in the vast stretches of Siberia, the same process is at work. These are lands intimately woven in with the lives of Indigenous peoples, known to their inhabitants in the way in which some people know their own bodies. They have been used to test nuclear weapons, to develop military strategies for war, and now they are slated for nuclear waste dumps.

In 1998 and 1999, an international corporation, Pangea, proposed an area of the Pilbara in Western Australia as a suitable site for nuclear waste. Because of lobbying by anti-nuclear groups, the proposal failed, but it is worth looking at the level of contempt Pangea displayed in even making the proposal.[83] This is one of a series of violations against Indigenous communities in Australia, from nuclear testing on Maralinga lands in the 1950s and 1960s to

---

82   See Klein (2007, p. 85) on the aftermath of economic shock in Chile and how public ownership of the copper mine, Codelco which was nationalised by Salvadore Allende, helped to save Chile from collapse.

83   It was a joint venture by British, Canadian and Swiss companies.

mining of Mirrar land at Jabiluka in the Northern Territory, and a number of sites in the Western Desert and Pilbara regions. The traditional owners of the Pilbara include

> ... a number of Aboriginal communities, among them Jigalong, Pangurr and Cotton Creek. This region is the traditional homeland of the Martu (Western Desert) people, and there are still significant numbers of people living in this area ... further south [are] the Bidjandjadjara people, who were very angry when Pangea flew a media crew onto their reserve without first seeking a permit (ANAWA, 2001).

In a later discussion of proposals by the (now defunct) Pangea company to bring nuclear waste to Australia, John Veevers was disparaging of the idea because of the dangers to the environment and public health. Writing in *Australian Geologist* he stated:

> Tonnes of enormously dangerous radioactive waste in the northern hemisphere, 20,000 kms from its destined dump in Australia where it must remain intact for at least 10,000 years. These magnitudes — of tonnage, lethality, distance of transport, and time — entail great inherent risk (Veevers 1999; Green 2015).

In 2019, a proposed nuclear waste dump was slated for several communities in South Australia. Both the Barngarla Determination Aboriginal Corporation on the Eyre Peninsula and the Adnyamathanha, traditional owners in the Flinders Ranges area, opposed the dump. The former lost a federal court case (now being appealed). Calla Wahlquist (2019), writing in *The Guardian*, highlights the restrictions on access to information about the dump by the people whose communities are close by.

While displacement has happened in past eras, sometimes on a large scale, the period from 1900 to 2020 has seen many more people displaced, killed in wars and turned into refugees than ever before. The UNHCR reports that in 2020 there are 70.8 million people forcibly displaced in the world today (UNHCR 2020). Vandana Shiva writes of the "freedoms that the 1% have created for themselves" while simultaneously enforcing their patriarchal ideologies and economies on the dispossessed. Those same 1% are "disconnected from the earth and humanity (including their own), and are trying to control every sphere of our lives" (Shiva and Shiva 2018, p. 2).

Over several decades I have asked myself whether there was a time when the people of this earth behaved differently. I think there was and I think the lessons we can learn come from Indigenous peoples of the present time and from prehistory, that far away time we are slowly increasing our knowledge about.[84]

Land as relationship

What is the counter argument to deterritorialisation? How can we prevent being made homeless in our own land and separated from the land, the food and medicines, the culture, the language that are all a part of one's being and a community's history?

Judy Atkinson, of Jiman and Bundjalung descent, puts it this way, "This land now called Australia was no wilderness" (2002, p. 27).

Marcia Langton, descendant of Yiman and Bidjara nations, argues that wilderness disrupts the "relationships with species and ecologies" (Langton 1998, p. 18). Max Oelschlaeger noticed that when the concept of wilderness does not exist because the place one lives in is home, then there is no possibility of being lost or becoming homeless (1991). Pueblo Laguna poet and activist, Paula Gunn Allen writes,

> Wilderness is not an extension of human need or of human justification. It is itself and it is inviolate, itself. This does not mean that, therefore, we become separated from it, because we don't. We stay connected if, once in our lives, we learn exactly what that connection is between our heart, our womb,

---

84   There are many publications on this subject. See for example Sjöö and Mor, 1987; Gimbutas 1989; Foster 2013; Beavis and Hwang eds. 2018.

our mind, and wilderness. And when each of us has her wilderness within her, we can be together in a balanced kind of way (Allen 1998, p. 61).

Haunani-Kay Trask, a descendant of the Piʻilani line of Maui and the Kahakumakaliua line of Kauaʻi in Hawaiʻi, connects the ways in which industrialists and those fighting for wilderness approach nature.

> Even the ecological/wilderness approach remains within the view of nature as a resource for humans. The only difference between this view and the industrialists' view is that the former fights for and preserves wilderness areas. Philosophically, however, the Earth is still seen as a resource (1986, p. 183).

Kim Mahood (2016), writing of resilience in the face of dispossession and about the theft of country asks,

> … how do you steal embodied knowledge? How do you steal the webs and tracks of Dreaming that tie the place to people, to culture to story? You can't roll up a piece of country like a carpet and make off with it in the middle of the night. You can move your stock over it, you can fence it in, you can steal the livelihood of a people, but you can't steal the memories and the family histories and the conception sites that connect people to their country. These things persist wherever the people themselves persist (2016, p. 121).

Wilderness environmentalists, such as Deep Ecologists, separate the wilderness from humanity, removing it from all contact with human existence, and this is emblematic of how non-human players in the world are separated out from humanity. The concept of wilderness is a construct of the western imagination.

Separating out 'wild lands', making them free of human endeavour, is suggested as a solution by some environmentalists. Anthropocentrism in the construction of nature is only part of the problem. Not only does anthropocentrism require separating humanity out from the biophysical world and creating a hierarchy where human beings are at the pinnacle, it also allows deep ecology thinkers to remove people altogether thereby ignoring the relationship between people and the land which has persisted for many thousands of years before people separated from the land and nature, and began destroying it. It is yet another way of dispossessing the people who lived on that land before it was colonised (by internal or external forces). Separation and disconnection are the processes that allowed anthropocentrism, and the domination of nature by humanity, to flourish as conquering philosophies. Indigenous peoples are resisting this ideology of separating human from the land, the land from the human. Indeed, they say that both land and people grow one another (Atkinson 2002, p. 29).

On 24 May 2020, the mining giant Rio Tinto blew up part of the Juukun Gorge, WA the location of 46,000-year-old artefacts belonging to the Puutu Kunti Kurrama and Pinikura people. It was blown up with West Australian government seal of approval and followed the finding of artefacts that are at least 46,000 years old. A comparable destruction, but nowhere near as old, are the Bamiyan statues in Afghanistan blown up by the Taliban in 2001 or the Temple of Baalshamin in Palmyra destroyed by Daesh in 2015. This erasure of peoples' history is carried out by fundamentalists — whether they be market fundamentalists (Rio Tinto) or religiously inspired fundamentalists (Taliban and Daesh).

In South Australia, the Ngarrindjeri have much to teach us about the ways in which the land and the body are connected. They speak of *ruwe* 'country' or 'land' and *ruwa* 'body' (Bell 1998/2014, p. 263). It is more than just a linguistic connection. Damage to the land can be experienced in the bodies of the people as Eileen McHughes, Isobelle Norvill, Sarah Milera explain in their reactions to the building of the Hindmarsh Island Bridge (Bell 1998/2014, pp. 266–268). The connection also goes the other way. As Deborah Bird Rose writes, "Country expects its people to maintain its integrity (Bird Rose 2000, p. 109). It is a reciprocal relationship and the reciprocity comes with responsibilities on the part of people to not damage Country.

Land as relationship in prehistory

Prehistory gives us many examples of people's attachment to land. Deciphered written sources do not exist, but many clues are to be had in the passing down of mythic stories, in the survival of artefacts and buildings from these periods. To give full expression to this would require another book. The work of archaeologist Marija Gimbutas and of pre-historian Harald Hartmann show the many ways in which the remnants of pre-historic cultures (that is, cultures who existed before writing) were deeply connected to the land, to their home in the land. Lynne Kelly's (2015) work on systems of mnemonics transmitted orally and Judy Foster's (2013) examinations of prehistoric artworks give these ideas a global scope. The work of Gimbutas is based in Europe from the Balkans to Lithuania, while Hartmann's focus is the Danube Valley. Traces of these appear in ancient societies in Mesopotamia; in the Indus Valley of India; in Egypt and other parts of Africa; in stories and artefacts from Minoan Crete and from the Etruscans; in Ireland and across the Celtic lands including Scotland and Brittany. What these societies show us is that fortifications did not exist or were very rare.[85] The likely reason for this is that warfare was rare. Until approximately 6000 years BP (Before Present), patriarchy too, was rare. I do not refer to these societies as matriarchal, because the assumption is that matriarchies are violent reversals of patriarchy. There is plenty of evidence to the contrary. Rather I refer to them as *gynocentric*. The rhythms of the seasons, the rhythms of the body work in conjunction with one another. I am sure there was conflict in gynocentric societies, but as there is no evidence of mass slaughter and deterritorialisation, we can infer from this lack, that the conflicts that arose were dealt with in other ways.

---

85 The anthology *Goddesses in Myth, History and Culture* edited by Mary Ann Beavs and Helen Hye-Sook Hwang (2018) is international in scope and includes essays that cover Korea and Old Europe, the Middle East, North and West Africa, Scandinavia and as well as Indigenous, Asian and Abrahamic religions.

I have been reading the literature in this field for around 40 years, so this is not a quickly drawn inference. Each year, there is new research, new findings that suggest that patriarchy is neither inevitable nor universal. Indeed, the words of contemporary Indigenous peoples resonate with the materials being discovered around the world. The dates of human migration around the world continue to be pushed back. But migration tens of thousands of years ago was not what we know of as colonisation. It was instead movements of people from one place to another because of changes in local conditions such as climate or availability of food or environmental disasters such as earthquakes.

Movement was slow and as peoples moved across the earth, they took with them knowledge of plants and animals, of the formations of stars, of the cycles of the moon and followed the ways in which these events changed or remained the same. The migration to Australia was a significant one because it involved an intentional trip of at least four to five days across deep waters. Upon arrival, many of the elements in the environment would have been quite different. The most recent date that is firmly established is 65,000 years, but it is likely to be earlier and Indigenous peoples often refer to 120,000 years BP.

The other migration that is remarkable in its success is that of Polynesian sailors whose navigational skills were well ahead of those of later European 'explorers' (Andrews 2004, pp. 253–290). In both these cases, the migrating people were moving into areas that had not been previously inhabited by humans. Of course, their arrival had an impact on the environment; every change is accompanied by further change. But from what we know, it was not disastrous change (and I disagree with Tim Flannery's thesis in *The Future Eaters* [1994] that the demise of Australia's megafauna was caused by Aboriginal hunters).[86]

---

86 Part of my disagreement is that the amount of meat in the diet of Aboriginal people would have needed to be huge; it is too unlikely a scenario for me to accept.

Trauma

As I argue in Chapter Three, the ways in which the military and the sex industry both recruit (mostly) young men and young women, respectively, are very similar to the ideology and practice of militarisation. In the chart that follows, one can readily see the ways in which the trauma of torture, of systematic rape in war and the trauma of colonisation — usually an undeclared war — operate in very similar ways.

Judy Atkinson, in her book *Trauma Trails, Recreating Song Lines*, writes of the results of her research on violence in Central Queensland between 1993 and 1998:

> The region has a violent history that is well documented. The coastal area where the study took place is located at the periphery of a semi-circle, the centre of which is the site of a series of massacres that occurred from the mid-19th century into the beginning of the twentieth century. There were large-scale dislocations of Aboriginal nations from their homelands both before and after that time. Consequently Aboriginal people subjected to these massacres and displacements moved and were moved across the country away from the milieu of the destruction, thus creating trauma trails running across country from the locations of the pain and disorder they experienced. Government reserves such as Woorabinda were created as places of forced removal to contain people who were traumatised outcasts in their own country. Within this region there are also two orphanages where children who had been removed from their families or who had been orphaned were placed. A prison presently run by Queensland Corrections is located several kilometres outside the major town in the region (Atkinson 2002, pp. 9–10).

Here we have it again *"people who were traumatised outcasts in their own country"*, made to feel a sense of homelessness inside their own country. This is very like the experience of women who were raped in Serbia during the war (1991–1995) as described by Lepa

Mladjenovic as "homeless in their own body" (Mladjenovic cited in Copelan 1994, p. 202). Judy Atkinson continues:

> In spite of the fact that colonisers have disregarded the rights of Indigenous peoples, and have used force to dominate, intimidate, subdue, violate, injure, destroy and kill, they do not consider their actions, either morally or under their law, to be violence. On the other hand, they have defined many of the functions of Indigenous disputing processes as violence, while at the same time categorising much contemporary Aboriginal interpersonal violence, which Aboriginal people themselves have spoken of as unacceptable behaviour transgressing the cultural mores of our societies, as customary practice (Atkinson 2002, pp. 11–12).

What is trauma? Trauma is the result of extreme distress, caused by violence, controlling behaviour, various kinds of dispossession including breaking ethical codes. It often exceeds the ability of a person to cope.

> Waves radiate across the surface of the pond from the point of contact, and under certain conditions there is some discernible impact along the shore of the pond. Trauma — the point of penetration — and its wake — the psychosocial repercussions — are normal reactions to extraordinary circumstances (Figley 1986, p. xvii, cited in Atkinson 2002, pp. 23–24).

Jeanne Sarson and Linda MacDonald (2019), commenting on their Canadian study into non-state torture, problematise the way in which trauma affects the notion of 'Self' for women who have undergone extreme violence in their homes or in intimate relationships. They write that Self, "… is comparable to having and owning a name. It works at answering the question, 'Who am I'?" (2019, p. 108).

And in the documentation of torture she experienced in Chile under the Pinochet regime, Consuelo Rivera-Fuentes ends her testimony with

I have broken my silence ... I have finally given voice to pain ... but in my terms ... By the way ... did I tell you that my name means consolation? I am Consuelo ... I am Consuelo ... am I? (Rivera-Fuentes and Birke 2001, p. 657; italics in the original).

Torture[87]	Trauma	Colonisation
Infliction of mental or physical pain through punishment of the body and the mind. The word torture here includes rape.	Pain inflicted on a person physically, mentally, psychically resulting in loss of Self, dignity, self-determination and control over her own body.	Infliction of pain through murder, stealing of land and distortion of meaning. Loss of family connections. Loss of children.
Clear message about who holds the power and includes acts of dominance, rage and violence (Seifert 1992, p. 55).	The result of injustice, unfairness and punishment that is not commensurate with the actions.	Unduly harsh methods of punishment make it clear who holds the power. In Australia, the number of Aboriginal people massacred is considerably more than the number of white settler invaders (Ryan, Colonial Frontier Massacres, Australia).[88]
Turning whatever the tortured person knows against her/himself. It is an attack on the Self.	The result of name calling, insults, hate speech, demeaning actions and violence which results in dissociation.	Criminalising the speaking of the mother tongue and using everything against the colonised person and her/his community.
Breaking the will and the spirit of the person tortured including the destruction of a person's culture and sense of Self.	The result of being broken. This can happen in childhood, in institutions, families and prisons. Schools can exacerbate this by erasing knowledge, culture and language.	Breaking the spirit of a people through dispossession and destruction of knowledge systems, culture and language. Destroying cultural meaning.

---

87   The column on torture is adapted from David Luban's seven specific evils of torture (2018).

88   Colonial Frontier Massacres, Australia (Date Range: 1780–1930) <https://c21ch. newcastle.edu.au/colonialmassacres/map.php>

Torture[87]	Trauma	Colonisation
Complete subordination and humiliation of the tortured person.	The result of subordination and humiliation.	Complete subordination of an entire people and humiliation that results in some people wanting to pass as members of the colonising group.
The tortured person is worn down by repeated violations and producing a sense of worthlessness.	The result of persistent and continuous expressions of hatred or diminishment of a person.	The colonised people are worn down by repeated violations against them and minimisation of their own worth.
The torturer becomes sovereign and has complete control over every intimate feeling and emotion.	The individual feels that s/he has no free will and that all actions and needs are determined by those with the power, whether an individual or some other entity. Loss of cultural and bodily sovereignty.	The coloniser imposes their sovereignty and has complete control over even small acts carried out by the colonised (e.g. methods of greeting or relationship designations).
The tortured person feels 'homeless in her own body'.	A sense of not belonging, alienation and isolation pervades the psyche of the traumatised person.	The colonised person feels homeless in her/his own land.

Torture is an experience no one wants to suffer, and the colonised — who understand the political ramifications — also express anger at past and present events. When a woman is raped by an enemy soldier or civilian, forced to carry a child to term and coerced into bringing the child up as a citizen of the enemy culture, the impact on the woman is not simply one act of rape, but a lifelong trauma that can be carried over to future generations. As Judy Atkinson writes:

> The layered trauma that results from colonisation is likely to be expressed in dysfunctional, and sometimes violent, behaviour at both individual and large-scale levels of human interaction, and these are re-traumatising (2002, p. 24).

A group who might experience multiple dimensions of trauma about which I am speaking are refugees and people who live in exile because to return 'home' is too dangerous. Refugees do not leave their homelands because they want a holiday abroad; they leave because they fear for their lives or threats to the lives of others in their families or circles. Some refugees have escaped from wars, from the burning and bombing of their houses and communities; some have seen relatives maimed, tortured or murdered; some have been threatened with violence and torture; some have survived and escaped from torture; some have left because 'peace' became too dangerous (Simiç 2014). In order to escape, many refugees have to travel over land, through forests, high mountains, cross freezing cold rivers, travel by boat across an ocean at the risk of their lives. Only a few are able to buy a plane ticket.

Refusing refugees

The history of colonised Australia is rife with tensions between peoples. Convicts were sent to Australia so England could be rid of poor people and political agitators, and it was this that began the process of dispossession of Indigenous peoples across the continent. The wars that decimated Aboriginal communities have been revealed in recent years (Dovey 2017; Pybus 2020; Ryan *et al.* 2018; Bradley 2020), but there remains a significant political class of people who refuse to acknowledge these wars. When the British Navy invaded and colonised Australia, according to the Australian Museum there were at least 700 languages in Australia (Australian Museum 2018). This number is now severely reduced to around 250 languages and a number of languages have only one fluent speaker alive. The elimination of languages is one clear result of warfare. The expected life span of Indigenous peoples and the mortality rate of infants are higher than that of non-Indigenous Australians. While more Aboriginal teenagers are completing school and some going on to university, we must beware Ama Ata Aidoo's warning about PhDs and Doris Lessing's 1971 Preface to *The Golden Notebook* about education:

Ideally, what should be said to every child, repeatedly, throughout his or her school life is something like this:

"You are in the process of being indoctrinated. We have not yet evolved a system of education that is not a system of indoctrination. We are sorry, but it is the best we can do. What you are being taught here is an amalgam of current prejudice and the choices of this particular culture. The slightest look at history will show how impermanent these must be. You are being taught by people who have been able to accommodate themselves to a regime of thought laid down by their predecessors. It is a self-perpetuating system. Those of you who are more robust and individual than others will be encouraged to leave and find ways of educating yourself — educating your own judgement. Those that stay must remember, always, and all the time, that they are being moulded and patterned to fit into the narrow and particular needs of this particular society" (Lessing 1973, p. 17).

Aboriginal people in Australia have suffered generations of trauma. The earliest generations suffered massacre; some saw children mutilated and violated; some were captured and taken to work on the colonisers' farms; some were given inducements to live close enough so that when pastoralists (invaders) needed more workers they were brought in, paid a pittance and often their wages secreted away in a bank account they would never see; women were captured, raped and taken 'into service' by single men; some became guides to the colonisers and in return suffered decimation. Any of these are enough to cause a person a high level of trauma. The conditions of trauma continue through the justice system. Charmaine Weldon in an interview with Anna Kerr 'Escaping Family Violence' says:

I am concerned that, increasingly, Aboriginal women who are victims of domestic violence are being identified as perpetrators when they defend themselves or respond to a long-term pattern of abuse. Aboriginal women are increasingly being arrested and incarcerated which can result in the loss of their children and perpetuate intergenerational trauma. This has to stop. Domestic and family violence legislation should be for the protection of women and not weaponised against them (Weldon 2020, p. 20).

In recent generations, the theft of children has been institutionalised and carried out in many different ways. A young woman — a former student of mine — was taken by authorities because as they said 'she could pass as white'. But she lost her family and the years of loss can never be regained. Her mother lost a child and was worried sick about what would be done to her.

Trauma, after trauma, after trauma: Aboriginal people from across many generations became refugees in their own country. The Australian government, in our name and in their name, is carrying out a new series of violations against refugees seeking asylum in Australia.

The similarity can be seen in the first-person stories told by people from both groups. Mary tells Judy Atkinson this about her childhood:

> I never used to have memories of myself as a child, well before I was about eight or nine. I didn't have memories except of a feeling of being frightened — no terrified — yeah, terrified is a better word. I was frightened of everything. Something happened around eight or nine that I do remember, all of it, every bit of it, almost frozen. It's as clear today as if it just happened yesterday … I've been trying to work this out in my head. I got raped. It wasn't sexual abuse, or molestation, it was rape (cited in Atkinson 2002, p. 99, p. 101).

Jamila Jafari, a Hazara refugee from Afghanistan, was five when she and her family arrived in Australia. She too remembers, while in the Woomera Detention Centre, a day of being frozen. Though the circumstances are different from Mary's, the resulting trauma is similar.

> I was skipping about and I noticed these vehicles on the other side of the fence. Like, rows of vehicles. I've stopped because

I am curious to see what's going on. The car doors open and I see these people dressed in black: black shoes, black pants, black shirt, black hat. They step out, they're staunch, and their figures are really dominating. I remember being so intimidated. I was doing nothing wrong, I was just skipping about. It was … crippling. I don't really know how to put it into words, but their presence was so scary that it made me want to crawl up into a ball. They stared me down and I burst into tears. I was frozen. I couldn't move. I didn't know what was going on! This image, it's always been in my mind, ever since that encounter (Green and Dao 2017, p. 70).

Meera Atkinson (2018), writing about the long-term effect of trauma caused by violence against women in the home notes, "All I have is a patchwork of random recollections without their broader context" (p. 50).

Margaret Bennett and Jennifer Maiden (2019) talk about ways of working through experiences of torture and trauma, including with a group of women refugees from Chile with whom they ran writing workshops. Their method begins with the ordinary lives the women lived prior to their imprisonment and torture only gradually progressing to writing.

Trauma is part and parcel of the system of power in patriarchy. It comes about because of war, colonisation, abject dispossession (of self or homeland or language), violence against the body and mind, exposure to extremely violent acts. It is as though the DNA of patriarchy consists of trauma. Even some of the powerful experience it, but those in poverty and those at the margins of society feel its most profound and prolonged effects.

Money

The wealth of the western world is built upon theft from the colonised world. Colonising nations massacred millions of people, they raped women, ravaged land, dug up and stole resources from the land; they stole valuable cultural artefacts including jewellery and precious stones and metals. These processes continue.

As mentioned earlier, Christine Stark, in her research on the trafficking of Native women in the USA concludes that Christopher Columbus made the rape, trafficking and sexual abuse of women and girls central to the colonising of the Americas. In Tasmania, Indigenous women were routinely captured by sealers and ex-convicts (Pybus 2020). Vandana Shiva compares Columbus to Bill Gates and says that he is the "modern day Columbus" (Shiva and Shiva 2018, p. 80). The colonising project has moved into the immaterial realm, but is no less real for that and its impact is just as traumatic and violating of those who are dispossessed.

It is impossible to estimate the riches stolen through colonisation over 500 years. Consider the following:

Beginning with the East India Company, Britain, until independence in 1949, accrued stolen riches that Utsa Pattanaik has calculated to be about £45 trillion (Merchant 2018).

"African countries received USD $162bn in 2015, mainly in loans, aid and personal remittances. But in the same year, $203bn was taken from the continent, either directly through multinationals repatriating profits and illegally moving money into tax havens, or by costs imposed by the rest of the world through climate change adaptation and mitigation" (McVeigh 2017). This is just one year. When one considers the centuries of taking, the huge resource losses and theft of archaeological items, the money equation is profit to Europe and loss to Africa (see my examples earlier about diamonds and rare earths).

In his classic book, *The Open Veins of Latin America* (1973) Eduardo Galeano documents the many ways in which the continent was pillaged over five centuries. It began with gold and silver and the enslavement of women. Then came the plantations of sugar which destroyed the forests. The latest is destroying the forests — in particular the Amazon — to farm beef cattle.

The history of theft in India and Africa is replicated in North and South America, across the Island Nations of the Pacific, Indian and Atlantic Oceans, in Asia and Australia. The question has to be asked, "Who owes whom and how much?"

Women trafficked and women in prostitution have had their bodies stolen by patriarchal governments, capitalist, socialist, religious and market-driven men. Who will ever compensate women for their losses?

The list is endless. It includes slavery, resource theft, theft of jewels, precious stones and metals; it includes theft of land and its productive capacity for agriculture and the building of cities; it includes the theft of rivers and waterways once used by people for transport and trade and the water dammed and stolen for the use of colonisers (see Chapter Eight); it includes the theft of creativity such as art, music, dance and story.

What systems could be put in place to end planetary theft?

- Recognise the history, calculate the debt and come up with ways of returning what is owed.
- Refuse practices of deterritoriality whether that be of land, language, culture or the body (including refugees and survivors of prostitution).
- Abolish torture and prostitution and make the penalties sufficiently high to keep the world's rich and powerful away.
- End the patenting of life, including plants, by corporations. End all immaterial ownership over the property of others.
- It is not sufficient simply to ban all these practices, educational and attitudinal shifts have to happen for stable change to occur. It means we need a multiplicity of movements to bring about these changes.

I cry. I cry for all. For all the women. For all the lesbians.
I cry because no one cries for us. In Kampala and Chicago.
We are shot and raped. We are thrown from the top floor
of a high building in Teheran and Mecca. When they arrest
us, they put us in cells with violent men who think nothing of
having their own 'fun'. In Melbourne and on the Gold Coast,
we are tossed from cars, rolled into a ditch. In Santiago we
are imprisoned and put on the *parrilla*. In Buenos Aires they
insist we accompany them to dinner outside the prison.
We are caught, used and banged away again at midnight.
On the Western Cape they come for so many of us that
even the media notices. But most of us remain hidden.
There are few reports of the crimes against us.
Fewer readers.

— Susan Hawthorne,
Dark Matters: A Novel
(2017, p. 52)

CHAPTER SIX

Colonisation, Erasure and Torture: Wars against Lesbians

n 2002, I am in Uganda for a World Congress of Women being held in Kampala. I learn a lot at this conference especially in the sessions on war and refugees. Wars in the previous decade have torn apart several nations in this part of Central and East Africa. The Lord's Resistance Army still has a presence in the north of the country. In the week preceding the conference, three of us have travelled together in a small van with a driver. He had spent time in a refugee camp in Kenya. He knew the ropes when soldiers at roadblocks waved for us to pull up. He passed over the required money, a kind of informal road toll.

On the last day of the conference there was a session on Radical Feminism in Africa. I went along to listen and find out what activism was occurring among radical feminists. Towards the end I asked a question about lesbians. I can't recall what I asked, but after the session a woman who'd been there approached me and said, "Be careful, be very careful. In this country they torture lesbians." Her name was Christine. I sat with this sentence for a long time and by the end of the day I had decided I needed to write about this. But where to begin?

In the summer of 2003, I began by entering lesbian plus torture into the internet. All that came up was pornography. I then read Consuelo Rivera-Fuentes and Lynda Birke's article which documents Consuelo's experience in Chile under the Pinochet Regime (2001). It remains one of the most important records of a lesbian's experience of torture. Amnesty International produced two publications, *Breaking the Silence: Human Rights Violations Based on Sexual Orientation* (1997) and *Crimes of Hate, Conspiracy of Silence, Torture and Ill-treatment Based on Sexual Identity* (2001).[89] While they include reports on the torture of lesbians, they do not give anything like equal space to lesbians. Is this because the reports are fewer, or were the researchers failing to identify cases of lesbians who were tortured?

In a third publication sponsored by Amnesty that focuses on torture of women — *Broken Bodies, Shattered Minds: Torture and Ill-treatment of Women* (2001) — lesbians are included in an appendix.

You say, "perhaps things have changed." Sadly they have not. Two books published in 2015 have similar gaps. Sarah Helm's important book *If This Is a Woman* about the Ravensbrück concentration camp, gave me hope when I read a review of it. I read the book avidly expecting that it would answer questions about what happened to lesbians. But there is no recognition that lesbians are treated differently, instead the author simply repeats abusive language used about lesbians. Helm does not ask pertinent

---

89 Note the shift in language from sexual orientation to sexual identity. Within ten years, sexual identity would change to gender identity. I suspect this change came about in the intervening years and by November 2006, when the meeting on developing human rights principles in relation to sexual orientation and gender identity, run by UNAIDS, was held in Indonesia, 'gender identity' had become the norm. *The Yogyakarta Principles*. 2007.

questions about lesbians as she does about other groups (Gypsies, so-called asocials, Poles, politicals, Jews, the old and the disabled).[90]

The book, *Rape: A South African Nightmare* (Gqola 2015) was likewise a callout to me that maybe here the issue of corrective rape, the targeting of lesbians in a country with constitutional protection for gays and lesbians, might be discussed. The author spends multiple chapters analysing rape, but only a few pages are devoted to the subject of corrective rape and lesbians are not mentioned as a specific targeted group. This is a significant gap. Reading the research in this field involves more than reading between the lines.[91]

Globalisation

There have been many analyses of globalisation in the last couple of decades. Some, like my earlier work, have focused on women, and although that analysis included lesbians and critiques of heterosexuality as institutionalised systems of power — including racism, classism, sexism, ableism, ageism, and marginalisation based on religion, ethnicity or culture, I did not single out heteropatriarchy. I also note that when I make such analyses and don't mention the institution of heterosexuality or don't mention lesbians, no one seems to notice the absence of sexual orientation from the debate. But when I speak of sexuality as central to my analysis, people do say, what about class, race, disability, age, culture, religion, ethnicity?

I want to begin by saying that what follows does not exclude these factors (and they are discussed in other pages of this book), but it has to be possible to put sexuality and lesbians at the centre

---

90 A more substantial analysis and documentation is available in Claudia Schoppmann's *Days of Masquerade: Life Stories of Lesbians during the Third Reich* (1996).

91 The research I undertook resulted in numerous conference papers, peer reviewed journal articles and several pieces of journalism. It also formed the basis of my novel, *Dark Matters* (2017).

of our thinking if we really want to understand what is going on around us. That then has to be set alongside other analyses, discussed, synthesised and new theories developed. My analysis draws on decades of theorising by radical feminists and lesbians; about interlocking oppressions which predates the concept of intersectionality coined by Kimberlé Crenshaw in 1989 (p. 140) but was more than akin to that concept. Sarah Lucia Hoagland in *Lesbian Ethics* writes about plurality, complexity, relationship and cooperative interactivity (1988, pp. 246–292). In *Wild Politics*, I write of refracting oppressions amplifying one another (2002, p. 12). Indeed the oppressed belong to a range of dispossessed groups encompassing sex, race, class, disability, sexuality, ethnicity, and some age groups and oppression works in similar ways across these groupings (Hawthorne 2019, pp. 30–39).[92]

One can't speak of globalisation without mentioning power. The superstructure of globalisation is built upon excessive imbalances in power, although the rhetoric is all about level playing fields, transparency, 'choice' and free trade. The reality is about impossible gradients, shifting targets and confusion, consolidation that reduces the range of products and often annihilates local assets and goods, and trade that is structured to benefit the powerful and the monied.

How does heteropatriarchy fit into this? If we want a feminist analysis, is it enough to speak of men, whiteness, wealth and mobility? I don't believe so, for inside this grid is a fifth element that comes into play in relation to all of these, and that is heterosexuality as an institution.

What do I mean by heterosexuality as an institution?

1. An institution formalises the relations between women and men and consequently controls and limits those relations between people in at least the sexual sphere.

---

92 While only published in full in 2019, the section on oppression and hetero-sexuality as an institution was written in 1976 when these statements were far ahead of what was considered the norm.

2. Particular tasks and roles are allocated to women and men within the institution. These differ according to the sex of the person. It is not generally acceptable for women to initiate sexual activity, whereas men are expected to. This preserves the respective subordinate / dominant positions of women and men. Flexibility within heterosexual relations is minimised.
3. Heterosexuality has authority over the people in the institution, including men, and it also affects people not involved in heterosexual relations because it is *the* acceptable model of relating (Hawthorne 2019, p. 45).

The institution affects not only personal and intimate behaviour; it affects global behaviour. Think of the images from Abu Ghraib. They exemplify the heteroreality of militarism. Iraqi men are feminised, dominated, treated just like all the women in all the porn you've ever seen. But when it is pornography, it is not viewed as torture because those subjects (the women) are pre-feminised by their sex. The horror only occurs when men feminise 'enemy' men, and or military women (even if under duress) feminise 'enemy' men (Clarke 2004; Hawthorne 2006). Vera Kurtić in her book *Džuvljarke: Roma Lesbian Existence* (2014) writes about the oppression of lesbians withing Roma communities and of Roma within the Serbian nation.

Unfair, says the liberal, war is always bad. Let's look at something that is marketed globally as good: development. Development is an interesting area and it is one that has changed its form significantly due mainly to appropriative moves by the big money spenders: the IMF, the World Bank, the UN and the on-ground workers, the women working in NGOs. There is now recognition that women make development projects more successful, and are also cheaper than comparable projects where men are involved. But when you look at the language of development, it is premised on a woman being part of a family, whereas development projects focused on men put the men at the centre. And when women want aid, they are first contracepted, when clean water, poverty alleviation and reduction of violence would help more (Akhter 1992).

Further, the woman is structured as part of a group. This is no bad thing, because, as I've argued elsewhere, relationships are central to human activity. But the relationship always assumed is that there is a man in the family — he may be kind, brutal, dependent, or absent — but his symbolic presence is key to development thinking. Imagine if the development institutions thought instead of communities of women — sisters, lovers, friends, aunts, mothers, grandmothers and daughters, with men at the semantic and symbolic margin. What if development institutions imagined single women? What if development institutions considered lesbians? Simply considering these questions creates a challenge. How would development projects look, if the assumed heteronormativity, which determines how money and resources are used, were removed from the development process (Bergeron 2006)? How would the visibility of women's economic and social relationships change? Such shifts would change what we see — and it would affect heterosexual women and lesbians as well as those who don't want intimate relationships.

The radical feminist group, The Purple September Staff, highlighted this in 1975 when they wrote about the normative status of heterosexuality and the very different effects of female and male conditioning:

> In male conditioning, male heterosexuality is linked to male prerogative of a human identity; in female conditioning, female heterosexuality is linked to the denial of that same identity (1975, p. 81).

When I first read this in 1975, I thought that by 2020 it would no longer hold. But today I look around and see girls wearing T-shirts with 'Porn Star', and heavy-duty sexualisation of girls at a younger and younger age (Caputi 2004; Tankard Reist 2009). And I see boys running about with pretend AK 37s under their arms (and in some places, real ones) and I see videos made by boys glorifying violence against and rape of girls. You might argue that I'm seeing select-ively. I'll happily admit there are happy and fulfilled heterosexual couples, but they are overwhelmingly unrepresentative of the cultural trend.

The politics of shame

In late 2010, I received an email about Millicent Gaika, a South African lesbian who had been subjected to 'corrective rape' on 2 April 2010 by a man she knew. The image of her bruised face and body as well as her recounting of what had happened to her, created the momentum for a global campaign against 'corrective rape'. It's an abusive term that refers to the rape and battery of lesbians to cure them of lesbian existence. The man who raped, beat and attempted to strangle Millicent Gaika said this: "I know you are a lesbian. You are not a man, you think you are, but I am going to show you, you are a woman. I am going to make you pregnant. I am going to kill you."

Millicent Gaika is not the first South African lesbian to be attacked in this way. In 2008, Eudy Simelane, a star of the South African women's football team, was gang raped and murdered.

In 2009, in an interview in *The Guardian*, Zakhe Sowello from Soweto, Johannesburg, said:

> Every day I am told that they are going to kill me, that they are going to rape me and after they rape me I'll become a girl … When you are raped you have a lot of evidence on your body. But when we try and report these crimes nothing happens, and then you see the boys who raped you walking free on the street (Kelly 2009).

South Africa is the only country in the world to constitutionally protect the rights of people based on sexual orientation. I think this has been a critical factor in the success of Millicent Gaika's Avaaz campaign, although no doubt it took enormous courage on her part, to present this as a breach of the South African constitution.

By May 2010, more than 140,000 people signed the petition for Millicent Gaika to uphold the constitutional rights of lesbians to state protection. By mid-June 2010, it had reached 939,905. But the increasing number of victims of violence is not new. So while I was pleased to know that finally these violations were coming to light, it's been a long wait.

How is it possible that violence against lesbians is such a non-headline? Because, although the Avaaz petition was signed by a lot of individuals around the world, it has not reached metropolitan newspapers. If you search for Millicent Gaika, the reports mostly come from activists and bloggers.[93]

Is corrective rape a new occurrence? No, it is not.

- In 2006, a mob of young men in Khayelitsha, near Cape Town stoned to death Zoliswa Nkonyana. They threw bricks and beat her with a golf stick.
- In 2007, Sizakele Sigasa and her partner Salome Masooa were raped, tortured and murdered in Soweto. I received information about this from a German friend, not through the media (Pers. Comm. 1 July 2007).
- Simangele Nhlapo was raped and murdered in the second week of July 2007. She was a member of a support group for HIV-positive people and her daughter was also killed (Ndaba 2007).
- A more high profile death occurred in 2008. Eudy Simelane was known because she was a star player in the national women's soccer team, Banyana Banyana. She did not hide her sexual orientation in her hometown Kha Thema, near Johannesburg. Indeed she was active in campaigning for equality rights. Eudy was abducted, gang raped and stabbed multiple times. She was 31 (Kelly 2009; Human Rights Watch 2009).
- Dudizille Zozo was murdered in July 2013; a toilet brush had been plunged into her vagina (*Cape Times* Editorial 2013).

---

93 A number of reports can be found at the LezGetReal site, for example this one: <http://lezgetreal.com/2010/11/the-shocking-truth-of-corrective-rape-survivors-speak-from-south-africa/>

This list of horror acts of violence against lesbians in South Africa shows just how ineffective the constitutional protections for lesbians are.

In March 2010, the then South African Minister of Arts and Culture, Lulu Xingwana, stormed out of an art exhibition at Constitution Hill, Johannesburg, claiming that photographs of black lesbian couples by Zanele Muholi were "going against nation building" (Pithouse 2011).

> Muholi has documented more than 50 cases of violent hate crimes against black lesbians living in townships. Half of these women were raped and some of them killed. In 2006, Zoliswa Nkonyana was stoned to death by a mob of young men in Khayelitsha for being an 'out' lesbian (Pithouse 2011).

Richard Pithouse names some of the murdered lesbians already listed here and says that the constitution did not protect them because black lesbians are "only protected on paper" (Pithouse 2011). It is this reality and not the fact that some women find love and share desire with other women that is perverse.

Zanele Muholi's photographs are regarded as meaningful within the black South African lesbian community because it gives meaning to their daily lives. Her work reflects the true meaning of the South African constitution.

Is life for lesbians safer in the USA? Victoria Brownworth has been documenting the murder of lesbians in the US for many years. In her article in the lesbian magazine *Curve* (2015), she writes about five young lesbians:

- Sakia Gunn was stabbed to death on 11 May 2003 because the men who were harassing a group of young women picked up that she was a lesbian. She was murdered as punishment for standing up for herself.
- Britney Cosby and Crystal Jackson were killed in 2014 by Cosby's father and Brownworth suggests this was an honour killing.

- Lisa Trubnikova was killed on 5 February 2015 because Adrian Loya was obsessed with her and said that if he couldn't have her, it was better that she was dead.
- Lizzi Marriot was murdered in October 2012 by Seth Mazzaglia because she was not interested in his advances (Hawthorne 2015).

What these women have in common is that the media ignored the fact that they were lesbians. As Brownworth writes:

> Like Sakia and Britney, Crystal and Lisa, there were no vigils for Lizzi. No hate crimes legislation authored in her name. No memorials. No reminders that lesbians are murdered all the time and have been for decades and we still pretend they weren't lesbians or we just ignore their murders altogether (Brownworth 2015).

The phallus and the penis

In her book, *Reading Between the Lines*, Denise Thompson states: "The feminist aim is to render the phallus impotent, to sever its connection with the penis, and to ensure that the latter is reduced to *nothing but* anatomy" (1991, p. 15; italics in the original).

Denise Thompson's distinction between the phallus and the penis is very important. Thompson does go on to say that the "selective recognition towards women and away from men, does not have to be a permanent state of affairs" (p. 15). Men of every generation make statements over and over that direct attention away from women permanently and universally and it hardly raises an eyebrow. I believe that the position of dominance that men hold — and that each person may hold in one or more parts of their lives — results in sloppy and uncritical thinking. And within the heterosexual worldview, it is easy to slide from lesbian to lesbianism (a state of illness), while heterosexual and heterosexuality is a given. And an assimilationist view is the prevailing one.

A lesbian feminist reading of globalisation brings another way of seeing the world. Indigenous women in many parts of the world are developing critiques of globalisation that reflect the ways in which they are being recolonised by bioprospectors and drug companies. Lesbians are being recolonised in different ways in different countries.

For example, same-sex marriage. I didn't join the women's liberation movement to fight for marriage, although I was furious when, in 2004, Liberal and Labor parties in Australia joined forces to create a new discriminatory law to prevent same-sex marriage.[94] But it isn't something I fought for in Australia in 2017 because I see it as a new form of normative heterosexuality. It is yet another Trojan horse. If only we could quieten down those rabble-rousing lesbian feminists and pretend that they don't threaten the social structure. To speak out on behalf of lesbians is somehow seen as passé, boring, not relevant to the real political fight. To that extent lesbians have become — and perhaps in the coming years will become even more — difficult to centre a campaign around. I believe that lesbian feminism is a threat to patriarchy, and should be, while simultaneously it is a positive and often joyous alternative. Nor will I go to the barricades to get lesbians into IVF. The discrimination is wrong, but the health outcome is not worth having because it comes with too many problems. If lesbians fight these battles for the privileges of heterosexuality, what energy remains to fight for those issues which put women and lesbians and lesbian feminism at the centre? How will it be possible to turn our attention to lesbians for long enough to create change?

Giti Thadani writes from India and the difficulty of what words to use to speak about lesbians. In her words: "... one can be, but

---

94 It's amazing what you can get away with saying in public about lesbians, and not be accused of discrimination or hate speech. In the lead-up to the federal elections in Australia in 2004, a Family First Party campaign worker made a joke about burning lesbians at the stake, and no media organisation objected. If such a bad joke were made about anyone from a marginalised ethnic group, voices would be raised in protest. All that happened was that the worker was later stood aside. See Hawthorne (2004).

only if one remains nameless" (Thadani 1996, p. 10). The same problem is raised by the use of overly inclusive language such as queer, LGBTIQ, same sex, alternative sexualities, diverse sexuality, non-binary, minority sexualities. The symbolic meaning of these terms is to keep turning our attention towards the phallus which is a part of all these terms. I like the word lesbian. It has oomph. Many languages do have equivalents for the word lesbian, and those languages that don't, are going to be the places where turning away from the phallus is particularly difficult.

In academia, any word except lesbian has become preferable — because the lesbian, the feminist, the lesbian feminist is unsafe ground for too many people in every department. We need a shift in the culture that recognises the tyranny at the root of this language. This is the result of globalised thinking that picks up the global and forgets the local, or to put it slightly differently, picks up the heterosexually acceptable language and ignores the intimate.

The LGBTIQ label is useful only to show a combined strength of numbers. It results in prioritising of some groups over others. Although L is at the beginning, it represents the group that others in the alphabet would rather ignore. In 2019, Angela Wild and other lesbians protested at Pride in London with banners which put lesbians at the centre including LESBIAN NOT QUEER, LESBIAN = FEMALE HOMOSEXUAL and TRANSGENDERISM ERASES LESBIANS. The protesting lesbians were saying that "lesbians have a right to sexual boundaries and self-definition" (Wild 2019, p. 6). But instead of respecting the needs and rights of lesbians, Pride in London referred to them as 'disgusting' 'bigoted' and 'transphobic'. These are much stronger terms than those on the banners.

Origins of patriarchy and violence against lesbians

What is it that makes lesbians feel real? Makes lesbians feel like citizens?

> It is crucial to remember ... that [many] 'creation' myths are not about the origins of the world at all, but about the origins of patriarchy which has, nonetheless claimed itself as the world (Caputi 1988, p. 9).

Jane Caputi's observation brings us back to basics. Who, in the mythology or the religion or the storytelling, gets the credit for creating meaning in the world? Most of the world's cultures have old stories that tell of times when women created the world, and then went on to create social meaning. The vast majority of these stories have been steam-rolled and steam-cleaned, but they can be found in 'mythologies' which are great repositories of women's knowledge. The Middle East, for example, is filled with ancient stories in which 'goddesses' — or as they were renamed 'demons' — populated the stories and were then torn to shreds, decapitated and violated. In Greece, the daughters of goddesses are raped, abducted and made hostage (Hawthorne 2018).[95] When the stories are retold, they are reframed as origin stories. This is comparable to the discovery stories of Europeans — the first [white] man to cross the mountain, the river, the desert, the continent, or attributing Captain Cook with the 'discovery' of Australia, when the continent had been inhabited for tens of thousands of years. They are stories

---

95 Graham, Rawlings and Rigsby (1994) argue that women's social relationship with men suggests a form of societal Stockholm Syndrome, that is that the institution of heterosexuality and the individuals who patrol it — men and apologists for men's power — who act as through women are *hostages* to men. The captive perceives the behaviour of the captors as ranging from extreme violence to kindness. The kindness creates a belief in safety in the midst of violence and abuse.

of remaking reality in the framework of the ruling class and the colonising class.[96]

In our contemporary global world, this is taking on new forms. The area of conquest now is the immaterial, it is *knowledge* that is privatised and sold at great profit. One of those stories is how to gain constant access to female bodies. Heterosexuality is ramped up to an ever-greater pitch. Little girls are dressed in bras and panties before they've learned to run. They might not all wear pink, but the expectations of satisfying masculine sexual drive is happening at the age when girls have the developmental advantage over boys (Tankard Reist 2009).

This is serious. How can a woman ever learn to move freely if she doesn't experience it in childhood? How can she sense the possibilities of her own power if adolescence gives no space for the girl within? If it becomes instead a lesson in self-denial? The global advertising industry, the sex industry, the trafficking-in-girls-and-women industry are about the institutionalisation of heterosexuality as dollars for tourism, and a way of providing for that group of highly mobile, cashed-up men who take for granted easy and constant access to women's bodies.[97]

The alternative, which could encompass female friendship, lesbian love, or solitary solutions, is simply not thinkable (Raymond 1986/2020). They are not advertised on billboards or in movies or on TV soaps because within the heteropatriarchal world, they are a nonsense. The lesbian cannot have meaning. It is so far off

---

96 Ngahuia Te Awekotuku (1991 and 2001) retells the story of Maori ancestor Hinemoa through a lesbian lens; Consuelo Rivera-Fuentes (2018) similarly retells the story from the Chilean Mupuche tradition of Millaray and Licanray.

97 The numbers of rich men who have been charged with trafficking, assault, rape and other crimes has escalated in recent years (think Dominique Strauss-Kahn, Bill Cosby, Roman Polanski, Jeffrey Epstein, Harvey Weinstein just to mention a few). In a recent article in *The New York Times* about the French writer and paedophile Gabriel Matzneff, commentator Pierre Verdrager says of France, "We're in a very egalitarian society where there is a pocket of resistance that actually behaves like an aristocracy" (Onishi 2020).

the planet as to be out of this world. Or as I write in my poetry collection, *The Sacking of the Muses*,

I am a nonsense
I do not exist

or if I do I am illegal
and should be punished

killed if need be

(Hawthorne 2019a, p. 72).

The violence carried out against lesbians is both symbolic and real. Lesbians *are* killed and tortured for whom they love. Men *do* use rape both to punish and to convert. All she needs is a good fuck and that will do it. The symbolic violence can be seen in any porn magazine or website where 'lesbian' eroticism becomes a turn-on for voyeuristic viewers. The world rightly protests the destruction of the 2000-year-old Bamiyan Buddhist statues in Afghanistan. Giti Thadani (2004), in her research of ancient lesbian sites in India, also records the violence against 5000-year-old sacred stone sculptures. Why have we not heard about how the breasts of these statues have been cut off? Why is there no international protest? Is it because the statues are symbolic of lesbian existence, not just now, but back in ancient history?

> On the one hand the lesbian is reduced to the Western other and declared not to be a citizen of the country within any socio-cultural-historical-cosmological context. But on the other hand the heterosexual business executive is very much the result of an economic order arising out of a 'Western' context, yet his Indianness is never called into question (Thadani 1996, p. 87).

Or, as a Peruvian lesbian says:

> When I speak of my right to my own culture and language as an indigenous woman, everyone agrees to my self-determination. But when I speak of my other identity, my lesbian identity, my

right to love, to determine my own sexuality, no one wants to listen (*ILIS Newsletter* 1994, p. 13).

Put differently, the paradox faced by lesbians in countries outside the west is this: To be a lesbian is to rebel against everything patriarchy demands of women. To be a lesbian is seen as kowtowing to western ideas. It is seen as being recolonised. But the colonising of women is never made visible and the suited businessman or businesswoman goes about doing his or her business within the context of western neoliberalism.

How lesbians are colonised	How lesbians are violated	How lesbians are shamed
Infliction of pain on lesbians including murder, torture (rape), imprisonment and unduly harsh methods of punishment. Lesbians are kicked out of the family, disinherited, not recognised (erased) and ostracised.	Criminalising lesbians: state violence by making it illegal to be a lesbian. Punishment can include the death penalty, long periods of imprisonment and torture, including rape and humiliating sexual violence.	Lesbian existence is considered shameful even when being a lesbian is not illegal. Passing as heterosexual or transitioning are adopted to avoid shame. The epidemic of transitioning lesbians documented by Shrier (2020) and by Brunskell-Evans (2020) are examples of this.
Erasure: the idea that lesbians are considered a non-sense. This denial of existence is a way of breaking the spirit. Even when lesbians are murdered, their sexuality is ignored.	Murder by non-state actors. This includes immediate and extended family members. Honour killings. Persistent rape so the lesbian becomes pregnant.	Shame is isolating and especially difficult for young lesbians in school who are taunted, ostracised and sometimes beaten up.
Destruction of lesbian knowledge and culture. Lesbians remain hidden in history. Intentional exclusion of up-front lesbian-centred work or policies.	Corrective rape: the false belief that raping a lesbian will turn her heterosexual. Used against political prisoners and executed by gangs of young men.	Lesbians are declared mad and incarcerated in mental hospitals, some die. This adds yet another layer of shame. Mixed wards in mental hospitals can be dangerous for lesbians.

How lesbians are colonised	How lesbians are violated	How lesbians are shamed
Heterosexuality is imposed and normalised (compulsory heterosexuality).	Lesbians are subjected to inferior medical treatment, not permitted to see their partner(s), the partner is not recognised as next of kin (except when married or recognised by law).	Lesbians who stand up for themselves publicly when called names are responded to with words that intensify shame or create the sense that anyone on the receiving end of such words *should* be ashamed.
Isolation: the lesbian (especially a young lesbian) feels as if she is entirely alone in the world.	Lesbians are treated as second-class citizens, find it difficult to get promotions or in the arts be recognised (there are some lucky exceptions).	Should a lesbian become famous, she will be remembered either only for her sexuality (her achievements hidden) or her sexuality will be hidden and her achievements remembered. These are the result of shame.

Nationalism and exile

In the 1920s, a young woman named Grace McDonald travelled to England. She lived there for the rest of her life and the only photos of her are with another woman called Peg. Grace was my great aunt. We never met, but she sent gifts at Christmas. It is only in the last few years, after discovering the photographs of her and thinking about exile in relation to lesbians that I have come to see that it is more than likely that my Auntie Grace was a lesbian in exile. I have been an activist and writer in this field for 30 years and it took years and an accident of photographic preservation for me to *see* this. Sue Ingleton, in her book *Making Trouble, Tongued with Fire* (2019) writes about the history of two remarkable 19th-century lesbians, Harriet Elphinstone Dick and Alice C. Moon. Without a number of serendipitous events, these women's lives would still remain hidden.

It is an indication of the great losses we have of lesbian history. While heteropatriarchy is rewriting our histories, while it distorts and dismembers whatever we have, while it severs those crucial lines of inheritance, we are left floating without that matrix of connection that most people take for granted. For those who don't have the connections, there is usually some recognition — even if it comes late — that it has occurred. Here I am thinking of the Holocaust, of refugee displacement, of the Stolen Generations, dispossession of Indigenous peoples and forced adoptions (Mackieson 2016; Arditti 1999; Çetin 2010). These are all horrific events. Could we try to be horrified about what has happened to lesbians (Hawthorne 2005b)? In 1976, under the Pinochet regime in Chile, Consuelo Rivera-Fuentes was tortured and fled to England as a refugee.

> *... no training session prepared me for this intense pain ... my pain ... the one I did not choose ... all this alienation, this empty vacuum ..., my body, my mind, my pain ... this is not happening ... I am a little speck in the universe ... which universe? ... the world is not anymore ... I am ... disintegrating ... bit by bit ... yell by yell ... electrode by electrode ... The pain ... all this pain here and there, down there in my vagina ... the agony ... where am I? Where is my I?* (Rivera-Fuentes and Birke 2001, p. 655; italics and ellipses in the original).

"*Where is my I?*" asks Consuelo Rivera-Fuentes after her experience of torture. She is also asking where is my lesbian I? Where is the centrality of the experiences of lesbians recorded and recognised? Where is the recognition that the violation of lesbians goes on day after day and no one speaks of it (Hawthorne 2006a)? She too, is writing in exile from England, not her native Chile. While she is now able to return to Chile, in a speech on a panel on 'Violence against Lesbians' (FiLiA 2019), Consuelo speaks about how she managed to escape from Chile under dire circumstances.

It was eleven years after her release when the country had returned to democratic rule. A policeman came into her work place at the British Commissariat. He said that she should come with him to the police headquarters and convinced her she had nothing to fear. After taking her through many parts of the building where she and others had been tortured, the policeman took her to a room where an officer sat at a table. He offered her a seat and a coffee and she refused. His apparent benevolent face and smile made it clear that he wanted her to know that they knew how to find her and she should be scared. He said he wanted Consuelo to have sex with his female lover. She asked him why. After some time they came to an agreement to meet in two weeks. He agreed that he would only watch. But what he didn't know was that Consuelo was flying to the UK in five days time to live there. Consuelo added that when she was arrested they already knew she was a lesbian and had targeted her because of that. At that time, they also threated to rape her (FiLiA 2019).

It took Aderonke Apata, a Nigerian lesbian activist, thirteen years to gain asylum in the UK. She was put in solitary confinement for a week in Yarl's Wood Immigration Removal Centre in 2012. The Home Office, headed at the time by Theresa May, accused her of pretending to be a lesbian in order to gain asylum. Aderonke is claiming that if she were returned to Nigeria where to be a lesbian is illegal, it would mean a long jail sentence. These are the same grounds on which other lesbians apply for refugee status. The bar is set so high that it is hard to imagine other applicants for asylum getting through. If an activist of Aderonke's status struggles to gain recognition, what of a lesbian who has no current partner? That means that a lesbian without a female partner jumps to the default position of heterosexual.

> Sitting amidst Aderonke's supporters in the gallery, there was something surreal about hearing counsel for the Secretary of State, Mr Bird, debate with the Judge about the 'genuineness' of a black lesbian woman's sexuality. Mr Bird argued that even if Aderonke self-identifies as a lesbian and sleeps with women, this does not make her a lesbian, because she has not always self-identified as a lesbian: by 'coming out' she has shown her sexuality is not an immutable characteristic (which is part of what she has to show to fall within a 'particular social group' in the definition in the Refugee Convention) (Blair 2018).

This was well countered by Aderonke's lawyer, Abid Mahmood:

> So for example a child seeking asylum cannot force themselves to be older so they are not at risk on return and likewise a lesbian asylum seeker cannot simply choose to change their sexuality. This is notwithstanding that a child will eventually grow up and that there may have been a time in her past where a lesbian woman had not identified herself as a lesbian (Blair 2018).

Refugees' status and exile are not chosen lightly. In the case of Aderonke Apata, she was in exile and could not return to her home country of Nigeria without the likelihood of persecution. For many lesbians, the possibility of ostracism, shame or a sense of not belonging might drive them into exile.

In Kakuma Refugee Camp in Kenya, lesbians are put in Block 13 which is reserved for LGBT people. But the conditions there are terrible, including high levels of abuse and persecution of lesbians within the camp (FiLiA 2020). They are also informed by the representatives of UNHCR that they should not be lesbians since no one likes lesbians.

Many a rural lesbian has made the move to the city, because it is simply too hard to live the way she wants in her own country town. Ask me. I grew up in rural NSW. Do I live there? Do they know who I am? Hardly. So, like my great aunt, most of my life has been spent elsewhere. I know this applies to many lesbians of my generation and earlier. Lesbians are a diasporic population. The connections zigzag down the generations, often through maiden aunts.

Lesbian existence resists nationalism. And what could it mean for a lesbian to be patriotic (Hawthorne 2006b)? I'm sure that oxymoron exists, but as challengers to the symbolic and actual power of patriarchy and heterosexuality, "Like oil and water/ lesbianlife and patriotism don't mix" (Hawthorne 2005b, p. 221). And Nicole Brossard writes, "A lesbian is *radical* or she is not a lesbian. A lesbian who does not reinvent the world is a lesbian in the process of disappearing" (Brossard 2020, pp. 96–97).

The lesbian, as Monique Wittig so astutely pointed out in 1978, is "not a woman" because her "relation to a man" falls outside the heterosexual obligation that occurs inside the institution of heterosexuality. What does lesbian motherhood look like in this context? Is it possible to have the generational connection while remaining outside the "personal and ... economic obligation" (Wittig 1992, p. 20) of heterosexuality? Or, as Nicole Brossard writes, "Amazons and lesbians are the only women not invented by Man" (2020, p. 116).

Just as lesbians are accused of disloyalty to family because we have left the places we come from, lesbians are also accused of disloyalty to their own culture. Vera Kurtić (2014) in a report on the situation of Romani lesbians in Serbia found that lesbians in Roma society are considered shameful and in turn Roma in Serbian mainstream society are victims of racism. The lesbian is an outsider; and the Roma is an outsider. She writes that Roma lesbians "... are completely dislocated from Romani communities" (p. 64). But when Romani lesbians try to go to the Pride March, they were not able to "... because it was visible we were Romani women" (p. 49). The women considered that their safety was under threat.

It is more than likely, that if we could find the connections, if we could find temples and statues and artworks as we can in India, we could begin to discover the ancient treasures that draw lesbians into focus. But would anyone support such a research project? Max Dashu has struggled to support the Suppressed Histories Archives which she founded in 1970, set up because she faced so much resistance from Harvard University on feminist scholarship (Dashu 2020). My own experience at La Trobe University and later the University of Melbourne in pursuing lesbian philosophy (1976) and new interpretations of the Homeric Hymns (1981)[98] reflects

---

98 Both of these took decades to be published. For my philosophy essay see Hawthorne 2019b; for my classics essay see Hawthorne 2018.

the same attitude towards feminist scholarship. Even within the feminist movement the ideas of the 1970s and 1980s are being sidelined from history and accused of destroying the women's movement. Sheila Jeffreys (1993) documents this in her book *The Lesbian Heresy*. She writes:

> The idea that lesbian feminists should be visionaries working towards a vision of a world in which women are not oppressed and indeed all oppressive hierarchies have become unthinkable was widespread in the seventies. Lesbians were not afraid to have visions (Jeffreys 1993, p. 161).

Jeffreys calls for a deep separation that "should be intellectual and ethical" (p. 169). She wants a world in which lesbian existence "will continue to be a heresy until the world has been changed to suit a lesbian feminist vision" (p. 170). A reconceptualisation of the world as I too am calling for.

When colonists first enter a country, they dispossess the people, not only of their land, but also of their culture. The colonists deny this possibility. They say, "The natives have no culture." What could we know of the colonists through many thousands of years ago who, upon 'discovery' of lesbians, have killed, raped, maimed and also denied their existence? So many families have their own colonists inside them (Machida 1996). How do we fight against this? And when our knowledge is digitised, who will use the word lesbian and in what context, and with what overtones?

Global recolonisation

In her book *Pedagogies of Crossing*, M. Jackie Alexander writes,

> Making the nation-state safe for multinational corporations is commensurate with making it safe for heterosexuality, for both can be recodified as natural, even supernatural. Thus tourism and imperialism become as integral to the natural order as heterosexuality, and are indispensable in state strategies of recolonization (2005, p. 26).

Afro-Caribbean writer, Jacqui Alexander, points to an interesting concept here, that of recolonisation. It is particularly apt in the context of the Caribbean, where western tourists flock to, and where you can be imprisoned for being a lesbian. The important element here is that colonisation is not a one-off event. Rather, it is a series of actions played out against those who challenge the stock knowledge of the dominant culture. It is like the movement of tectonic plates, simultaneously sliding across one another in several layers.

As I write in Chapter Five, the land is taken and the colonised are killed, enslaved, violated and disconnected from their language and culture. Then the products of the land and the people are stolen: the land is mined, it is farmed wastefully, forests, rivers and seas are plundered, the land and seas bombed and used as dumps, the material goods and arts are commodified, made safe for tourists and people in other countries (they are watered down). More recently, the knowledge and the cell-lines of people are being stolen, but this too has happened in different ways over many years. All of these things continue to happen simultaneously.

In the context of lesbians, these days most lesbians have no land to plunder, indeed in too many instances that connection has been sacrificed. Lesbian bodies are violated in various ways: murder, torture, suicide, rape and most recently surgical violence (see Chapter Seven). They are all justified as necessary. Gays and Lesbians of Zimbabwe (GALZ),[99] was the very first organization to be attacked in Zimbabwe for dissenting in 1995 (Tiripano 2000). But who protested for Tsitsi Tiripano in 1995? I would suggest that when lesbians become victims of attack, they are a signal. They are the canaries in the mine. And if the perpetrators get away with it, then other attacks will follow. So we need to be protesting every attack on lesbians, because it is a sign of hatred in the social

---

99   GALZ was established in 1990, and came to prominence in 1995 when it attempted to enter the Zimbabwe International Book Fair, which had as its theme, Human Rights and Justice. Permission was refused. For more information, see <http://www.galz.co.zw/cp_bookfair.html>

system. If lesbians are not protected, then people who don't fit some other social dimension will not be safe from attack either. Keep your lesbian sister safe and watch the effect it has on society. Following 1995, anyone in Zimbabwe with a dissenting voice was under attack. Many fled into exile. It is a huge challenge because as one Zimbabwean woman said: "How can we expect our black lesbian sisters to find their voice in our society when they cannot even speak for themselves within their own families?" (Amnesty International 1998).

In Zimbabwe in the mid-1980s, Tina Machida was violated at the instigation of her parents in an effort to 'cure' her of her lesbian existence. She writes:

> They locked me in a room and brought him every day to rape me so I would fall pregnant and be forced to marry him. They did this to me until I was pregnant (Machida 1996, p. 123).

In Sierra Leone, on 29 September 2004, FannyAnn Eddy[100] was found dead after being repeatedly raped. She had testified at the UN Commission on Human Rights just a few months before her death.

> Silence creates vulnerability. You, members of the Commission on Human Rights, can break the silence. You can acknowledge that we exist, throughout Africa and on every continent, and that human rights violations based on sexual orientation or gender identity are committed every day. You can help us combat those violations and achieve our full rights and freedoms, in every society, including my beloved Sierra Leone (Eddy 2004).

She had been working in the offices of the Sierra Leone Lesbian and Gay Association on the day she was murdered (Human Rights Watch 2004; Morgan and Wieringa 2005, p. 20).

---

100 See her testimony, Eddy (2004) at the UN Commission on Human Rights just a few months before her death.

Some governments are supported by religious ideologies. Nazanin, an Iranian lesbian says, "The punishment for lesbians is most definitely execution. Before execution they are raped, which is a mental torment worse than death" (Parsi 2002, p. 4).

She goes on to explain why the families are silent about the rape and execution of their daughters. It is, "to save face for the families involved ... it is a cause for disgrace" (Parsi 2002, p. 4) and it is considered '*haram* and blasphemy' (Parsi 2007, p. 3, italics in original).

Rape, torture, silence, shame and hatred all combine so that no one ever hears of the violations of lesbians' human rights. It's invisible; it's as if it doesn't exist. Just as lesbians don't exist.

Shame takes on a huge shape for lesbians. Even the most political of lesbians suffers from shame. It comes in many guises: as silence within families as Nazanin and Tina Machida note; when lesbians put their needs last in political campaigns, that too is shame because who will support a political campaign if lesbians are its leaders, so just keep quiet until the revolution is over.

The problem is that lesbian oppression is based on women's sexuality. It is a given in patriarchal societies that women must not be able to have any freedom around sexual pleasure. Sexual pleasure for women (and here I am not speaking about pornography — that is men's idea) is so totally unthinkable in some instances that the idea of two women deciding to have sex, to have a sexual and emotional relationship is enough to send them straight to hell. Such women should feel shame. If they don't, then they are pressured to feel ashamed. As a result some lesbians commit suicide, including double suicides. Such women are called unnatural. It is obvious that women would only do such a thing if they were desperate, hence the line: 'All she needs is a good fuck.' And out of that, all of the above human rights abuses flow: corrective rape; gang rape; torture; forced marriage; forced pregnancy; diagnosis of madness; diagnosis of neglect of children; punishments such as beatings and murder. And if none of the above works, pull out the camera and turn lesbians into porn stars. Heterosexualise lesbian sex, and sell it to men.

And what of the lesbians who have died, for want of good medical treatment? Gloria Anzaldúa, dead at 61, because she couldn't afford the American health system. Lisa Bellear, who died far too young, at age 45, from a preventable illness. And what of the mostly young women who die in double suicides and whose deaths do not prompt families (like the Montagues and Capulets of *Romeo and Juliet* fame) to consider their part in their deaths. Giti Thadani (1996, p. 101), in her research on lesbian existence in India, found many examples of lesbians committing suicide. She cites the cases of Malika and Lalita, both twenty years old, who attempted suicide by drowning together when one failed an examination that would mean separation; also of Jyotsana and Jayashree, who jumped in front of a train because they could not bear the separation caused by their respective marriages; of Saijamol and Gita, who committed suicide in a joint poisoning; of Gita and Kishori, both 24-year-old nurses who hung themselves from a ceiling fan in the hospital quarters (Thadani 1996, p. 104).[101] Although at the time of these deaths, India's Section 377 did not name lesbianism as a crime, it was nevertheless used to harass lesbians and put pressure on them to enter heterosexual marriages (Voices Against Section 377 n.d., pp. 31–32). When the pressure to heterosexualise lesbians is extreme, lesbians suffer and some, as indicated by the above examples, are driven to suicide.

Surgical violence against lesbians can now be counted alongside the violence meted out to lesbians in the 'mental health' system. Gender disorientation is a 'medical tag'. Interestingly, disorientation is a method of torture. Lesbians are among the earliest to name this as violence (see Raymond 1980; Jeffreys 2003; Gage 2008). There is an epidemic of lesbians opting for surgical removal of their breasts as a way of entering the trans-sphere. A sense of 'being in

---

101 Giti Thadani writes about a number of cases of double suicides by lesbians in India (1996, pp. 101–104).

the wrong body', but a sense created through social media and a massive propaganda campaign against young people, the latest form of conversion therapy (Brunskell-Evans 2020, pp. 159–163; see Chapter Seven).

There is nothing new about propaganda directed to sexual stereotypes. Nicole Brossard writes about how men actualise themselves through

> … the military apparatus, the rise in the price of gold, the evening news, pornography, and so on. The man in power and the man in the street know what it's all about. It's their daily reality, or the 'how' of their self-realization. You know — life!
>
> On the other hand, we can also say that women's reality has been perceived as fiction. Let us name some of those realities here: maternity, rape, prostitution, chronic fatigue, verbal, physical, and mental violence. Newspapers present these as *stories*, not fact (2020, p. 54).

Nothing has changed in the four decades since Nicole Brossard first wrote these words in 1980, except that violence has gone viral and is now also spread electronically. In Argentina, Eva Analía Jesús, known as Higui, is on trial because she defended herself against a man who had attacked her for being a lesbian. She has been charged with homicide and no account was taken of her testimony of self-defence against corrective rape (Listening to Lesbians 2020).

These are global realities. They are global issues and they are issues that should be visible in our communities. They are in fact the same issues that every group battling globalisation confronts. There is a great deal of fear around the word 'lesbian'. As has been shown in Zimbabwe, Iran, Argentina, Serbia and India, if lesbians remain outside the scope of social justice reform, then everyone's civil and political rights remain in jeopardy. If campaigns for the safety of lesbians cannot be shaped — and many of us have borne the brunt of attacks from both our enemies and those we thought were our allies — then what are we fighting for when we take up any social justice issue? Are we wanting just partial freedom? Freedom for some, and not others? If this is so, what are we changing? Are we serious?

Lesbian refugees

I have included above the stories of lesbian refugees including Consuelo Rivera-Fuentes and Adironke Apata and the successful campaign on behalf of Millicent Gaika, and there are many more, but they rarely make the news.

In 2007, when Iranian lesbian Pegah Emambakhsh was about to be deported from Britain, there was an email campaign that stayed her deportation, but on the whole lesbian refugees have not even hit the radar of refugee activists or as in Kenya's Kakuma Refugee Camp, they become targets of violence and persecution (FiLiA 2020).

A recent successful campaign was on behalf of Brenda Namigadde, a Ugandan lesbian living in the UK who was due to be deported on 29 January 2011. Around 60,000 people signed the petition to put a stop to her deportation on the grounds that she was in danger of her life. The danger was reinforced by the murder of gay activist, David Kato, just two days earlier.[102]

An unnamed lesbian refugee from Iran says of her experience: "In Kashan they tied me to a car and pulled me across the ground. What should I say, who should I say it to? ... Why doesn't anyone listen to us? Where is this 'human rights'?"(Darya and Baran 2007).

In 2007, when US gay congressman Jared Polis visited Iraq and Jordan to see for himself the situation of gays, lesbians and transgenders he had this conversation with a Jordanian woman engaged in refugee work. "Why they help lesbians? Widows and orphans need help, and they help lesbian?" (Polis 2007).

Using the word 'lesbian' provokes what Indian writer Maya Sharma calls a "discourse of catastrophe" (Sharma 2006, p. 38). This

---

102 I received the news about David Kato's murder from *Pambazuka News*; For updates, go to <http://www.allout.org/brenda>

is a softer form of the lack of respect for lesbian civil and political rights, but no less damaging than the idea that lesbian existence is a nonsense or the 'symbolic annihilation' Alison Hopkins (2008, p. 276) alludes to in her study of the representation of lesbians on New Zealand television.

Part of that brittle silence is one's own self-censoring behaviour which is particularly evident in cultural settings that are not one's own. The silence shifts between 'personalised silence' within a social, political and cultural context as well as the self-silencing of the person coming in from outside that context. A lesbian from Zimbabwe, Angel, was confronted by a series of questions from the Home Office in the UK which were contradictory to say the least. They wanted to know when she knew she was a lesbian. A question that is hard to answer, but in an environment in which you feel it must be hidden, even more difficult. And what of her child, her abusive husband and the rape intended to "straighten her out"? And if she was a lesbian why hadn't she had much in the way of relationships in Zimbabwe (it was impossible to be an open lesbian)? And in the UK, why hadn't she had relationships with women when there was no reason to hide? (Brewer 2020, pp. 1–2). She had been arrested by police in Zimbabwe when found naked in a bed with another woman. She fled across the border to South Africa and via France and in the back of a lorry from Calais to Dover (p. 7). Her 2015 refugee status was refused and it took until 2019 for asylum to be granted.

Within the LGBTIQ community, lesbians keep being marginalised. Our sexual orientation and our feminist politics are ignored and very frequently turned against us with name-calling, no platforming and hate speech directed against us.[103] Lesbians resist the dominant hegemonic position in multiple ways — some of which are specific to lesbians and not the whole of LGBTIs who will each have their own specific forms of resistance.

---

103 For a useful guide to the terms used against lesbians see Wild 2019.

I suggest that marginalisation occurs whenever an all-encompassing term is used. There is a need to speak broadly in some fora, but that need should not be used as an excuse to silence the lesbian feminists who have done the most to challenge gender normativity. Is it, as Monique Wittig argued, that "lesbians are not women" (Wittig 1992, p. 20),[104] or, as popular discourse would suggest, that homosexuals are not lesbians?[105]

Lesbians are not the political priority of any well-funded policy-making organisation, including UNHCR (FiLiA 2020).[106] Moreover, they tend to be invisible both in policies of governments and in agendas of social justice organisations. When it comes to campaigns on violence against women, lesbians are either left out or included only in a footnote or in passing in the terms *sexual orientation* or *same-sex relationships* or *sexual minorities*. None of these specifies lesbians.

Extreme violence against lesbians occurs under every kind of political regime. In so-called developing countries it can result in state-sponsored executions. In the west, postmodern and market-driven libertarian philosophies are used to invisibilise and justify both linguistic and physical violence. But who cares? Do you?

Money

The money trail is less obvious here at least until recently, when drugs and surgical procedures for young women who say they feel they are in the 'wrong' body have opened a lucrative business opportunity (Brunskell-Evans 2020, see Chapter Seven). But if one considers all the ways in which women are denied a life, are denied

---

104 Her point is both interesting and radical. It is so because it gives clues as to why lesbians are so threatening to patriarchal heterosexist society.

105 For an interesting analysis of the similarities and differences between the experiences of violence by lesbians and gay men, see Ohms and Stehling (2001, pp. 190–222). For the German-language version, see pp. 17–52.

106 This is so in Australia and internationally. In Australia there is the Coalition of Activist Lesbians (COAL), the only formally registered lesbian NGO, but all its work is done on a shoestring and in a voluntary capacity.

freedom to be and do what they want and that when women who step out of line as lesbians and demand independence are raped, tortured and killed, the impact is significant. Since lesbians in nearly all arenas are almost impossible to count, then it is difficult to count money funded, spent, gained or lost.

The money trail by its absence is a clue. Organisations established and run by lesbians are rarely externally funded, although occasionally short-term funding is available. I know of several organisations for lesbians over 60 that have been able to continue because of bequests from lesbians who have died.

In the US, Old Lesbians Organizing for Change (OLOC) was founded in California with a conference in 1989 for lesbians over 60. Included in the1989 statement of purpose is: "We refuse to lie that it is shameful to be an old woman. We are here to meet each other, build community and find new ways to combat ageism, sexism, and racism" (Old Lesbians Organising for Change, 2020).

In Australia, Matrix Guild of Victoria Inc. has a focus on care and accommodation needs for older lesbians and invites members over 40 years of age (Matrix Guild of Victoria Inc. 2020).

Similar organisations exist in other countries such as Lilac in Aotearoa/New Zealand and in Germany where the name Graugänse (Grey geese) is used for a very successful social media page.[107]

But these organisations continue in spite of no funding or very limited funding from their own pockets. Lesbians want to be in control of our lives from youth to old age. We want to be able to speak on our own behalf, rather than have others who know nothing of our experiences to speak as if they knew. Indeed, as you'll read in Chapter Seven, many groups want to silence lesbians altogether. Lesbians call for nothing less than what other oppressed groups call for.

---

107 No websites are listed for these organisations.

Guidelines for officials interviewing lesbian refugees[108]

- It should not be assumed that women presenting for asylum are seeking asylum simply because their spouse or another male family member is doing so; they might need asylum in their own right, and for very different reasons, *including persecution on the basis of their sexual orientation.*
- Some women may however be persecuted because of their association with men who are under threat. If they are lesbians, their level of risk may be increased.
- It should not be assumed that a married woman cannot be a lesbian. In some countries marriage is the first level of protection a lesbian might seek.
- Lesbians seeking asylum are likely to be politically active, but even lesbians who are not politically active come under threat in some countries.
- Do not assume that because a woman does not use the word lesbian to describe herself, that she is not a lesbian. It may have been too dangerous for too long for her to be able to speak the word lesbian (or the equivalent in her language) out loud.
- Do not assume that because there is no word for lesbian in any particular language that there are therefore no lesbians in that society or linguistic group.
- Do not assume that if a woman comes from a country where it is not illegal to be a lesbian, that she is therefore not able to claim having been tortured or in danger of torture or other external harm to her self.
- Do not assume that your interpreter is open to her experience. The interpreter may be hostile to her claim.
- Lesbians who have been tortured will find it difficult to speak of their experience. Speaking to a stranger is difficult, speaking

---

108 The idea for this list came from a similar list of guidelines contained in *Agenda: Women, the Invisible Refugees* (Magardie 2003, pp. 81–87).

to a strange man might be impossible. Uniformed men may precipitate reliving the experience of torture.

- As a result of trauma, some lesbians may be unable to relate the experience at all, or may appear detached and emotionless. This should not be read as evidence of fabrication.
- Lesbians who are refugees might also be in danger from their families, in particular from the men in their families. Her confidential interview should not be shared by asking questions about her sexual orientation of other family members.

Queer theorists see the intimate connection between biological sex and oppression and they react by dismantling the notion of biological sex; feminists see the intimate connection between biological sex and oppression and they react by dismantling oppression. That's the fundamental difference between liberals and radicals; one sacrifices truth to avoid confronting power, and one confronts power to avoid sacrificing truth.

—Jonah Mix,
'Playing the Intersex Card'
(2017, p. 5)

CHAPTER SEVEN

Breaking the Spirit of the Women's Liberation Movement: The War against Biology

studied Zoology and Genetics at university as well as attending the first courses in Women's Studies in Australia in the 1970s. It was an exciting time as I was also diving deeply into feminist history and philosophy where we discussed Freud's statement, "biology is destiny." We read Simone de Beauvoir and we turned Freud's statement on its head, "biology is not destiny", we roared. Under patriarchal rules, "one is not born, but rather becomes, a woman."[109] We sang Helen Reddy's song *I Am Woman* loudly and passionately. We believed that the future would be better and freer. We could not have imagined a time in which biology would not only be denied, but *still* used against women.

We talked of sex-role stereotypes and some of the texts were *Sexual Politics* by Kate Millett (1970), *The Dialectic of Sex* by

---

109 Brownyn Winter begins her talk at The IQ2 Ethics Debate during Mardi Gras in Sydney 2016, with a reference to Simone de Beauvoir's quote above. See The IQ2 Debate 2016.

Shulamith Firestone (1970), *The Female Eunuch* by Germaine Greer (1972), *The First Sex* by Elizabeth Gould Davis (1971) and *Female Sexual Slavery* by Kathleen Barry (1979). In French there was *Le Deuxième Sexe* (*The Second Sex*) by Simone de Beauvoir originally published in 1949 and in English in 1953.[110] In German there was *Sexismus* by Marielouise Janssen-Jurreit (1976). Here was biology at the centre of debate. Hundreds of books were published with the words 'woman', 'female', 'mother', 'sex', 'sexual'. Until the publication of Judith Butler's *Gender Trouble* (1990), we were free to discuss women's bodies and women's biology. We hardly mentioned the word 'gender' — a term that Ann Oakley began to use in 1972. The word 'gender' was used to refer to 'feminine' and 'masculine' ways of behaving. There were only two genders and they lie at the extreme ends of the masculine/feminine binary.

< masculine -----

most human behaviour is found in the middle

----- feminine >

In 2020, the Australian Academy of Science has taken on the definition of woman as "anyone who identifies as a woman" (Lane 2020). The Chief Scientist, Alan Finkel, backed this re-definition. I wondered whether any of the scientists had studied biology, or indeed used their common sense. Madeleine Beckman, a Sydney University professor in the field of evolutionary biology, asks whether her scientific female colleagues have heard of the new definition. She goes on to point out that "biological sex could be a key variable in health and medical treatment, as shown by the higher male mortality rate from COVID-19" (Lane 2020).

What if we had followed the UK Green Party Women in 2016, using the word non-men to refer to women: non-men's liberation![111]

---

110 This translation by H.M. Parshley is now considered rather poor; a new edition translated by Constance Borde and Sheila Malovany-Chevallier was released in 2015. It includes many passages that were cut in the 1953 translation.

111 This was meant to be an act of inclusivity and instead excluded 50% of the population, that is women. As one subhead in *The Independent* put it, "'One

Would anyone have understood us? Would anyone have joined us? (See Wright and Hilton 2020; and Elliot 2020.)

Trans vs cis

> Trans is most easily explained by using the alpine analogy: trans-alpine means across the mountains; cis alpine means this side of the mountains (Hawthorne 2019, pp. 8–9).

Transgender therefore refers to someone who believes they are the sex on the other side of the binary (which they refer to as gender); cis refers to women and men who were born female and male respectively, but it does not mean they conform to the gender stereotypes of masculine and feminine, as trans activists claim. The term 'cis' is almost always used of women and in its use it turns the sex-class of women from an oppressed group into a privileged group. Because men are already a privileged group, adding cis makes no difference to men's status.

Those trans ideologues who are changing the language are clearly well educated and versed in Latin. The other change is to suggest that Ms and Mr are insufficient. Mx is one of the alternatives used. But the -ix ending in Latin indicates a feminine ending. You find it in words like creatrix and matrix. Our words are being taken from us.

How everything has changed. Simply using the word woman gets you into trouble these days. The slogan, 'Woman: adult human female', taken from the *Oxford English Dictionary* has caused uproar.[112] This meme, also available as a T-shirt, was put out there by Posie Parker (2019) in response to the slogan 'Repeat after me, Trans women are women' projected on the Justice Ministry Building in London in July 2018.

---

is not born, but rather becomes a non-man,' as Simone de Beauvoir didn't say"(Beale 2016).

112 See Posie Parker's site at <https://www.standingforwomen.com/>

Trans vs intersex

The category intersex is frequently used as a justification for transgender people to access treatment. But the organisation Intersex Human Rights Australia (IHRA) states the difference very precisely:

> Intersex is not a part of the trans umbrella (such as transgender or transsexual) nor is intersex a form of gender diversity, because intersex is not about gender, or transition. Intersex is about bodies; about congenital physical differences in sex characteristics (IHRA 2011).

In order to understand this definition, one needs to understand the difference between sex and gender. Briefly, sex is what you are born with and is visible in primary sex characteristics, or in the case of intersex of ambiguous primary sex characteristics.[113] Just as intersex is not about gender, nor is sex, that is female and male are sexes not genders. Gender is not visible on the naked body. Gender is a socially produced stereotype and includes statements like 'girls don't play football' or 'boys don't cook'; it is coded in niceness for girls and strength for boys; it is using people who are intersex as a 'vehicle' for the trans lobby (Graham 2019); it is the constant colour coding of pink and blue which is reflected in the nursery blue, pink and white flag of the transgender movement. According to trans philosophy *gender is a feeling*. But as a woman the only feeling I have about gender is that it is prescriptive and in patriarchy limits the full participation in life for women. It also limits men by expecting them to behave in masculine ways (unfeeling, strong, provider). Or as a Facebook meme has it: "sex is why women are oppressed; gender is how women are oppressed."[114] The trans lobby has appropriated intersex and hijacked it for the political ends of

---

113 The term 'disorders of sex development' (DSD) is sometimes used instead of intersex (see Graham 2019).

114 For a slightly different discussion on biology and identity see Hawthorne 2019, pp. 4–12.

transgender ideologues. Some claim it is a third sex, but this is just another language game. There is no third sex.

Trans vs lesbian

The abbreviation LGBTIQ[115] is widely used in the media as a shorthand. Let me unpack that: Lesbian, Gay, Bisexual, Transgender, Intersex, Queer. The first three LGB refer to sexual orientations of women and men, their sexual desires and intimacies; Intersex, as noted above refers to physical manifestations of xx and xy bodies with chromosomal variations and it does not reference sexual orientation; Transgender is a feeling of not being in the right body and has nothing to do with sexual partners; Queer is an academic philosophy with claims of inclusivity. Because of the use of the abbreviation LGBTIQ, most media organisations have no idea of how to separate the threads. Mostly it is read as 'whatever works for T is fine for all'. But TRAs[116] have invented language to erase women and to isolate lesbians. The needs of lesbians are not only left out, the discussion never happens.

I pointed out in Chapter One that it is the sex of women that has kept women's pay low. A number of 'transwomen' who claim to speak for women got all their promotions while they were living as men. For example R. W. Connell (Robert/Raewyn) was appointed Professor in 2004 and began publishing under the name Raewyn in 2005. By 2011 he was the Australian 'feminist' keynote speaker at the Women's Worlds Congress, in Ottawa-Gatineau, Canada. If the wages of trans people dropped subsequent to transitioning this would be a case of discrimination. This is not unlike the 'transwomen' competing in women's sport after they have grown up in male bodies.

---

115 LGBTIQA+ is used by some. I will use a range of variations of this abbreviation according to context.

116 Several years ago I began using the abbreviation TRAs because I noticed many similarities in their philosophy and that of Men's Rights Activists (MRAs). I think I was the first to do so.

Lesbians have been on the front line of this conflict for more than two decades. Two decades in which we noticed how the media picked up the trans side and ignored concerns of lesbians and of its impact on women more broadly.

In December 1992, the Sydney Lesbian Space Project was launched with the aim of raising $250,000 to purchase a building in Sydney's inner west (Parker 1993). It did not come to fruition even though sufficient funds had been raised to purchase a building because some of the lesbians on the organising committee wanted the Lesbian Space Project to be trans inclusive. It split the fund-raisers and the community and the building had to be sold and funds returned. Elsewhere, in Adelaide, a group called Sappho's Party, set up so that lesbians could meet privately. It was shut down because membership was for lesbians born female only (Redgold 2007); in Melbourne, where I lived at the time, the WOMAN Network — a transgender lobby group — threatened the existence of the Lesbian Festival and its ability to employ women-born-women.[117]

By 2012, the term 'cotton ceiling' had entered the language. You would think in an era of #MeToo that concerns about rape would be taken seriously. The term 'cotton ceiling' puts a lie to that. It was invented "to describe the difficulties faced by men who identify as 'trans lesbians' in being accepted as a 'real lesbian', finding lesbians reluctant to choose them as sexual partners" (Wild 2019, p. 5). And, as Angela Wild points out, the norm today is that most transgenders who grew up male "remain genitally intact males" (Wild 2019, p. 5). The men who still have a 'lady dick' (sometimes called 'lady stick') consider it transphobic to refuse their sexual advances. Rape is rape. How is it that when a trans activist says that he is offended, this counts for more than the rape of women?

---

117 The Victorian Civil and Administrative Appeals Court granted the LesFest 2004 an exemption allowing for the festival organisers to employ and advertise the festival only for female-born lesbians. However, the Australian WOMAN Network, a transsexual lobby group, complained that the term female–born is offensive. See also Hawthorne 2006c.

Lesbians are always aware of the threat of rape as I discussed in Chapter Six.

A 'transwoman' can never be a lesbian. And the harassment doesn't end there. Lesbians have been taken to court, including (perhaps especially) lesbians with a long history of activism. Among them, businesswoman and Black radical feminist activist, Linda Bellos OBE and former Labour Party (UK) activist Venice Allen were put on trial in the UK (Two Hare Court 2018). Journalists, Julie Bindel in the UK (Denham 2013) and Meghan Murphy in Canada, have received death threats (Lane 2019). All these women have been outspoken critics of the transgender lobby. But free speech has not been granted to them under the new rules of 'inclusivity'. It is clear that 'inclusivity' is used selectively and lesbians, radical feminists and gender critical feminists are outside the pale. They are vindictively charged with hate speech for standing up for their rights and for the rights of women as a group.

Trans vs women

All women are threatened by the trans lobby. But radical feminists and women who stand up to the bullying have copped it most. Maria McLaughlan, a 60-year-old radical feminist was punched in the face in Hyde Park, London in 2017. Women in prisons have been raped by 'transwomen' with a history of sexual violence. Rapist 'Karen' Smith was sent to a women's prison, in spite of his history of sexual offences against women and boys (Evans and Davies 2018). Although convicted, the report by Evans and Davies refers to Karen White as 'she'. He has had at least two previous identities. As David Thompson, he was found guilty of indecent exposure to a 9-year-old boy in Leeds in 1989, sexual assault of a 12-year-old boy in Leeds in 2001, and multiple rapes of a 23-year-old woman which caused her internal injuries. The report also states he was originally from the Manchester area and went by the name of Stephen Wood.

Midwives in the USA have been told to change their language to be more 'inclusive' with the result that there is no longer a 'mother', only pregnant parents (Woman-Centred Midwifery 2015).[118] The vagina is renamed the front hole; breast feeding becomes chest feeding (Wild 2019, p. 3). Trans activists want to access the services that are tailored to women such as access to refuges set up by women, for women who fear for their lives.[119] There are also trans activists who push the line ever further, such as the infamous case of balls waxer, Johnathan Yaniv (Jessica).[120] They want access to women's colleges and prizes; they want the sporting awards and records. Then there are the statistical distortions: when a 'transwoman' is arrested and categorised as female, the crime statistics change. Women are becoming more violent, says the latest woke media report. 'Transwomen' want to be treated as 'women' by doctors (did these doctors ever study biology?). But if a 'transwoman' patient is recorded as female what will this mean for the accuracy of information about reactions to drugs? The consequences are immense. Women's bodies are biologically different from men's and no amount of redefining women will change that.

The language confusion was made stark for me when doing an online search on the costs of gender reassignment surgery in Australia. I came across the following Google question: How many Australians are trans? The answer provided is: "According to the 2016 Census, there were around 46,800 same-sex couples

---

118 Glosswitch (2015) in an article responding to "inclusive transgender language around pregnancy" notes that "gender-neutral pregnancy starts to feel akin to John Major's 'classless society'. It's a way of using language to create the illusion of dismantling a hierarchy when what you really end up doing is ignoring it."

119 See Chapter 8 in Jess Hill's *See What You Made Me Do*, 2019.

120 "A 32-year-old male who claims to be a woman and describes himself as a 'proud lesbian', Yaniv is internationally notorious for filing more than 16 human rights complaints against Vancouver-area beauticians for refusing to wax his genitals, as well as for widely disseminated online social media messages that reveal his disturbing interest in young girls" (Laurence 2020).

in Australia." This is an incorrect answer to that question since it includes lesbians and gay men who far outnumber trans.

Lesbians and gays are not trans. Nor is sexual orientation the same as gender identity. These terms are not in the same category. Sexual orientation refers to women of the same sex attracted to or having sex with women (lesbians); and men attracted to or having sex with men (gay); and men and women attracted to or having sex with both women and men (bisexual). In many instances these individuals and groups challenge patriarchal gender normativity. The term 'transgender', by contrast, refers to individuals who want to perform the stereotyped behaviours of the opposite sex: cross-dressers (men dressing as women), 'transwomen' (men who claim to be women but share none of the culture of growing up female and living in a female body). What transgender people who take on feminine gender do, is to reinforce gender stereotypes. Among 'transmen', similar behaviours result and some women partners of 'transmen' express their anger at the misogynist behaviours some 'transmen' take on (Krishnan 2018, pp. 442–453).

Indeed, many trans undergoing gender transition (or a declaration to be of a different 'gender') do so because they feel uncomfortable being lesbian or homosexual.

> My best reading of the situation of men wanting to be women is that some men have decided to escape from their compatriots who have become too dangerous for them because they are challenging the norms of masculinity (Hawthorne 2019b, p. 87).

The language slippage, however, is distorting their fear of punishment from masculinists and the liberal mainstream seems unable to grasp the difference. The entry of aggressive and violent trans rights activists complicates it yet further.

Women's Circus

I was a member of Melbourne's Women's Circus when in April 2000 a 'transwoman' wrote and asked if he could join the Women's Circus. The circus was formed in 1990 in order to work with women who had suffered from sexual abuse or rape (Liebmann *et al.* 1997). I joined in 1994. Circus is a place of physical and emotional trust. There is bodily intimacy in balances, in double aerials acts. There is one balance in which the flyer puts her head between the legs of the base; there are aerials movements that involve hands between thighs or on breasts. This takes trust. Over the next six months, his application was talked about by members of the circus. To my knowledge no other applicant was ever accorded this privilege. It was a privilege because in the past, membership was either accepted or denied.[121] In his case there were clear boundaries for denying it. He was not a woman who had been subjected to sexual abuse or rape. The issue of boundaries was raised, to which I answered in an open letter:

- Women living outside of the state of Victoria are not permitted to join.
- Women under the age of 18 are not permitted to join.

Is the boundary 'woman' any less difficult to define than these rather arbitrary boundaries which are already in place? (Hawthorne 2000).

I also suggested that he be asked to withdraw his application. It took more than a year for this to happen. In the meantime, the circus was divided. Six months later, with the issue unresolved, I decided that I could not continue or be part of the end-of-year show. In late September 2000, I wrote the following in another open letter.

---

121 The suggestion was made that he be invited to speak to members of the Women's Circus. I thought this an incredible breach of protocol, since no one else ever had a right of reply to membership application (Hawthorne 2000).

Since speaking out about the transgender issue in April I have felt extremely isolated. I know a number of women feel like I do, some have said so and I appreciate that. Almost no one else, with the exception of the Dialogue Action Group women, has discussed the issue with me. I no longer feel the trust I have always felt in other women of the circus, partly because I do not know any longer what you think (I except from this about eight women who have said what they think including those whose view is the opposite of mine). For several weeks after that initial meeting in April I felt like an alien walking into the Women's Circus space, and though this feeling has lessened over time it has not gone away. I feel that for the most part I have hit a wall of silence … I have always thought the Women's Circus a most marvellous organisation. Inspiring. Dedicated. Irreverent. Fun. But I now have another series of words to add to the list. Disillusionment. Sadness. Anguish (Hawthorne 2000).

The result of my Discussion Paper on the circus was that a significant number of women over 40 years of age (another target group for admission to the circus) felt so uncomfortable that they left and never returned. I did return a year later after he withdrew his application, but the 2001 show was to be my last. I was punished by exclusion; on at least one occasion my contribution of a show text was rejected without explanation. I had contributed many songs, poems and scripts during my eight years in the Women's Circus. I no longer felt welcome in a place where previously I had felt at home; I had felt trusted and able to trust others. I had lost an entire community, friends and a fabulous way of keeping fit.

Oppression

As we've seen in earlier chapters, a number of features create oppression. They are used intentionally by the oppressors against those whom they dominate.

- *Silence*: silence has a multifaceted purpose. It separates the oppressed from one another. It makes it difficult and sometimes impossible for them to speak, for example forbidding speaking the mother tongue and in the case of lesbians enshrouding all words to do with lesbians in shame. The use of 'queer', generalised use of 'gay' and the LGBTIQ label has the effect of homogenising and of erasing lesbians. The same is the case for people with disabilities or those made homeless and stateless.

- *Trauma*: the oppressed are traumatised in multiple ways. Slaves are dehumanised and humiliated as well as being subjected to violence, often extreme; women experience many kinds of trauma and it is notably sexual trauma or related to shame.

- *Hatred*: while related to trauma, hatred of the oppressed is rewarded. Various kinds of bigotry, whether it be racism, poverty, misogyny, homophobia or meted out to anyone made different through disability or ethnicity. Hatred acts as a tool of suppression and makes it difficult for those who become objects of hate to be able to respond effectively.

- *Breaking the spirit*: this is a key feature of all kinds of suppression and domination. It creates an environment in which people are cut loose though dispossession of land, language, culture and a sense of community.

- *Theft of a future and a past*: when prisoners of war are taken, it plays out differently for women, men and children. Women are almost universally raped and sexually abused; men are tortured and too frequently killed or dehumanised by being treated as women; children, if they survive, are often kidnapped and raised as members of the winning side. This act steals their past and dislocates their future. It also prevents the continuation of the losers' culture.

- *Commodification*: alongside the above dispossessions, it is almost normal for the powerful to make their living from the commodification of these groups. Women are prostituted and pornified; their bodies and body parts sold to surrogate brokers as egg 'donors' or to carry a pregnancy for baby buyers; the poor are ravaged by having their organs removed which are sold on to the wealthy; the colonised or the defeated in wars are captured and sold into slavery.

Postmodernism and queer theory

How do the above-mentioned features play out in the battle between transactivists (TRAs), queer and postmodern scholars and radical feminists, lesbians and gender critical theorists?

For the purpose of this analysis, I am writing about transgender as a philosophical approach and as an ideology supported by postmodern and queer theory.[122] This ideology is played out in behaviours and it plays out differently for 'transmen' (born female) and 'transwomen' (born male). When referring to both, I use the word transactivists or TRAs. I use the pronouns he and she as they represent the original sex. I do not use the singular they. The explosion of inclusive words has become ludicrous and does not assist in clearly communicating with one another.[123]

In her book, *Gender Hurts*, Sheila Jeffreys sums up the use of the female pronoun nicely:

The female pronoun [is] an honorific, a term ... due to women as members of the sex caste system that have survived subordination and deserve to be addressed with honour. Men who transgender cannot occupy such a position (2014, p. 9).

---

122 See Raymond 1979/1994; Bell and Klein 1996; Jeffreys 2003, pp. 133–137; Jeffreys 2014; Jeffreys 2020; Jensen 2016; Krishnan 2018; Brunskell-Evans 2020.

123 "Males and females are in the problematic column. An array of unproblematic alternatives is listed in the column marked preferred: Cisgender men, cis men, cisgender women, cis women, cis people, cis allies, transgender men, trans men, transgender women, trans women, transgender people, trans people, gender-fluid people, gender-nonconforming people, gender-expansive people, gender-creative people, agender people, bi-gender people, genderqueer people. If in doubt, the authors suggest, use the word humans" (Cater 2019).

Silence

As discussed throughout this book, silencing and erasure are significant measures used to keep the powerless down. For lesbians, silencing has been extreme. While lesbians are more visible than ever with TV series and films with upfront lesbian characters and there are even politicians who are out, this is very recent. When I came out in the 1970s, it was easy within the Women's Liberation Movement but difficult outside that (a few brave women were out in earlier decades). Furthermore, there remain many limitations and mainstream (married with children) and queer lesbians are far more visible than radical lesbian feminists. Indeed, the latter, when visible, are almost always vilified. They are also shouted down and called names. The most frequent name-calling comes from transactivists who use terms like TERF (Trans Exclusionary Radical Feminists). When J.K. Rowling tweeted in support of Maya Forstater, who was sacked from her job because she said trans-women were not women (Fair Play for Women 2019), Rowling was vilified; she was called 'old' in an insulting way — a standard ageist attack. These are well known silencing tactics and many people including women and lesbians are too scared to speak in support of gender critical feminists.[124] Between 6 and 8 June 2020 under the tag #suckmydick, J.K. Rowling was further vilified by tweeters who think it's reasonable to make such comments. Subsequently, on 10 June, J.K. Rowling wrote back. She wrote "I was transphobic, I was a cunt, a bitch, a TERF, I deserved cancelling, punching and death" (Rowling 2020).

Such abuse has become frequent and much of it is not only misogynist but also colonising. One extract reads,

> We decide what being a woman means now. Cis bitches need to pick a new gender, because womanhood is off limits to them now. Your bathrooms belong to us. Your parades belong

---

124 For more on silence and erasure see the anthology, *Female Erasure* (Barrett 2016).

to us. Your clubs belong to us. Your bodies belong to us. We've already won (Facebook 2020).

I wish that this were an infrequent sentiment. But sadly I have seen many variations online and my response is to call for an end to the mass dehumanisation of women from this movement.

Trauma

Learning to survive when you are a young person who does not fit into the expected roles of your sex, your race, your ethnicity, your class, your place in the family and the world is hard. These are difficult experiences for adolescents. There are services provided to help cope with most of these adolescent hurdles. But recently the service has *become* the hurdle. For young women and men who feel challenged by 'gender expectations' the 'service' has turned on them by offering the diagnosis of gender dysphoria. Judith Herman describes dysphoria as "a state of confusion, agitation, emptiness, and utter aloneness" (Herman 2015, p. 108). An echo of the empty vortex. External trauma, such as child abuse, anorexia and autism are turned into an internally generated cause. Like so many women in the past punished not for what they do, but for who they are, these young women are offered a way out. They are offered puberty blockers, then cross-sex hormones and later irreversible double mastectomy surgery. Young men are offered similar irreversible options. Both are told that this will free them from trauma and they can go and live 'normal' lives. In fact, these are *normalised* lives, lives made to fit gender stereotypes. Anyone who has read from Chapter Two onwards in this book would recognise that this is not the positive step that it is made out to be in the public domain (Moore and Brunskell-Evans 2019; Brunskell-Evans 2020).

The resisters to the TRAs are those who have been most affected, some say most duped by the ideology of the transgender movement: the detransitioners. Jesse Singal in *The Atlantic* in 2016 spoke to women who believed that they were men. Once transitioning began, however, they found that this was not the case.[125] Carey Callahan, one of the women interviewed has spoken publicly about detransitioning and been attacked on numerous occasions for doing so.

> In a video accompanying the article, Callahan explains that when she was a child, she felt like 'a tomboy,' and when forced to wear a school uniform as a teenager that included a kilt, she started to be sexually harassed by men. "It felt so unfair to me that I had to wear this ridiculous outfit," she says. Once in college, she — like so many young women — was sexually assaulted, which she says "contributed to this feeling that I wanted to take my body off." In other words, what trans activists frame as 'gender dysphoria' was in fact the regular old sexism most women and girls experience in a patriarchal society. After living as a trans man for four years (which included injecting testosterone for nine months), Callahan realized that transitioning hadn't resolved any of her struggles. *"This is not a trans thing, this is a trauma thing,"* she says, adding that she now regrets transitioning, though luckily she had not yet gone so far as to get surgery as part of her transition (Murphy 2018, my italic emphasis).[126]

Hatred and shame

Surviving trauma is difficult enough, but when adolescents are subjected to hatred by being vilified as bull-dyke lesbians or sissy boys, or simply have the slur 'gay' hurled at them negatively, the layering of homophobic bigotry is hard to take. Hatred from the outside turns in on itself and it seems that it will never end. But a new heaven is offered, namely not gay, not lesbian, but trans. Suddenly the child or adolescent is the most popular and cool

---

125 For more from the voices of detransitioners see Brunskell-Evans pp. 77–81 and pp. 159–163.
126 There is a link to the video in Singal 2018, p. 22.

person in the school. No wonder they want to transition. The power of peer group pressure is immense.

Hatred by peers can cause shame. Many people who are outsiders experience shame. Shame is a powerful emotion and when young people experience homophobia, they understandably want to escape the psychological discomfort it causes. When I joined the Women's Liberation Movement in 1973, the first thing I was encouraged to do was to join a consciousness-raising group. All across the world, women were doing this. We did not ask for expert help, we'd already seen the harm caused by that. We talked and we listened. We all learnt from one another and we discovered that we were not isolated in our feelings, but rather that these experiences were systemic and structural. We began to understand oppression, power, domination and how we might extricate ourselves from the patriarchal system.

Today, instead of offering consciousness-raising groups and political activism, young people are psychologised and medicated. They are told that if only they transition all will be well. Initially, it appears to be celebrated when children and adolescents announce that they are transitioning. The pro-transition advertising/propaganda creates this ambience. Who would want to be gay? Who would want to be a lesbian? These categories are too old school, too passé for today's media-driven generation.

But this is only the beginning. For an adolescent to come to grips with themselves they need to be both loved and challenged. The friendships I developed through the feminist movement enabled me, for the first time, to talk about having epilepsy. Before that, like the dysphoric adolescent, I felt disconnected and isolated. But by confronting and processing my own fears, I became less alone. It was my peers who enabled me to reveal my secret and in doing so reduce its power. Young lesbians fear the label lesbian, and even more they fear that they will be disowned by family and relatives and called insulting names by their peers. They are vulnerable and this is not the moment to offer irreversible hormones and operations.

Breaking the spirit

By breaking the spirit, the trans lobby has created an inducement for young people to go down the road of conversion therapy which is called 'transitioning'. But it often does not work. The anguish does not go away or it re-surfaces and is worse. Suicide is often raised as a reason to transition adolescents (Withers 2019, p. 149) but detransitioning has saved lives (Patrick 2019).[127] The number of female detransitioners has skyrocketed in recent years and there have been many who have told stories of regret. Transitioning, instead of being a great boon, has become a burden, a terrible mistake. Many detransitioners talk about how they were just too young to be making this decision:

> Then I had chest surgery. It was botched and I was left with terrible scarring; I was traumatised. For the first time, I asked myself, "What am I doing?" I delayed the next steps of hysterectomy and lower surgery, after looking into phalloplasty and realising that I was going to need an operation every 10 years to replace the erectile device. Trans issues were starting to be written about in the media, and I understood that people would always be able to recognise me as having transitioned. *I just wanted to be male, but I was always going to be trans* (Anonymous 2017, my italic emphasis).

This anonymous writer eventually saw that the oppression of women was at the core of her decision to transition. She has come off testosterone and regrets that drugs and surgery were the only course of action offered for her unhappiness.

Mothers have been maligned when they try to protect their daughters and sons from predatory organisations who can see only the profit margins.

---

127 Robert Withers (2019) notes that there were four suicides of trans people in the UK over a period of ten years, and they were not adolescents; Patrick (2019) writes that after transitioning he made several suicide attempts and then when he decided to detransition, he found it a beautiful process (2019, pp. 195–199).

Fifteen-year-olds are considered adults for purposes of what is sometimes called sex change surgery; so called 'health providers' are immune from parental lawsuits if the provider can say they surgically altered a kid without the parent's permission, but did so in 'good faith'. Kids can be seized from parents who want therapy for them instead of surgery and hormones (Herman 2019).

The process of transitioning is a colonising one; it is intended to break the spirit of young lesbians and young gay men.[128] Corinna Cohn, a transsexual, writes that in a recent conversation with a former partner, they "agreed that our experiences as teenagers in the trans community was akin to grooming" (Cohn 2020). Breaking the spirit and grooming reinforce 'gender' stereotypes. Even the trans flag does this with its nursery blue and pink stripes. No amount of additional colours can change that basic premise of holding to 'gender norms': stereotypical blue for males and pink for females. Or as Donym writes:

A recent proposed change to the classic rainbow flag features a black and brown triangle, with the trans flag in the middle, placed on top of the rainbow. It looks like an invading force establishing a beachhead (Donym 2018, p. 12).

The visual shift from the rainbow flag to the trans flag is immense. On the one hand the rainbow flag represents a challenge to heteronormativity and the idea of gender; the trans flag reifies gender normativity. There is an urgent need to disentangle sexual orientation and gender identity. The two are utterly different.

Theft of a future and a past

In war, children are stolen. Colonisation results in the theft of children and their acculturation to the colonising culture. The trans movement is engaging in precisely the same ideology. Young

---

128 In the Money section of this chapter, I identify the colonisers.

children, children far too young to make lifelong decisions that will affect their physical and mental health, are being stolen once again: this time by the patriarchal medical system in the guise of transactivists. This is yet another Trojan horse sent by the ruling class. The sources of power and funding are such that the ideology has rampaged across the neoliberal west. While 'transwomen' come out and are visible, 'transmen' remain hidden (Krishnan 2018). Those who grew up as girls, can they ever speak of their childhoods? Or are they further excluded, for example from conversations about their past?

Children caught in this neoliberal cultural revolution underpinned by queer theory, lose not only their past (interrupted by massive numbers of medical and psychological appointments which makes them medically dependent for life), but also their future. We hear from detransitioners how they have regained their sense of self after escaping the trans industry. But we also hear how hard this has been and how so many facets of their original selves are lost forever (e.g. detransitioned women will forever keep a deep voice because of the irreversible effects from testosterone treatment).

Commodification

The profit mongering associated with trans ideology is mind-boggling. Imagine an exponential rise in young women transitioning in a decade and the cost of that. Each young woman — or her parents — forks out money for diagnosis; for ongoing psychological appointments; for puberty blockers over several years; for hormones for the rest of their lives; for top surgery (double mastectomy), bottom surgery (phalloplasty, and an operation every decade), the hospital stay and post-operative treatment; for further psychological services while transitioning. The cost is huge in time and money. While it is not possible to be precise about the total cost over a lifetime, because in the UK and Australia some of this is covered by the public health system, even rough estimates make it hugely expensive; in the US transitioning needs to be either privately funded or undertaken as part of a research program which provides the researchers with free guinea pigs. The costs begin at around $20,000 and can easily escalate to $50,000. This figure accounts for just the beginning; over an entire lifetime it could amount to hundreds of thousands of dollars.[129] Donym (2018) does her figures on the cost of taking Lupron, a puberty blocker, from age ten to sixteen. At $1200 per month over six years it comes to $86,400. Jennifer Bilek, two years later, estimates that in 2020 it costs USD $95,000 per year to have regular use of puberty blockers (Bilek 2020e). For each child transitioning, the profit margins in prescriptions for Big Pharma are high. Bilek goes on to cite Market Watch (2020) that predicts that by 2024 growth will be more than USD $968 million.

This suggests that most of those deciding to take this option are either very well-heeled (they can pay the full cost) or are poor enough to be able to access a health card or underwriting from social services. Or they are being used as research and surgery guinea pigs (WPATH Open Letter 2018). No wonder the TRAs want to be able to self-declare their gender (e.g. under the Gender Recognition Act in the UK and in Australia, under Victorian law) and thus avoid any treatment including operations.

Strategies used by the trans lobby

In 2020, after losing the 2019 General Election in the UK, the Labour Party insisted that all members sign a Trans Rights pledge that called "for sex-based rights campaigners to be expelled from Labour" (Kaufmann 2020). By sex-based rights campaigners, they are referring to gender critical people and radical feminists who for years have fought for women's rights (women like Linda Bellos,

---

129 Abigail Shrier reports that in some US colleges it is possible to begin transitioning for as little as $10.00: "At Yale, the cost of a course of testosterone for a natal girl under the student health plan is ten dollars a month — less than a standard Netflix subscription" (2020, p. 156).

Julia Long, Sheila Jeffreys, Julie Bindel and many others). The Labour Party vowed to "organise and fight against transphobic organisations such as Woman's Place UK, LGB Alliance, and other trans exclusionist hate groups" (Kaufmann 2020). In other words they vowed to fight against feminists, gays, lesbians and bisexuals. The UK Green's Party has faced similar problems over identity politics in their ranks. Political commentator Beatrix Campbell resigned from the Green Party in July 2020. She writes:

> … if a man is a woman because he says he is, then the category woman is emptied of meaning. How can we address the fact that women everywhere in the world are put upon, discriminated against, oppressed, under-paid, unpaid, raped and disrespected because they are women (Campbell 2020).

Hannah Arendt noticed in her book, *On The Origins of Totalitarianism*, when commenting on the nature of elites:

> The elite is not composed of ideologists: its members' whole education is aimed at abolishing their capacity for distinguishing between truth and falsehood, between reality and fiction. Their superiority consists in their ability immediately to dissolve every statement of fact into a declaration of purpose" (Arendt 1951/2017, p. 503).

If, like Maya Forstater, a woman uses male pronouns when referring to 'transwomen', she is accused of hate speech, bigotry and an intention to act violently. Her words are taken as 'a declaration of purpose'. The elites in this case are the funders of the transgender lobby, the transgender NGOs and acolytes. What hope have young people going through the usual adolescent confusions about the real world?

The accusation of hate speech, that is, harm intended by the speaker and expected to be felt by the hearer, has become a major strategy of silencing by TRAs. No amount of explanation preceding a speech (for example) is listened to. Women have been no-platformed, sacked, cancelled, attacked legally and physically.

These are women who refuse to kowtow to the trans agenda; those who use the word woman; those who deadname (use the pre-transition name of men who purport to be women); those who use the 'wrong' pronoun. All of these things 'hurt' the male ego so much that they lash out and punish the women. It is almost always women who are punished. As Heather Brunskell-Evans writes:

> Transgenderism is the attempt to wrest female biology from women and in that process not only violates women's agency but our collective capacity for resistance. We need the language of sex difference if patriarchy is to be challenged and resisted (Brunskell-Evans 2020, p. 31).

The trans lobby is quite sophisticated in strategic planning. Like many reactionary political groups, appropriation is a key feature. This is seen in the appropriation of women's spaces, of words for women, of women's bodies. It doesn't ever stop at appropriation. As I argue in *Wild Politics* (2002, pp. 92–93), appropriation is followed by incorporation, commodification, distortion, homogenisation and dislocation. These are familiar strategies we have seen throughout this book and there are other interesting ways that the TRAs have made their propaganda even more effective.

- Incorporation: using the LGB acronym and adding to it: T followed by a host of others (I, Q, A, P, +).
- Commodification: transitioning to transgender is a lucrative money earner (see below) for medical, pharmaceutical and psychological services.
- Distortion: not only is it lucrative, it is marketed as an end game in which transgenders are bound to be more popular than L, G and B.
- Homogenisation: the transgender flag with its pink, white and blue stripes indicates that transgenders are following the stereotypical gender script of feminine and masculine norms and will therefore fit into normalised gender stereotypes.

- Dislocation: young gay and lesbian people are shifted out of their communities into a new social norm. Their historical lives are erased.

The invasion of women's spaces has been going on for decades, but in the past few years even speaking about women's spaces is enough to be accused of evil motives. My book *In Defence of Separatism* (2019b) is based on work I originally did in 1976 when the discussion within the Women's Liberation Movement was less divisive. I write about the importance of women's spaces as a political strategy, a strategy that is widely used by many oppressed groups in order to create social and political cohesion and understanding among the oppressed. The difference is that oppressed groups might sometimes share houses with the oppressor, but they are not expected to love them. When men, calling themselves women, break into women's spaces it is like a black face claiming to belong to the Black community or the community of People of Colour. All the oppressive characteristics work in exactly the same way. But apart from radical feminists, no one seems to understand this.

Violence against trans people

Since 2018, I have seen articles about the massive numbers of murders of trans people. Murder is a vile crime and one that should be punished. But the media outrage is significantly overhyped and often untrue. Amnesty International has been running a campaign to highlight these crimes.

But the reality is that in the United Kingdom:

- Over the last decade there have been 7 homicides of trans people, all biologically male; there have been 12 homicides perpetrated by trans people, all biologically male.
- There were 71% more homicides perpetrated by trans people, all biologically male, than against trans people (all biologically male). Women are perpetrators of homicide at 18% lower rates than we are victims. Males are perpetrators of homicide

at 8% greater rates than they are victims. Trans people are perpetrators of homicide at 71% greater rates than they are victims (Ingala Smith 2018).

Comparable figures, gathered by the Femicide Census, for women killed by men in the UK show that at least 100 women per year are killed: 139 in 2017 (Women's Aid 2018); 149 in 2018 (Bindel 2020b). That means that in a decade approximately 1000 women were killed.

In 2018, a UN Report showed that around the world 50,000 women were killed every year globally by intimate partners and family members (Cole 2018). Across the board, men kill women, and men also kill 'transwomen'. The TRA lobby could better spend its time advocating for an end to violence by men. The Human Rights Campaign, an organisation that funds transgender advocacy has estimated that "globally 1,700 transgender murders have been reported in the *past seven years*, according to Arcus data" (Donym 2018, p. 13; italics emphasis by Donym). Arcus is another generous funder of transgender advocacy.

That is 242 murders per year, probably the lowest murder rate of any statistical category; not the 50,000 women murdered annually. One question this raises for me is why prostitution is made out to be a 'safe choice' of career by the funders (when the statistics show the opposite)? 'Transwomen' are said to be facing a trans murder epidemic? Of the 27 transgender people killed in the US, the majority were black prostitutes (Donym 2018, p. 14). The racist element in these attacks is not highlighted. The Open Society Foundations since 2010 has funded the Trans Murder Monitoring (TMM). The figures across four years from 2008 to 2011 show that globally 831 transpeople have been murdered across 55 countries; that is slightly more than 200 per year (Balzer *et al.* 2012, p. 22).

Institutionalising trans laws

A major international law firm has helped write a lobbying manual for people who want to change the law to prevent parents having the final say about significant changes in the status of their own children. That manual advises those lobbying for that change to hide their plans behind a 'veil' and to make sure that neither the media nor the wider public know much about the changes affecting children that they are seeking to make. Because if the public find out about those changes, they might well object to them (Kirkup 2019).

The IGLYO *et al.* (2019)[130] report has many flaws including ignoring the need to discuss the long-term health consequences for teenagers wanting to transition. The report asks for the elimination of the minimum age requirement as well as being in favour of self-determined change of identity as quickly as possible. None of this takes account of the possibility of infertility, cancer, bone density loss and other as yet unforeseen health impacts. But these big media companies (Reuters), large law firms (Dentons) and organisations that used to have the words lesbian and gay in their names and their mission statements now pander almost solely to the 'needs' of the transgender lobby.

The UN is complicit in this; *The Yogyakarta Principles* (2007) opened the door to these so-called universal recommendations that take no account of women, nor of lesbians. The principles drawn up by a meeting of the International Commission of Jurists, the International Service for Human Rights and other experts from around the world met at Gadjah Mada University, Yogyakarta, Indonesia from 6–9 November 2006. Throughout the Principles, 'sexual orientation and gender identity' are tied together. In some

---

130 IGLYO *et al.* 2019. IGLYO originally stood for International Gay and Lesbian Youth Organisation. It has been changed to International Lesbian, Gay, Bisexual, Transgender, Queer and Intersex Youth and Student Organisation. Of these three — L, G and B — are sexual orientations; Transgender is an identity; Queer is an academic discipline; Intersex individuals can be female or male.

of the clauses to do with Economic, Social and Cultural Rights (Principles 12–18) there are contradictory statements including some in which lesbians and transgender women are written about as if the two groups have the same needs and face the same hostilities. What they do have in common, as mentioned above, is that both groups are subjected to violence from men. But there are no protections for lesbians whose sexual autonomy or lesbian-only spaces are invaded by transgender 'women' (see my discussion above on the 'cotton ceiling'). [131]

Funded by billionaire philanthrocapitalists[132] who have appropriated organisations that were previously gay and lesbian focused but have been sneaking new laws through via same-sex marriage campaigns and the like leaves gays and lesbians in the lurch. The transgender lobby in many places has financially supported same-sex marriage laws. The philosophy of normalising lesbian and gay marriages along with following the norms of gendered behaviours (the stereotypes of feminine and masculine) has helped the push for marriage and heteronormative models for living. Same-sex marriage law campaigns also benefited from injections of money and the mobilisation of the masses.

I recall hearing about *The Yogyakarta Principles* when they first appeared and there was excitement that finally there was an international instrument which could be used in protecting the rights of lesbians and gay men. And while the claims for this remain, their usefulness is far more apparent for trans rights than for gays, lesbians and bisexuals. The trans umbrella has become

---

131 In March 2019, a group of three women came together to prepare the *Declaration on Women's Sex-Based Rights* to counter the effect of the Yogyakarta Principles. It begins: On the re-affirmation of women's sex-based rights, including women's rights to physical and reproductive integrity, and the elimination of all forms of discrimination against women and girls that result from the replacement of the category sex with that of 'gender identity', and from 'Surrogate' motherhood and related practices (*Declaration on Women's Sex-Based Rights* 2019, p. 3).

132 This is Vandana Shiva's word for the billionaire club she writes about in *Oneness vs the 1%*, some of whom overlap with the funders of trangenderism (Shiva and Shiva 2018).

so broad that it has lost its definitional power. As Sheila Jeffreys points out (2014) lesbians and gays "are not 'trans' because they do not fetishise gender in any form, but simply choose to live without it" (p. 149). The element of fetishisation appears in an odd condition that has developed in recent years, labelled Body Integrity Identity Disorder (BIID) (Gottschalk in Jeffreys 2014). It is to disability what transgenderism is to lesbians and gays: it appropriates a social and political system — the sex caste of women and the disability rights movement — and turns it into a diagnostic disorder requiring medical treatment and social and political support.[133] The similarity between transgenderism and transablism is apparent in the sexual satisfaction achieved through body modification. Would the social system feel comfortable providing scarce resources for transableists like Chloe Jennings White (he is also a man who identifies as a woman)? He uses a wheelchair and presents as a paraplegic but does not have a disability (Jeffreys and Gottschalk in Jeffreys 2014, p. 179). This 'performance' is more akin to being an imposter. If it shakes our perception of need and rights, so too should accepting men who claim to be women, as women, when they insist on using services that have been fought for, and developed by, women, especially by radical feminists.

The techno fix that is at the root of transablism shares a philosophical base with the push toward transhumanism, that is the crossover between humans and digital technology including Neurolink, an investment by Elon Musk in experimental links between human brains and computers (Bilek 2020i). Bilek also points to the transhumanist activities by Martine Rothblatt, a lawyer and entrepreneur who has been at the forefront of transgender law reform and recognition through the UN and other major entities, including his influence on the development of the *Yogyakarta Principles*. Rothblatt was the founder of United Therapeutics and earned a great deal of money in the biopharmaceutical industry.

---

133 BIID includes those who want amputation and extends to blindness, deafness and paraplegia.

He also runs a xenotransplanation farm where animals such as rats, mice, monkeys, rabbits and pigs will 'become heart and lung donors' for humans.

As Renate Klein in her poem 'Hope' (2018) writes about the response of a pig whose heart is being removed for the Big Master:

> 'I will', it said, 'not obey the Big Master for he is not the Master of the Heart.'
>
> 'I will,' it said, 'shrivel and turn yellow and putrid as is the Master's flesh.'
>
> 'I will, above all, cry' (Klein 2018).

What is happening is a tragedy as it divides radical feminists from young 'woke' feminists and left-liberals who are pro-trans. It is a tragedy because we should all be on the same side. It is similar to the tragedy that occurred in the 1930s, when communists felt they had to defend Stalin. Many communists outside of the Soviet Union were ignorant of the violent acts carried out by Stalin. As I have indicated earlier in this book, there are many similarities between totalitarian systems and those being used by the TRA lobby. In totalitarian Russia, Hannah Arendt points to the breakdown of the classes, a gap in understanding between the generations and atomisation of the society (Arendt 2017, pp. 412–417). In the current climate, the breakdown of what is seen as the 'gender system', a similar lack of understanding between second-wave feminists, the postmodern philosophy of individualism and the 'woke' generation has a similar trajectory. Today, most liberals feel compelled to defend trans because they are unaware of the violence being carried out mostly on young people's bodies and minds. Most people are uninformed about what is happening to young people; most are also uniformed about the attacks on radical feminists, among them death threats. Hannah Arendt also notices the misuse of science in promoting totalitarianism. Reflect on the statements of Australia's Chief Scientist mentioned earlier

(Arendt 2017, pp. 437–445).[134] The mainstream media is, in the main, propagating a pro-transgender line.

But the excuse 'I did not know', like that of defending Stalin, is beginning to wear thin. It is also like the divisions between people who used to be neighbours but have turned inexplicably on one another because a new distortion has entered their relationship, one based on lies and violence, often rigged up through notions of fundamentalism. The examples are numerous and are the foundation of wars between and within nations: the wars between Bosnians, Croats and Serbs in the former Yugoslavia in the 1990s (Simiç 2014); between Pakistan and India over what was formerly known as the Princely State of Jammu and Kashmir (Butalia 2000). Fuelled by Partition in 1947, the conflict between Hindus and Muslims has, under the leadership of Prime Minister Narendra Modi, intensified.

Fundamentalism is never good for women as I wrote in Chapter Three.

Money for astroturfing and transgender causes

Astroturfing is a very 21st-century means of advocacy. Organisations mask their sources of funding to give the appearance of being a grassroots organisation. Just as astroturf is fake grass, astroturfing refers to organisations that are fake grassroots, i.e. a phoney movement. Astroturfing is especially prominent in the US, but has spread around the world and is prominent among transgender and 'sex work' advocates.[135] A number of researchers have delved into the funders of the transgender movement, among them Jennifer Bilek (2020c; 2020g; 2020f; 2020h), Jody Raphael

---

134 This section of Hannah Arendt's *The Origins of Totalitarianism* has the thought-provoking section title 'The Temporary Alliance Between the Mob and the Elite'.
135 Just as the transgender organisations are well-funded, so too are prostitution rings.

(2018), Austin DeVille (2020) and the obviously nom-de-plume Sue Donym (2018). They all highlight the contributions of the following billionaire philanthrocapitalists:

George Soros
The man behind the Open Society Foundations is funding an enormous array of organisations who have lobbied governments, changed laws, and been a force to reckon with in the United Nations to change the language of human rights. Open Society Foundations (OSF) can be found supporting a wide range of organisations, among them the American Civil Liberties Union (ACLU), Human Rights Watch and Amnesty International which are also engaged in supporting the decriminalisation of prostitution and funding organisations who push that line (see Chapter Three).[136] George Soros also has connections to drug company Pfizer and to Monsanto (now Bayer). Other organisations funded by the Open Society Foundation include the Human Rights Foundation (HRF),[137] Freedom for all American (FFAA), and Planned Parenthood (PP). Austin DeVille (2020) includes transgender lobby groups such as Gay Straight Alliance, the Los Angeles Gay and Lesbian Community Center and the Global Action for Trans Equality. You might recall that Open Society also funds pro-sex work groups and is fully engaged in promoting the sex industry (see Chapter Three).

---

136 Around 2007, I had an ongoing argument with Amnesty International because they were ignoring instances of lesbians being tortured. My arguments were long and fruitless and I now suspect their motives had to do with lesbians falling outside the LGBT ambit.

137 A major corporate partner of HRF is Pfizer, the pharmaceutical company whose profits dropped significantly after Hormone Replacement Therapy (HRT) was found in women to lead to strokes, thromboembolism, endometrial cancer, and breast cancer (Coney 1993). Menopause created a market for women between 50 and 70 years of age; transgender treatment creates a hormone market from childhood to old age (if it doesn't kill them first). Long use of testosterone also has adverse effects such as elevated heart attack risk, stroke and blood clots (Donym 2018, p. 31; Brunskell-Evans 2020 pp. 46–50).

Jon Stryker

Jon Stryker owns Medical Corporation as well as the Arcus Foundation. The foundation is named alongside OSF as a major funder of Transgender Europe, together with the Government of the Netherlands and the German Heinrich Böll Foundation. Stryker's medical and surgical supplies for life-long medical treatment needed by trans people is a very useful corporate cover for making immense profits. Jennifer Bilek writes that he:

> ... funds his "LGBT" NGO from the coffers of his medical corporation worth [USD]$13 billion. Arcus is at the root of all the global programs driving this mythology through schools. They fund the ACLU, HRC, PFLAG, GLSEN, Gender Spectrum, OUT for Safe Schools, the National Center for Transgender Equality, and many many others (Bilek 2020e).

Jennifer Bilek (2020i) argues that the move by Arcus into Southeast Asia to assist in humanitarian projects, only needed because of deterritorialisation followed by impoverishment, is opening doors for Stryker to further colonise through the spread of transgender industries. These industries rely on a system of bodily dissociation and the need for long-term profit.

Through the Arcus Foundation Jon Stryker also funds the Gill Foundation and Transgender Europe, among others (DeVille 2020).

His sisters, Ronda and Pat are also engaged in pouring money into the LGBT lobby. Ronda does so through the Greenleaf Trust, whose chair is her husband, William Johnston. Pat Stryker is working closely with the Tim Gill Foundation, funded by the sale of Gill's computer software company, Quark (Bilek 2020g).

Col. Jennifer Pritzker (born James Pritzker)

Owns the Hyatt Hotels chain and runs the Tawani Foundation. Jennifer Bilek, writing about the Pritzker family, unpacks the family relationships.

JB Pritzker, is the Governor of the State of Illinois. The Pritzker family controls billions of dollars and they appear to have chosen the transgender cause as a major recipient of their money.

James Pritzker is a cousin of JB Pritzker, and now goes by the name Jennifer. Jennifer Pritzker is the richest transgender person on the planet. His wealth is estimated to be USD$1.8 billion. He claims to be a trans 'lesbian'. He transitioned in 2013, is the recipient of the fortune from the Hyatt Hotel and he funds Republican, far right and transgender causes. Among them is a transgender youth clinic in Chicago (Donym 2018, pp. 15–16; Kenobii 2020). A former military man, Jennifer has donated USD$25 million to Norwich Military College and USD$13 million to transgender organisations over three years. He has supported a children's hospital, one that delivers increased access to mental health services for children and youth. This is the first step in providing 'treatment' for dysphoria (Goldberg 2019).

Penny Pritzker, another cousin of Jennifer, was a part of the Obama administration and Penny's brother, JB Pritzker

> [in] 2014, JB donated [USD]$25 million to Obama's early childhood development initiatives, after JB's sister, Penny got Obama elected and during the same year *The Advocate* was touting Obama as the most Trans-friendly president ever (Bilek 2020d).

So while the Pritzkers mostly support Republican and right-wing causes, when it's expedient or when a family member supports the Democrats, the money still moves in the same direction, that is towards funding the transgender movement.

Peter Buffett
Peter, son of Warren and Susan Buffett, runs NoVo Foundation. Jennifer Bilek (2020d) writes that along with the Pritzkers, they too were at Obama's early childhood summit. The Buffetts "have committed billions of dollars" to the NoVo Foundation. Further:

NoVo in partnership with Arcus Foundation, the largest "LGBT" NGO in America, which is having enormous global impact pushing "transgender" mythology, donated [USD]$20 million dollars for "transgender" causes in 2015 (Bilek 2020d).

They are all responsible for a massive increase in funding to transgender organisations who themselves often hide behind the label LGBTQI (but the vast amount of proceeds go to T organisations).

The amount of money that has been put into supporting the transgender lobby is mindboggling. From 2010 to 2016, transgender funding in the US increased from $3 million to $22 million (Donym 2018, p. 4), that is, a seven-fold increase.

After doing the research in this area, I realised that it needs a book of its own but these brief pointers towards the funding juggernaut will have to suffice here.

Why sexual orientation not gender identity?

- Sexual orientation is a relatively straightforward description of the desires and actions of people. When there are two sexes there are four ways of expressing sexual orientation: women with women (lesbian); men with men (gay); women with men (heterosexuality); women with women and with men, men with men and with women (bisexual).
- Sexual orientation challenges gender normativity.
- Political groups have formed to challenge T inclusion, such as 'Get the L out' and the LGB Alliance.
- The difference this makes in the lives of women and lesbians is that the rights of those born female are protected.
- Given the rates of murder of women (both lesbian and heterosexual) by men globally, the rights of women deserve protection. (I am not unaware of men's violence against men, especially of black men and men in oppressed groups, including

trans people. Instead of the power discrepancy between sexes, reasons of race, class, religion, ethnicity lie at its core.)

- Imagine a world in which the bodies of women are not objectified; not expected to be young, thin, beautiful; imagine a world in which women could walk through a park, along a street in the day or night and not be afraid; imagine a world in which men were aware of their power and sense of entitlement and used that understanding to behave with respect towards women (not follow a woman down a street or a park; and refrain from attacking her wherever she is).

- Imagine a world in which young lesbians and young gay men felt comfortable in their bodies and the words 'lesbian' and 'gay' were not used as insults nor as objects in pornography (nor should trans be used as an insult). The excessive funding of transitioning — which keeps people indentured to the industrial medical industry — is no better than any previous system of indenture.

- Radical feminist resistance to the trans lobby has been both longstanding and consistent. The analysis has been structural and anti-capitalist. It includes analyses of racism and poverty. It includes a critique of patriarchy and sex role stereotyping (gender). It appears that the radical feminist critique is gaining some success with stopping the Gender Recognition Act from being rewritten in the UK. One can only hope that increasing awareness of the inherent misogyny of self-declaration laws will gain traction elsewhere.[138]

- By contrast, gender identity is a useless and nebulous concept that has nothing to do with sexual orientation.

---

138 For a lecture that is both historical and current see Sheila Jeffreys on 'Men's Sexual Rights versus Women's Sex-Based Right. WHRC Webinar 18th April 2020. Sheila Jeffreys — YouTube. Also see Jeffreys 2020 for her take on the development of a lesbian feminist analysis from the 1970s to the present.

Timescale

Take a trip to the tropics:
lie on the beach, snorkel the reef, walk the rainforest
it can all be done in just a few days—
you see and you think you see
but only time brings other ways of seeing

—Susan Hawthorne,
Earth's Breath (2009, p. 2)

CHAPTER EIGHT

Breaking the Spirit of the Planet: Climate Catastrophe

The previous seven chapters have dealt with systems which are human-centred and which are responses to groups of people oppressed by the powerful and through systems under patriarchy which marginalise them politically, socially and culturally. There are intersections between humans and the natural world in previous chapters, but in this chapter my focus is on the way in which the natural world is changing in response to human action. Catastrophic climate change is caused by humans, but it is more than that: it is caused by patriarchal systems — some capitalist, some communist, some monarchist, some feudal, some libertarian. The traditional and Indigenous peoples around the world have had little impact, in fact as we will see they have much to teach those in the 'west'; and while there are rich women capitalists (Gina Rinehart, for example) they are few in number as women are the poorest of every poor group.

In this chapter I look at the crisis of patriarchy that we are seeing in the planetary vortex that is upon us. It has taken a back seat as we deal with the pandemic which is having a profound effect on the world, which, as Arundhati Roy notes, "in the richest, most powerful nations in the world, bringing the engine of capitalism to a juddering halt" (2020). In the meantime, millions of people have become sick, hundreds of thousands have died and been displaced in ways that at the beginning of 2020 we could not have imagined was just over the horizon.

> Adults keep saying:
> "We owe it to the young people to give them hope."
> But I don't want your hope.
> I don't want you to be hopeful.
> I want you to panic.
> I want you to feel the fear I feel every day.
> And then I want you to act.
> I want you to act as you would in a crisis.
> I want you to act as if our house is on fire.
> Because it is
> (Thunberg 2019, p. 24).

And as Arrernte woman Lorrayne Gorey says in her video:

> We finally need to treat the climate crisis as a crisis. It is the biggest threat in human history and we will not accept our extinction. We will not accept a life in fear and devastation. We have the right to live our dreams and hopes. Climate change is already happening. People did die, are dying and will die because of it, but we can and will stop this madness (Gorey 2019).

Breaking the spirit of the planet

When profit is everything, nothing else matters: not teenage climate strikers; not Indigenous peoples; not the bodies of women; not the largest living organism in the world; not ancient rainforests that have never before burnt; not koalas; not anyone; just the profit to be obtained from fossil fuels, shonky investment schemes, people's bodies, industrialised farming, fishing and forestry, and endless prescriptions of lifelong drugs: Big Coal, Big Weapons, Big Medicine, Big Porn, Big Agriculture, Big Pharma.

In February 2017, Scott Morrison walked into the Australian House of Representatives and held up a piece of coal; he justified it by saying that coal would keep the lights on and keep power bills low. Since that time, he has changed jobs from Treasurer to Prime Minister. The debate over the Adani coal mine in Queensland has gone on no matter how much the government would like it to stop (but unfortunately, to date, they have not stopped the proposed Adani coal mine). Extinction Rebellion rallies have been held in major cities as well as school-age children participating in the School Strike following the lead of Greta Thunberg. The most recent event, which has made that chunk of coal more chilling, was the massive fires burning across eastern Australia from September 2019 to March 2020. By December 2019, 4.6 million hectares had burnt (Evershed and Ball 2019). But this was just the beginning.

In the weeks immediately following that, the figures continued to rise. By 1 January 2020, 5,900 million hectares had burnt. By 17 January 2020, the figure had jumped to 10.7 million hectares. And by 4 March it stood at 18.6 million hectares.[139] Thousands of buildings and homes have been destroyed and 34 people have died. The number of animals killed is also heart wrenching, jumping from 500,000 to more than a billion. These figures are hard to stomach. The level of grief in the Australian community has skyrocketed.

When the Amazon rainforest was on fire in 2018, approximately one million hectares burnt. Forests in the Greater Blue Mountains World Heritage Area in Australia that were listed by UNESCO in 2000 have burnt for the first time in 2019–2020. It is an area with a huge diversity of eucalypt forest and endemic to the area are non-fire-resistant Gondwana-era species. By mid-January more than 50% of Gondwana rainforests in world heritage areas had burnt. Like the Amazon rainforest, this is a precious heritage. We cannot afford to be losing this level of biodiversity. The number

---

139 Every time I revised this chapter, the figures had changed yet again.

of trees is countless considering the understory, the nesting holes, all the microhabitats that make up forests and grasslands. People retreated to beaches, but even there ember attack made beaches unsafe places; breathing, because of thick smoke clouds that lasted for weeks, became arduous for many.

In the heat of Australia's summer with pyrocumulonimbus clouds entering our vocabulary along with the threat of fires started by lightning strikes, that piece of coal appears even more obscene. When Scott Morrison finally interrupted his Hawai'i holiday on 21 December 2019, hundreds of homes had already been lost and three fire fighters had died in one week. In subsequent days, thousands of people fled fires along the South Coast holiday area of NSW. In Mallacoota, the navy was called in to evacuate people stranded on the beach (McGuire and Butt 2020). Vast stretches of alpine grasslands across the NSW and Victoria border region have burnt; Kangaroo Island in South Australia has been devastated with around half of the island burning.

The house called Australia began burning in September 2019 and it was late December before Prime Minister Morrison noticed that only the chimney remained standing along with a few sheets of corrugated iron. As Greta Thunberg said almost twelve months earlier on 26 January 2019, and Australians in burnt out areas were saying to Scott Morrison, "We want you to panic. The country is on fire and you have done nothing. In fact, everything you have done has provided more fuel for the fire."

This is the background against which I wrote this chapter. Politicians, the fuel and energy industries and the big coal miners all claim that climate change is not caused by their actions. They use terms like clean coal, carbon capture and storage, nuclear power and most recently 'a gas-led recovery'. But these words are meaningless. They are the Trojan horses of climate change. The fake promises of fossil fuel barons are pretending they are somehow clean energy sources equivalent to renewables.

It is not only fires. There are massive problems around the politics of water, the survival of river systems and the Great Barrier

Reef. According to Earth System scientist, Will Steffen (2020), the catastrophe is already upon us. Underwater heatwaves have killed about half of the corals and sea grasses on the Great Barrier Reef. In April 2020, marine scientist Terry Hughes reported on the third mass bleaching in five years (Readfern 2020b) and the worst yet on record.

The flood that inundated Townsville in North Queensland in early 2019 destroyed large areas of a city rarely hit by flood. In southeastern Australia, a highly productive agricultural area, drought is causing farmers to abandon their farms and to send stock to market because there is insufficient feed for them. Cities around Australia, amongst them Sydney, Melbourne and the nation's capital, Canberra have suffered such intense smoke pollution that the air was almost unbreathable. Dust storms followed by rain have caused tanks to fill with mud instead of water.

These cascading weather events are a sign that worse is to come. The wastage caused by coal mining, by so much investment in and use of fossil fuels, is creating a future 'Hothouse Earth' with temperatures 5–6 degrees higher than in the pre-industrial era (Steffen 2020). It is not as if information on these dangers is not available. Listening to what Aboriginal people across Australia have to say would make a difference. Bill Gammage's 2012 book, *The Biggest Estate on Earth: How Aborigines Made Australia* won enough prizes to be required reading for all politicians. *Dark Emu* by Bruce Pascoe (2014) and Victor Steffenson's *Fire Country* (2020) should also join that list. These and other books show the ways in which land management was a central part of how the Aboriginal people of Australia acted over tens of thousands of years. They also tell us what we should do today.

Temperate zone: bushfires

bushfire four months after

headlights flash burnt tree trunks
standing like dead sentinels on a battlefield
the skyline is red the air is silent
no one sings here no bird flies overhead

between the blackened trees plain brown soil
as barren as a napalmed forest
my eyes are red my breath stilled
no animal feeds here where no plant grows

(Hawthorne 2009)

I wrote the poem above after the Black Saturday fires in Victoria in 2009. Friends lost their houses or came very close to losing them. Young people died when they could not escape. 173 people died in those fires. So, while some lessons have been learnt about how to save human life, several iterations of Australian governments have not listened and in fact have introduced policies that only intensify the problem. In April 2019, 22 former emergency and fire service chiefs from across Australia tried to set up a meeting with the Prime Minister Scott Morrison. Not only were they ignored, they were criticised and belittled (Mullins 2020).

The idea that climate change is an emergency does not seem to have sunk in for politicians. Elaine Scarry in her book *Thinking in an Emergency* (2011) sets out what is required in an emergency and it looks very different from the Australian government's reaction. In order to prepare for foreseeable types of emergencies early deliberation is required. The reason for this is that when the emergency eventuates, swift action must be taken. A government in denial about climate change is a government working against itself. Another requirement is practice. There are good reasons for the volunteer fire services around the country to regularly meet and practise skills when there are no fires. When the fires do come, they need to be ready for well-practised immediate action. Politicians arguing about whether the fire is a result of climate change are not practising for action in an emergency. While politicians recognise the need for action in an emergency, they are seduced to stop thinking. They think that action is all that is needed. But action under these circumstances could be worse than inaction.

This is where Australia stands in the grip of the emergency in early 2020, an emergency that governments could have been preparing for and practising for at least 30 to 50 years. In 2008, the Australian states commissioned Ross Garnaut to write the Garnaut Climate Change Review. It was presented to the Prime Minister and the State Premiers in September 2008. At that time there was strong support from both the federal Labor government, led by Kevin Rudd, and the federal Coalition Opposition led by Malcolm Turnbull. A series of leadership changes, particularly with the Liberal Party's Tony Abbott winning the leadership spill in December 2009 just ahead of the Copenhagen Conference, meant that Australia no longer had bipartisan support for the Review. Four years later, when Tony Abbott became Prime Minister in 2013, all the important policy moves went backwards even though the 2011 Review had been acted upon by Julia Gillard's Labor government. Indeed, as Ross Garnaut states, "it left an incoherent climate and energy policy legacy" (2019, p. 34).

Since 2013, the Coalition have been a government looking away from the looming disaster. And with the 2020 fires extinguished by heavy rain in February, the hope many held for action on climate change has come to naught. Instead, we hear that billionaire miners like Twiggy Forest are putting money towards projects that will show the "science was incomplete" on the link between fossil fuels and climate change (Bourke 2020). Of the $70 million dollars he said he was donating for bushfire relief, $50 million of that is not for victims of bushfire, but for research that will help to clear more forests.

Such misleading 'donations' echo ideas expressed by Scott Morrison and his government who would like to see National

Parks opened up through clearing and resort investment and more thinning out of forests. They claim that these actions will reduce the hazard of fires. But ecological and scientific research shows that reducing the number of trees leads to increased drying out of the forest floor and that logging debris results in increased fuel (Lindenmayer 2020).

The government and the coal industry are responsible for exacerbating climate change, for doing nothing to reduce emissions and nothing to help reduce searing temperatures across the Australian continent.

On 18 December 2019, the average temperature across Australia was 41.9°C or 107.4°F. The previous hottest day on record was the day before (Readfearn 2019).

Anyone living in Australia during this period understands just how hot it has been. The most severe consequence has been the bushfires that have devastated Australia. In addition to the 1.25 billion native animals that are estimated to have died, an estimated 100,000 farm animals have also died. The economics of this is revealing. Farmers who lose stock to natural disasters can expect some compensation for that loss, either through insurance or from government schemes to assist farmers recover. The people who look after native animals, ordinary locals in an area who feed the remaining animals, who grieve for their loss, get nothing. It strikes me that this is comparable to the way in which women's work is not counted (Waring 1988). As Suzanne Bellamy, an artist whose studio near Braidwood was threatened with fires five times during the past fire season wrote:

> I had a phone call this morning from the Agriculture and Livestock Board, a very pleasant woman from Goulburn. Did I have livestock impacted by the fire? I told her my land is native vegetation inhabited by native animals, and yes it has been impacted. Doesn't count, not commercial, no assistance. I do understand the distinction, and I feel for the cows and sheep and the farmers. I thanked her for the call. Still, it frames the dilemma of the land, money, usage, status and value. So

we will cut up the carrots and sweet potato, scatter the bird seed and put out the water. We begin to let out the depth of mourning for our beloved friends with soft paws, square poo, spikes, slithery skin, feathers, pouches, ancient lineages and wild stories, beyond value so it seems (Suzanne Bellamy 17 January 2020).

Just as women's unpaid and necessary domestic work is not counted in the UN System of National Accounts, nor are forests, grasslands, rivers, mountains and shorelines. The native animals who render their own kind of service to land are erased and given no value. I am not suggesting that counting will *solve* the problem, but we need to *recognise* the problem and come up with different systems. A generation has passed since Marilyn Waring (1988) wrote that the system was broken. It is still broken and the bushfire crisis is also a crisis of patriarchy and of capitalism.

For decades, Aboriginal peoples across Australia have been talking about traditional systems of land management. Indigenous peoples from around the world have a range of different practices such as prohibitions on felling certain trees (Hawthorne 2002a, p. 225 ff). Darkinjung woman, Vanessa Cavanagh (2020) gives a sense of this in her moving essay about the impact of seeing an important grandmother tree near Colo Heights, northwest of Sydney, lost in the Gospers Mountain fire. There are many new calls for cultural burning, a system that allows for low intensity fires to be used in areas that could come under threat. It would require the forestry industry (and misinformed corporates and governments) to cease adding to the fuel load through thinning and clearing of forests.[140] An area that burnt in the 2020 fires, Kangaroo Valley in NSW south of Sydney, is an area that Bill Gammage writes about. Throughout his book, he outlines the multiple ways in which the land was burnt and how it has changed since 1788. He says,

---

140 For an extended discussion on forest management see Hawthorne 2002, pp. 218–230 and pp. 249–254.

> Without fire this is climax rainforest country; some is rainforest now, including under giant eucalypts. The valley required at least four distinct fire regimes, but confined and located the plants and animals of almost every conceivable local habitat (Gammage 2012, p. 232).

Victor Steffensen (2020) learnt his fire practices from two elders who had been brought up in traditional ways in the area around Laura in Far North Queensland. The men taught him how to read country in a context sensitive way (pp. 19–20). This is in stark contrast to hazard reduction and back burning carried out by Queensland Parks and Wildlife Service (QPWS) with flame throwers and no understanding of what kind of fire is appropriate for particular ecologies (pp. 20–22). Steffensen shows just how different the approach to burning is by Aboriginal people steeped in their traditions from the approach of those who are meant to conserve our National Parks.

Bruce Pascoe, writing about Aboriginal fire practices, suggests that it was intimately connected to farming (2014, p. 49). Farming in any sense is about land management and in Australia he suggests this could go back as far as 140,000 years. When we understand what poet, Mary Gilmore, noticed in 1934 — that burning had to do with spiritual practices — we need to ask more questions.

From my decades-long research into ancient cultures it is quite clear that ecological protection and spiritual and ritual practices go hand in hand: an important river or series of waterholes; a small copse of fruit trees; a plant or animal species; a cave that gives shelter; a mountain with particular species. These connections become more and more evident. The dismissal or ignorance about such important ecological and cultural sites is at an all time high in our current global culture that homogenises everything and ignores detail. The destruction of the Juukan Gorge site in the Pilbara region of Western Australia by Rio Tinto in May 2020 is one such example. Considered a sacred place by the Puutu Kunti Kurrama and Pinikura peoples, it contained artefacts that were at least 46,000 years old. Biodiversity is protected only when there is strong local knowledge of place, of country and appropriate respect, protocols and laws with teeth to ensure such places are protected (Koolmatrie 2020; Walhlquist 2020).

Dry zone: drought and water wars

Water fits land like a glove fits a hand.
It follows the lay of the land — pools

in hollows and flows between inclines.
Water and land are intimate—

they shape one another. Water seeps
through the soil, jumps down cliffs—

rocks bounce through streams—
clatter along shorelines.

In this time of separating land
from water, glove from hand

drought scrapes the surface
but it is our unsettling

that chops out the fingers
to claw at earth's innards.

(Hawthorne 2008, pp. 8–9)

I grew up along the Murrumbidgee and my brother and I were constantly walking its banks. We came to know its seasons, the odd pools where the water eddied; we swam in it and built small barriers so the water moved in new ways. And when the flood came in 1974, we heard it break its banks and watched as it flooded the paddocks in front of the house. The cattle had to be moved to high ground and we were isolated on the farm for some days. Fences were broken, the road was broken and the only way to drive on it was with a tractor. This force of nature was well beyond what I had expected when we heard that the river was expected to flood.

My father arrived just before they closed the road. He saw the flood front coming, put his case on the roof of the ute and climbed a tree in the long driveway. He strapped himself to the tree with his belt. Thirteen hours later, a small boat with provisions was navigating its way up the driveway and they heard his shout. He said later that the force of the water was so strong he could not have made it. His case was found five kilometres away. These stories enter the body. The sound of the river breaking its banks is with me forever. When threatened by a flood, I cannot sleep or rest until I am in a safe place.[141]

The Murrumbidgee is a beautiful river. On the planes near Wagga Wagga it is wide and full of birdlife. It is a critical part of the town. It has been used for irrigation and even while that irrigation remained relatively low key, the river had changed in massive ways in the preceding century. In 1881, journalist and adventurer George Ernest Morrison wrote of the Murrumbidgee,

> I saw three emus close to the water, disturbed 10 wild turkeys and put to flight any number of swans and native companions. In every little bay were pelicans by the score, singly, in pairs and by the hundred, mountain ducks in small bands, wood ducks, teal, blue cranes, black and white cranes by the hundred, white cranes by the thousand; ibises, both the ordinary kind and the all-white, in immense flocks, feeding in the long water-covered grass; great black shags (cited in Bellamy and Hawthorne 2008, p. 1).

By the 1960s, when I was swimming in, or wandering the banks of the river, only the ducks remained in any numbers.

Australian rivers by and large are episodic in their flow. This can range from massive flows of floodwaters across kilometres of flood plain to a completely dry riverbed with just a few pools of water.

---

141 It's not the only flood I have been in. I have written about floods in several books, the latest of which is *Limen* (2013).

1967 was a drought-stricken year in the Riverina. I recall a conversation with my mother in the summer of 1967 and I remember the sentence she spoke, *Oh, it breaks my heart so* (Bellamy and Hawthorne 2008, p. 5). The paddock was bone dry. Not a single blade of grass. Drought was not an uncommon visitor in my childhood years, but the drought that ran from 1957 to 1968 broke the spirit of many people. Some suicided. Some left farms they had worked and lived on for decades. Some just gave up. In country towns after a long drought you can see the loss of spirit. The drought is in their mouths. The Millennium Drought from 1995-2009 in Australia has been called the 'one-in-a-thousand-year drought'. The current drought, which began in most areas of Australia in 2017, while not yet as long, has exceeded all others in temperature.

Drought is not only about temperature, but high temperatures exacerbate drought because feed for animals is reduced on farms. Native animals are more resilient having evolved with the Australian landscape, but they too can be affected when temperatures are high and food is scarce. Rivers begin to dry out and flow is reduced. At the same time as the 'one-in-thousand-year drought', Australia's biggest river system, the Murray–Darling, was coming under pressure not only from the weather, but even more severely from industrial agriculture. Cotton farmers at the head of the Barwon–Darling River system were using excessive amounts of water for an unnecessary crop, cotton. Charles Iceland (2015), in a brief article about seven droughts on different continents, indicates quite clearly that in addition to surface water, the depletion of groundwater around the world is happening at an increasing rate and the consequences of this will be severe in coming decades. Just at the time we will most need good water supplies, they will be under even more stress. Groundwater is a global backup system. It can take millions of years to replenish. What are the current threats?

The number of recent fish deaths in the Murray Darling Basin in 2019 (occurring in the Lower Darling section) is estimated from anywhere between hundreds of thousands to three million.

The MDBA Report [Murray Darling Basin Authority] shows that a combination of factors associated with climate change and corporate water theft are the likely cause of the fish death.

In sum:
- 2018 was the 8th driest year on record.
- 2018 was the hottest year on record.
- Inflows to NSW rivers dropped from 4,000 Gigalitres to 30 Gigalitres (less than 1% of the usual inflows) (Vertessy *et al.* 2019)

While the report acknowledges the Barkandji people who have lived in the region for thousands of years, there is no serious attempt to take on board the knowledge they have of the river.

In 2006, in an article 'Unbundling water from land' I worried about the separation of land ownership and access to water licences:

Separating water from land is just the first move in a number of legal rewritings which we can expect to see in coming years. If you think Howard's move [the then Prime Minister] on saving the Murray–Darling Basin is important, look closer, read the small print, look out for separations. They are markers of far worse things to come (Hawthorne 2006d).

That prediction has come true with "70% of water allocations in the Murray–Darling Basin owned by two corporations: Webster, and Ron and Peter Harris of Ravensworth Agriculture Company" (Garcia 2019). In 2015, Peter Harris was charged with illegally taking water from the Barwon-Darling River (Davies 2019).

Maryanne Slattery, now a Senior Water Researcher at the Australia Institute had formerly been "in charge of assessing the unimplemented policy measures" at the MDBA. There are many convoluted parts to the implementation of policies within the Murray–Darling Basin. Four states, all with different policies, fight over the access to water along thousands of kilometres of rivers and tributaries; there are dams and weirs in place to regulate the variable flows. There are users of the water for a range of uses from human usage, to stock watering, to irrigating and environmental flows. Slattery, with some sense of irony, points out that

> The Australian ecology evolved in response to water variability and environmental watering aims to reinstate some level of natural variability. But governments have committed to achieving this within the regulatory framework designed to remove variability in the first place (Slattery 2018, p. 1).

The problem is not only bureaucratic and political. The plan is caught in a system with players who wish for contradictory outcomes. Three major concerns Maryanne Slattery has are:

a. The large volumes of new floodplain harvesting licences that are being issued under the NSW floodplain harvesting policy;
b. The purchase (by both environment and irrigators) of previously underutilised licences which are becoming fully utilised; and
c. The decline in reliability of water in all the valleys (Slattery 2018, p. 6).

These are serious issues that even a person without expertise in the area of water management can see are going to result in severe consequences. Those consequences are going to be felt by the land itself as it becomes ever drier; the fish and other aquatic animals who live in it; wetland birds and any animals who rely on water to survive; farm animals and those who farm them; food crops and those who farm them; humans who rely on the products and foods of farmers; humans who rely on water for survival.

The flaws in the Murray Darling Basin Plan are not just errors of numbers, of the amount of flow, of gigalitres — they are errors of judgement, ethics and vision. Some examples:

- climate change is not included;
- groundwater is not included, so the impact on the Great Artesian Basin is made invisible and uncountable and groundwater can continue to be pumped;

- the MDBA comes under Commonwealth jurisdiction, but water is controlled by the states with different laws;
- in Queensland floodplains don't count so large industrial farms like Cubby Station can continue to take water from the floodplain before it reaches the rivers;
- the Menindee Lakes in NSW only come under Commonwealth jurisdiction when the lakes reach a certain depth; NSW ensures that this depth is never reached;
- the amount of water needed to flush the Murray Mouth in South Australia is well under what is needed to move the two million tonnes of salt and pollutants each year;
- the MDB fails to acknowledge that the most knowledgeable people are those who have lived on and managed the land for thousands of years;
- the contradictory laws, the mismanagement, the lack of understanding about anything other than the great profits to be made from water licences and water trading are obstructing any genuine plan for a sustainable river system;
- the MDBA Draft Plan lacks any sense that such plans will affect the lives of future generations.

As Diane Bell so rightly asks in her submission to the Proposed Murray Darling Basin Plan, where is 'the imagining of Australia that underpins the plan?' (Bell 2012, p. 6).

It is not only the fish undergoing death throes. Farmers are struggling too. A drought can be survived, but not when it rolls on year after year. Some farmers are tackling the challenges in new ways. Just as Aboriginal peoples have a context-sensitive approach to fire, so too land is considered a relationship, not a possession. Such a view results in an utterly different approach, one in which "country is located firmly within a metaphysical system of knowledge, one not tied to individual ownership, but rather to spiritual continuity which includes the well-being of the land itself" (Bell 1981, p. 356).[142] The well-being of the land can be seen in systems of regenerative farming in which interdependent systems operate simultaneously. Charles Massey writes about this and the ways in which sun, water, soil, ecosystems and humans work together (Massey 2017), or what I have called ecosocial systems.

In Western Australia, near Murchison, David and Frances Pollock have been repairing their dry and rangeland property Wooleen. One of their strategies has been to integrate dingoes into their land management. In many parts of Australia dingoes have been labelled enemy number one. The Pollocks have discovered that dingoes self-manage their numbers and are good for the land (Pollock 2019, p. 307).

In other parts of the world, similar farming systems are being explored. Farida Akhter (2007; 2019) has written extensively about Nayakrishi Andolon and other agricultural methods; in Europe, Veronika Bennholdt-Thomsen and Maria Mies (1999) write of farming and subsistence. Ecological survival means listening to these advocates and farmers. In many cases, women are leading the push for change (Shiva 2015); Indigenous peoples and farmers steeped in long agricultural traditions are protecting biodiversity and creating change across Asia, Africa and Latin America (GRAIN 2016) and resisting colonisation (La Duke 2015).

---

142 For more on Kaytej land systems and women's role see Bell 2003. And for a longer discussion on land as relationship and land as possession see Hawthorne 2002a).

Wet zone: coral death, cyclones, floods

> Butterflyfish and seamoth float as you turn
> fullcircle undersea. The sea is lucent green
> the day you become a fish.
>
> The ocean is the first and last frontier when storms approach
> as sea scales grow to wavelets, from horse-crested waves
> to turbo white foam, froth and spray.
>
> Dugong shelter in bays like rocks among the seagrass
> coral lies exposed at the reef's edge
> as vulnerable as damselfish with sweetlips.
>
> (Hawthorne 2009, p. 11)

The Great Barrier Reef Marine Park Authority was established in 1975. It was the result of many years of activism on the part of artists, poets, ecologists and students. They were called cranks, crackpots and worse, but today we can see the results of their activism in something very precious: the Great Barrier Reef Marine Park, the first such national park in the world.

It wasn't until 1981 that the Great Barrier Reef was selected for inclusion as a World Heritage Site. This meant that because it is a significant and unique place, one that should ensure continuity for the future, it should not, therefore, be turned into an industrial theme park, dotted with oil wells, dumped with polluting substances or overused in such a way as to threaten its existence. In 2006, it was included in the Australia's Biodiversity Action Plan.

I live next to the Great Barrier Reef and in my time here (close to twenty years) I have come to understand just how important the reef is. I have snorkelled the waters in several places and once about a decade ago was thrilled to dive into its depths. An experience I won't forget. The extraordinary colours, the velvet texture of giant clams, the complex shapes, the exhilarating freedom of weightlessness, something I've often longed for.

Judith Wright in her book *The Coral Battleground* wrote, "… the Great Barrier Reef is still the closest most people will come to Eden." She describes what she saw wandering along shoreline pools on Lady Elliot Island:

> I myself had seen only a very small part of it, in the fringing reef of Lady Elliott Island many years before the battle started. But when I thought of the Reef, it was symbolized for me in one image that still stays in my mind. On a still blue summer day, with the ultramarine sea scarcely splashing the edge of the fringing reef, I was bending over a single small pool among the corals. Above it, dozens of small clams spread their velvety lips, patterned in blues and fawns, violets, reds and chocolate browns, not one of them like another. In it, sea-anemones drifted long white tentacles above the clean sand, and peacock-blue fish, only inches long, darted in and out of coral branches of all shapes and colours. One blue sea-star lay on the sand floor. The water was so clear that every detail of the pool's crannies and their inhabitants was vivid, and every movement could be seen through its translucence. In the centre of the pool, as if on a stage, swayed a dancing creature of crimson and yellow, rippling all over like a windblown shawl.
>
> That was the Spanish Dancer, known to scientists as one of the nudibranchs, a shell-less mollusc. But for me it became an inner image of the spirit of the Reef itself (Wright 2014, pp. 187–188).

In the 1970s, the forces of destruction had plans to drill for oil on the Great Barrier Reef. It was the 'cranks and crackpots' who stopped that. In 2013, with the Queensland state government led by neoliberal Campbell Newman and the federal government under ultra-conservative Tony Abbott as Prime Minister, new threats emerged. Inside the Great Barrier Reef Marine Park around 3 million cubic metres of seabed were dredged in order to build three shipping terminals as part of the prospective coal port at Gladstone on the Central Queensland coast and the development of Abbot Point near Bowen as the proposed port for Adani's export of coal. Since then governments and people have been split on the proposed Adani coal mine. Governments by and large have supported the Indian Adani coal mine, but a movement of people has been vocal in the Stop Adani protests across Australia. The Australian Labor Party (ALP) supported the coal industry through the repetitive mantra of 'jobs and growth'. But 'jobs and growth' is a three-word slogan that can be used by the conservative Liberal and National parties and very effectively by the coal industry itself. In 2009, the Labor Party in Queensland was courting Gautam Adani for its Coal Plan 3030. The reef was already under pressure with a major oil spill in April 2009. All the effective activism of the 1970s was being ignored and new ways of exploiting and destroying the reef had to be found. It was not only spillages from oil tankers, but changes in the climate itself which, with increased sea temperatures, was resulting in coral bleaching.

J.E.N. (Charlie) Veron has been diving and researching the Great Barrier Reef for more than 50 years and, at the Royal Society in 2009, he underlined the threat to the reef in a talk called 'Is the Great Barrier Reef on Death Row?' After watching the lecture one can only conclude that by 2035 the coral will be suffering mass bleaching year on year. That means there will not be enough time between each bleaching for coral to recover and therefore the reefs will become extinct. In the eleven years since his lecture, the situation has not improved and governments and corporates are simply making it more and more likely that the earth will face coral extinction within the lifetimes of people already living.[143]

In public discussions about climate change there is always a question mark in the air above the heads of the people like Prime Minister Scott Morrison. He sometimes claims to believe it, but you can hear it in his voice that he does not really mean it. Not so for Charlie Veron. He writes:

---

143 J.E.N. (Charlie) Veron is the foremost scholar of the Great Barrier Reef on the planet. At the end of his speech he remarks that he based his lecture on more than 3000 peer-reviewed articles by more than 1000 colleagues. You can watch his lecture here: <https://www.youtube.com/watch?v=xHo4vb-lPDQ>

> The predicted demise of the GBR [Great Barrier Reef] and most other reefs, first from mass bleaching and then from the irreversible acidification will occur this century (Veron 2009, p. 220).

The cause, he says, is not questionable but rather it is clear that greenhouse gases created by humans is the cause. More than a decade ago he wrote that in the next ten years we can decide to take one path to prevent climate change or the other to disaster:

> If we do not act, or do not act fast enough, marine and coastal ecosystems will be set on an irreversible path of extermination that will eventually see a meltdown in coastal economies with devastating cost to natural environments and human societies. When this is combined with terrestrial effects of climate change, the combination is catastrophic (Veron 2009, p. 231).

Part of the Great Barrier Reef lies alongside the UNESCO World Heritage Area, the Queensland Wet Tropics. In 2006 and again in 2011 respectively, two Category-5 cyclones, Larry and Yasi, hit the Mission Beach area, the same place where John Büsst, Arthur Fenton, Len Webb, Judith Wright and others began their fight against the drilling of oil on Ellison Reef just off Bingil Bay near Mission Beach. The level of destruction by both cyclones in 2006 and 2011 was immense.

After the cyclones, people set up feeding stations for wildlife, especially the southern cassowary. The cassowary plays a pivotal part in the health of the rainforest. As the local Djiru people say, *no wabu, no wuju, no gunduy / no forest, no food, no cassowary.* The cassowary eats forest fruits and distributes the seed throughout the forest. The forest in turn provides food for the cassowary. It is a beautiful virtuous circle.

Watching the fires, the fish deaths, the droughts, the floods I am reminded of the emotional impact of large natural catastrophes; reminded of the sound of a river breaking its banks; the turbine sound of a Category-5 cyclone as it passes over; the roar of a fire and the silence that follows — or in the case of a drought — that endures as the land falls still. It is, as Rachel Carson so presciently pointed out in her book *Silent Spring* in 1962, something that we should consider for our combined future. She was writing about the silence after pesticide poisoning and the use of DDT. Do we want to live in a world without birdsong? The pesticides, the coal mines, the clear-felling forestry industry, the industrial farmers are destroying the earth with their insistence on profit. But what point is profit on a dead and silent planet?

Money

The money trail here is quite obvious. Coal mine owners like the Adani Company are not in it for the good of the planet. It is all about profit.

In 2013, Monsanto acquired a company called Climate Corporation and in 2014, a soil data company Solum Inc. They will not provide resources for farmers facing climate change, rather together they sell data. More data is collected through spyware used on farm machinery such as John Deere tractors. As Shiva points out "[Monsanto] is buying IT firms not just to make farmers more dependent on them, but increasingly, on surveillance (Shiva and Shiva 2018, p. 78). The Bill and Melinda Gates Foundation, which is usually referred to as a donor to 'good causes', is in fact profiting from investments in companies such as Monsanto and Bayer.[144]

One of the shocking aspects of the money made by massive corporates lies in their origins. In 1954, Monsanto and Bayer were involved in a joint venture under the name of MOBAY. It was part of the then company IG Farben. IG Farben was the source of Hitler's Zyklon-B used as a poison in the gas chambers during the Holocaust. Zyklon-B was an extremely poisonous chemical used as

---

144 For an extensive discussion of Gates' problematic investments see Shiva and Shiva 2018, pp. 94–120.

a pesticide against rats and insects. Monsanto has its own history of producing chemical warfare products such as Agent Orange.[145]

Warren Buffett, father of Peter Buffett who runs the pro-transgender NoVo Foundation we met in Chapter Seven, runs a company called Berkshire Hathaway. Vandana Shiva and Kartkey Shiva point out that the Gates Foundation invested USD$11.8 billion in Buffett's company in 2014 and that Warren Buffett is a trustee of the Gates Foundation. In turn Bill Gates is a board member of Berkshire Hathaway (Shiva and Shiva 2018, p. 44).

Vandana Shiva and Kartikey Shiva also take to task billionaires Gates, Buffett and Zuckerberg for their part in fuelling the money machines which are "programmed to bulldoze, destroy, aggregate and accumulate, externalise and excavate" (Shiva and Shiva 2018, p. viii) to the detriment of those in poverty, those facing environmental cataclysm, the dispossessed and oppressed. These two corporations — run by Gates and Buffett — are numbers one and three respectively on the Top 100 Moneymakers according to Forbes in 2017 (Shiva and Shiva 2018, pp. 32–37). It is interesting that the main commodity that Buffett trades in is cotton. Cotton farming has proven to be a destructive monoculture export commodity that uses excessive amounts of water (it appears in the Top 100 Moneymakers chart seven times).[146]

We can see in just this small list of some in the billionaires club how they cross invest with one another, building and supporting destructive investments. To summarise, Bill Gates is connected to Bayer-Monsanto and its history in crimes against humanity. Warren Buffett and Bill Gates sit on one another's company boards. As Vandana Shiva notes in an interview with Amy Goodman on Democracy Now, Bill Gates is simply 'collecting rents'. This refers back to her comment that the richest man on the planet has not produced anything, but rather trades in data. This is a

---

145 For a comprehensive history of Monsanto prior to being made invisible by hiding behind the name Bayer see *The World According to Monsanto* by Marie-Monique Robin (2010).

146 For more on Warren Buffett see Shiva and Shiva 2018, pp. 44–46.

terrifying prospect. Consider the data on people with disabilities and how that can be misused in eugenics programmes that will echo the eugenics of earlier eras (Place 2019). Think of the ways in which data can be used against any group of people considered troublesome: the poor and afflicted, refugees and other displaced peoples, enslaved peoples from across the globe and the descendants of slavery. Think of how it could be used to track those in the sex trade, against lesbians, indeed against anyone who is gender critical. These are not the conclusion of paranoia — they are indeed possible. Whether they occur will depend on the decisions made by people and by politicians.

A handmaid in developing eugenic systems is the relatively new CRISPR technology. Bill Gates and thirteen other investors put up the first USD$120 million for EDITAS a company focused on CRISPR and gene editing (Shiva and Shiva 2018, pp. 101–105).[147] Renate Klein explains the method of gene editing using CRISPR-Cas9. It is

> … a fast and inexpensive technology that can exchange single genes or whole DNA sequences with a scissor-like cut-and-paste action in plants, animals and humans (Klein 2017, p. 170).

CRISPR can therefore be used as a eugenic tool on humans; in plants it can be used in digital farming processes thereby reducing biodiversity; it can also be used in animal breeding programmes such as cows increasing their 'productive capacity', that is producing more milk or meat.[148] Such processes denature and decontextualise living beings. It removes all creatures and plants out of living communities. Tree scientists are now discovering that biodiversity

---

147 The other thirteen were Deerfield Management, Viking Global Investors, Fidelity Management & Research Company, funds and accounts managed by T. Rowe Price Associates, Inc., Google Ventures, Jennison Associates on behalf of certain clients, Khosla Ventures, EcoR1 Capital, Casdin Capital, Omega Funds, Cowen Private Investments and Alexandria Venture Investments (Herper 2015).
148 See the section on Digitised and Globalised Farming in Hawthorne 2002, pp. 236–249.

leads to more communication between plants (Wohlleben 2016, p. 11).[149]

Breaking the heart of the planet

How long for recovery?

Every grief is simply layered
on top of the last. And the last.

Does the earth feel that way too?
How many griefs must we ply and

plough? How many layers before
the sadness breaks the earth's heart?

(Hawthorne 2008, p. 5)

What I have experienced over my lifetime is an intensifying grief for the earth. It is these huge events that reach into the guts that never really leave. But we cannot give up. Just as the firefighters keep going, just as Rachel Carson, Charlie Veron and Judith Wright have always fought the powers that be, so too must we. Grief combined with anger has taken root in many of us. For some it extends only to the environment; for others it encapsulates all the issues I have discussed in this book: racism, misogyny, dire poverty, the pain of exclusion for people with disabilities, the ignorance about lesbians and the violence suffered by them, the endless layers of colonisation. The grief we experience is felt also by the climate scientists who have tried to change the zeitgeist, but instead find themselves experiencing more grief than five years ago (Readfearn 2020).[150] The grief from racism; of the battles being fought on the ground against Indigenous peoples of the Wangan and Jagalingou in Queensland over the Adani mine; the Wet'suwet'en in Canada

---

149 I say more about this in Chapter Nine.
150 To read the letters by scientists in 2014 and in 2020 see <https://www.isthishowyoufeel.com/>

over the 670 km Coastal GasLink pipeline in British Columbia; the Mapuche people in Chile fighting against fracking, lithium mining and the copper mining industries; African Americans facing unremitting police shootings after years of protests against racism and police profiling. The entrenched grief caused by police violence against Aboriginal women in Australia; the trafficking of Indigenous women on the border between Canada and the USA. The sheer numbers of women killed everywhere around the world by men; domestic violence which is more properly called domestic terrorism. The criminalisation of refugees fleeing war and torture and the cheap trick of decriminalising women in prostitution; both groups are rendered homeless. The grief experienced by lesbians who see how violence against them is minimised, ignored, erased including corrective rape and murder; the grief of people with disabilities who see laws passed that display their second-class status, that show just how easily they too could be erased.

In my book *Wild Politics: Feminism, Globalisation and Bio/diversity* (2002) I concluded that we needed a structural change to the system, one in which we change the spirit of the culture. The maxim of capitalist, corporate, patriarchy is profit (and yes it extends beyond capitalist nations now). Many people around the world are suffering a loss of spirit or the breaking of spirit as I have called it in this book. We sorely need a new inspiration, one which makes it impossible to ignore the consequences to the spirit. The foundation of that inspiration, I argued, is biodiversity. If one truly cares about the future, it should be one in which both the biology and the culture are rich in biodiversity. Biodiversity is a complex self-sustaining system of an ecological niche in a particular locale. The details cannot be universalised, but the behaviours that sustain it can be.

Ngarrindjeri elder, Tom Trevorrow had this to say about the management of the Murray Darling River Basin:

> Our traditional management plan was don't be greedy,
> don't take any more than you need and respect everything

around you. That's the management plan — it's such a simple management plan, but so hard for people to carry out (cited in Bell 2012, p. 23).

We must stop all wars and every industry associated with them. That includes industries of hatred, industries that kill people, animal, plants, rocks, seas and air. They are far too numerous to list. Critics will say the economy will dive. It will for a while, but not as much as it will if all the living creatures and plants die. There are imaginative ways of countering some of that. Different tax regimes including a Tobin tax, that is, a tax on international financial transactions. It is targeted at speculative currency exchange transactions. These transactions have increased with the ease of digital banking. If the tax were a very low 0.1% ordinary mortals would hardly feel it and the big money merchants would begin to pay their fair share of tax on short-term speculative international cash flows.[151] A Universal Basic Income could also be implemented along with universal health care.

We need new imaginings that take account of the long history — geological, ecological, biological, cultural — of Australia. We recognise that fire is an essential element in the growth of some plants (such as banksias), but that the intense fires we are experiencing now are not the same as the low intensity mosaic fires which Indigenous peoples have used for millennia. We recognise that mangroves bulldozed for resorts are erasing the fish nurseries along the coast. We acknowledge that wetlands and swamps are living centres which the Ngarrindjeri call 'nurseries' (Bell 2012, p. 16).

It is the least visible that are under threat. The underground water of the Great Artesian Basin not acknowledged by the MDBA; the undersea treasures of the Great Barrier Reef; the vast grasslands and forests under threat from future fires as well as flood and drought, the water that might be mined on Mars, or 'unfrozen'

---

151 An informal name for the Tobin tax is the Robin Hood tax: taxing the rich to pay the poor. For more see Kagan 2019.

from the poles. We have a government that is incapable of vision. Incapable of anything that does not prop up the coal industry, fossil fuels and the billionaire profit makers. This has to change.

Sibyls

Phemonoe the poet
says it is time to cease
prophesying

the future is now
time is
turned on itself

there
then
here
now

the known a memory
the knowable invented
our million mouths singing

—Susan Hawthorne,
Lupa and Lamb
(2014, p. 147)

CHAPTER NINE

Sovereignty and the Spirit of Nature

n this chapter, I want to detail a few hopeful things on the horizon. They are virtually invisible to the mainstream world and I am sure there are many events and projects happening out of sight run by those not in the media or in the spotlight.

- Home gardens are burgeoning in suburbs and small rural plots, even in the inner city and on high-rise buildings.
- Rooftop solar panel installations have increased massively in Australia, some but not all prompted by government rebates.
- Extinction rebellions have affected many and there is a huge increase in people reducing meat consumption, becoming vegetarian or vegan.
- #BlackLivesMatter protests have created reflection by ordinary people and even some corporates.
- #MeToo is shaking up some very old institutions including the legal and medical professions.
- There is an increasing number of animals sharing houses with their companion humans, sleeping with them and being recognised as an integral part of the family when climate disasters like fires, floods, and cyclones occur.

These might look like small changes but they are indicators of ways of living differently. They point towards incremental changes in attitudes. It is attitudinal shift that creates long-term and stable changes in societies.

Uncultivated

My introduction to the concept of 'uncultivated' was in Bangladesh. Travelling with Farida Akhter, the Director of UBINIG,[152] an NGO with a focus on agrobiodiversity, she began talking one day about the plants growing around a small pond. These were the uncultivated plants which the women use for cooking and medicine. Someone will say that uncultivated sounds like an insult. It is not, it is about recognising those plants that grow around you without interference and which do well without all sorts of externalities like fertiliser, pesticides, GMO seeds and the like.

In an interview with the NGO GRAIN, Farida said about Nayakrishi Andolon. "The main capital is not cash, but farmers' knowledge. It is about restoring 'culture' in agriculture (GRAIN 2002)." It is a system based on knowledge of local conditions by people keeping long-tested systems of food production combined with an understanding of biodiversity.

Farida Akhter also speaks of the importance of songs to Bangladeshi farmers. In song are to be found many methods of sustenance, of well-being, systems of memory relating to seasons, weather, shifts in conditions as well as information on when plants should be sown and harvested.[153]

---

152 Unnayan Bikalper Nitinirdharoni Gobeshona which translates as the Policy Research for Development Alternative. For more on UBINIG and Nayakrishi Andolon (farming for happiness) see Hawthorne 2002, p. 307 and the UBINIG website <https://www.ubinig.org/>

153 Lynne Kelly (2015; 2016) details the ways in which accurate memory is passed down through multiple generations in societies where orature is important. Song is one of many methods.

Song, storytelling, dance, music and visual art play a critical part in maintaining traditional cultures around the world and keeping the information accurate. Bruce Pascoe in his boundary breaking book *Dark Emu* (2014) takes the development of human technologies in Aboriginal Australia back thousands of years: baking to 30,000 years (p. 30); milling techniques to 18,000 years (p. 47); fish traps on rivers to at least 40,000 years (p. 57); fish smoke-houses to 8,000 years (p. 63). Pascoe's close reading of the notes of European explorers, his understanding of the land and the underlying cultural fabric has made his work an important contribution. His lack, however, is in not noticing the devastating impact of patriarchy on the planet.

But men too, can learn from feminists and some have. In his book *The End of Patriarchy* (2016) Robert Jensen writes that facing the difficult reality of cascading ecological disaster was helped by his earlier research on pornography. That both are so difficult to think about, that doing so helps to engage the mind and to attempt to climb that steep slope of understanding. Jensen writes, "Pornography is what the end of the world looks like" (2016, p. 160).

Pornography fuels violence. It fuels the prostitution industry; it fuels torture among state actors in war and among non-state actors in families; it fuels the enjoyment of domination whether that be of foreigners, of women, of animals, of the environment; it fuels the infantilisation of anyone who is different: people with disabilities, the colonised, women; it fuels the wish to dominate and conquer people in other countries; it fuels greed for colonisation and theft; it fuels the breaking of the spirit of the planet and its inhabitants.

Acknowledging the intergenerational effects of violence is part of recovering from trauma and recognising the sovereignty of people who have experience of colonisation, slavery, dispossession and being forced to flee wars and occupation by an external (sometimes internal) power.

The dispossession of people (slaves, women, refugees etc.) happens on many levels and in many different ways. It includes the stealing of children, the forbidden use of the mother tongue.

It includes deterritorialisation and humiliation of peoples through framing their knowledge as humbug or blasphemous or heretical. We see this across all the deprivations I write about in this book whether it is about disability, lesbian existence, the enforcement of transculture on young women; whether it is about displacement of refugees or a people of the 'wrong' culture, skin colour, religion or sex as in the witch-hunts.

Sovereignty

Sovereignty is a word that used to mean power over others or over land and its products. But in the contemporary world the meaning of sovereignty has broadened. Indigenous peoples have taken up the word as a way of speaking of their relationship to land and community. Indigenous societies are working hard to protect their lands from further decimation. Farida Akhter speaks of sovereignty in relation to food produced and she writes of the ways in which 'rice is interwoven with Bengali culture' (2019). The attempts by transnational corporates to turn Bangladesh into a country producing hybrid or GMO rice are not only misplaced but are deeply threatening to Bengali culture. She criticises the Bill and Melinda Gates Foundation for their grant of USD$10 million in order to develop Golden Rice varieties (Akhter 2019; also see Shiva and Shiva 2018, pp. 90–94). These are new kinds of occupation by colonisers that involve appropriation and theft. Land that is used to grow 'occupying rice' cannot be used for growing the many varieties of native rice.

Bodily sovereignty has also entered the lexicon. Women and children need bodily sovereignty because men have dominated the lives of women and children and literally — as well as meta-phorically — penetrated them. Bodily sovereignty is about respect for another person and not entering territory without an explicit invitation.

The transnational corporates and foundations are attempting to change the way the world works, both environmentally and bodily. As mentioned in earlier chapters, bodily dissociation is encouraged in the sex industry, the military, by transgender clinics and purveyors of surrogacy and organ trafficking. Along with the medical industrial system, Big Pharma and the sellers of seeds and patents are based on a system of breaking down bodily sovereignty.

Around the world, funding for women's services to protect and help women recover from violence is falling. Women are murdered every minute of every day. Women's bodily sovereignty is not only under attack from men in intimate partnerships, but also under attack from political parties and neoliberal lefties who care more for feelings of hurt than for physical, emotional and psychic survival.

In the contemporary global world, we are all in the same boat. Our political and environmental catastrophes are all heading us up the proverbial shit creek without a paddle! But when we reciprocate, when we treat one another with human compassion, empathy and kindness, we discover our commonalities. Community spirit rises during catastrophe as is evident in the response of people to bushfires, floods, cyclones and earthquakes. Harder to achieve is continuing those behaviours into daily life and into the ways we structure our economy, our laws and our systems of communal governance.

Following the bushfires, Fijians donated money to Australia to help people recover because Australia was the first to assist after Cyclone Winston in 2016. The Foreign Minister, Inia Seruiratu, maintained the importance of addressing "the underlying causes of changing climate" (McDonald 2020).

In the 1990s, Suzanne Simard from the University of British Columbia in Vancouver began to look into the ways in which trees communicate with one another. They do so using pathways created by roots and the mycelium of fungi. As we walk on the earth, beneath us are huge networks of biological material that create a living web. It is not restricted to trees but also grasses and low shrubs. As Farida Akhter intuited, the uncultivated plants are in communication with other plants around them. Simard also found out that on farms "the vegetation becomes very quiet. Thanks to selective breeding, our cultivated plants have, for the most part, lost their ability to communicate above or below ground" (cited in Wohlleben 2016, p. 11).

Just like people and animals, when plants lose their ability to communicate they are much more susceptible to attack by pests. What could help us to bring these living webs back to life? We could straightaway protect the grandmother trees under threat (Cavanagh 2020). Likewise, in Victoria the Djab Wurrung Embassy set up camp to protect grandmother trees, birthing trees, grandfather and direction trees. They believe that the roots of these and other trees are connected.[154] The rationale for killing these trees: the duplication of the Western Highway (Jacks 2019).

Connectedness, not dissociation, is what we need to be developing. This can be the connections between people or between people and their local environment. Connectedness means acknowledging who we are and the integrity of our bodies. Relationship with the land and with one another is central to our future. This might mean spending less time making profit, extracting and exporting. It must allow for differences without simultaneously turning differences into weapons. As I write in my poem:

You can never get enough

from capitalism
from tech
from porn
from prostitution
from industrial farming
from the animals and plants you want to turn into
    super producers

---

154 You can see some beautiful photos of these trees at <https://www.theage.com.au/national/victoria/saving-our-sacred-trees-20190824-h1heqe.html>. One day after this report the Victorian government decided to cut down the grandfather tree. The effect of this is to erase an oral tradition — or songline — of the Djab Wurrung people. There is no author of this article but photos are by Justin McManus.

from animals in transhuman experiments
from forests
from the drying rivers
from the oceans and land you intend to mine
from underground artesian basins
from war-torn countries whose oil you want
from prisons for profit
from the bodies injured by technical advances
from the defeated whose women and children you want
from the body you want to harvest or transform
from all of us
from the planet the sky the air we breathe

(Hawthorne 2020)

The fires and the cyclones are all connected; the rivers and the forests are all connected; the farmlands and the grasslands are connected by histories and stories, songs and dances; the saltwater and the freshwater are all connected as is the runoff from mines and industrial agriculture and forestry. This is the planet. It is how it grows and thrives.

All can learn from the land, from the way in which recovery occurs in the natural world. I know that the advent of feminism changed my life and following that a series of challenges provoked more change. For many who participated in those changes, they are permanent. They did not break me; instead they created new ways of being and thinking. My hope for the future is that mass movements can recreate the world in new ways. My hope is for a world enlivened by meaningful relationship, with freedom from violence in all its forms including epistemic violence, for decolonisation and recognition that the colonised have never ceded their lands and cultures. I hope for a world in which women can walk the streets without fear at any time of the day; that men will call out members of the male sex when they threaten women in any way; that children grow up to be the adults they want to be without the strictures of gender. I hope that the world will be a friendlier place for those with disabilities and a recognition that disability is something that occurs in most living beings at some time in our lives. My hope is that the richness of many cultures and languages can become a way of life and that the learning of more than one language becomes the norm, alongside access to creative expression through the arts. I also hope that many readers' voices will add to these small hopes and bring their own cultural depth, texture and knowledge to this currently fragile world. Let us wish that we can tip in the right direction.

References

ABC Radio National. 2019. 'Stop Everything, Interview with Terana Burke'. 15 November. <https://www.abc.net.au/radionational/programs/stop-everything/me-too-tarana-burke-josh-thomas/11705212>

ABC-TV (Australia) Q&A. 3 February 2020. <https://www.theguardian.com/media/australian-broadcasting-corporation>

Australian Bureau of Statistics (ABS) 2020. <https://www.abs.gov.au/ausstats/abs@.nsf/Lookup/by%20Subject/3302.0.55.003~2015-2017~Media%20Release~Life%20expectancy%20lowest%20in%20remote%20and%20very%20remote%20areas%20(Media%20Release)~15#:~:text=The%20life%20expectancy%20at%20birth,Bureau%20of%20Statistics%20(ABS)>

Ahmed, Nadia. 2005. 'An Iraqi Woman's Journal'. *Le Monde* (Paris). 4 February. <http://www.lemonde.fr/web/article/0,1-0@2-3230,36-396901,0.html>

Aidoo, Ama Ata. 1977. *Our Sister Killjoy or Reflections from a Black-eyed Squint*; pp. 86–87. London: Longman Group.

Akhter, Farida, Wilma van Berkel and Natasha Ahmad (eds.). 1989. *The Declaration of Comilla*. Dhaka, Bangladesh: UBINIG.

Akhter, Farida. 1992. *Depopulating Bangladesh: Essays on the Politics of Fertility*. Dhaka: Narigrantha Prabartana.

Akhter, Farida. 1995. *Trafficking in Women and Children: The Case of Bangladesh*. Dhaka: Narigrantha Prabartana.

Akhter, Farida. 2007. *Seeds of Movements: On Women's Issues in Bangladesh*. Dhaka: Narigrantha Prabartana.

Akhter, Farida. 2019. 'Sovereignty and Rice'. *NewAge*. 15 December. <https://www.newagebd.net/article/93731/sovereignty-and-rice>

Alexander, M. Jackie. 2005. *Pedagogies of Crossing: Meditations on Feminism, Sexual Politics, Memory and the Sacred*. Durham: Duke University Press.

Allen, Paula Gunn. 1986. *The Sacred Hoop: Recovering the Feminine in American Indian Traditions*. Boston, MA: Beacon Press.

Allen, Paula Gunn. 1998. *Off the Reservation: Reflections on Boundary-Busting, Border Crossing, Loose Canons*. Boston, MA: Beacon Press.

Alvaredo, Facundo, Lucas Chancel, Thomas Piketty, Emmanuel Saez and Gabriel Zucman. 2018. *World Inequality Report*. <https://wir2018.wid.world/>

Améry, Jean. 1980. *At the Mind's Limits: Contemplations by a Survivor on Auschwitz and Its Realities*. Bloomington: Indiana University Press.

Amnesty International. 1997. *Breaking the Silence: Human Rights Violations Based on Sexual Orientation*. London: Amnesty International United Kingdom.

Amnesty International. 1998. 'Appeal Cases: Zimbabwe: Threats to Homosexual Rights Activists'. In *Why Are We Still Waiting: The Struggle for Women's Human Rights*. Country Dossier: Zimbabwe, March: E 43 (Amnesty International Library, London).

Amnesty International. 2001a. *Crimes of Hate, Conspiracy of Silence, Torture and Ill-treatment Based on Sexual Identity*. ACT 40/016/2001.

Amnesty International. 2001b. *Broken Bodies, Shattered Minds: Torture and Ill-treatment of Women*. AI Index: ACT 40/001/2001.

ANAWA, Anti-Nuclear Alliance of Western Australia. 2001. 'The Pangea Proposal for an International Nuclear Waste Dump in Outback Western Australia'. 7 December. <www.anawa.org.au/waste/pangea.html>

Andrews, Munya. 2004. *The Seven Sisters of the Pleiades: Stories from around the World*. Melbourne: Spinifex Press.

Anonymous. 2017. 'Experience: I regret transitioning'. *The Guardian*. 4 February.

Arditti, Rita, Renate Duelli Klein and Shelley Minden (eds.). 1984. *Test Tube Women: What Future for Motherhood?* London: Pandora.

Arditti, Rita. 1999. *Searching for Life: The Grandmothers of the Plaza de Mayo and the Disappeared Children of Argentina*. Berkeley: University of California Press.

Arendt, Hannah. 1951/2017. *The Origins of Totalitarianism*. London: Penguin Random House.

Asafu-Adjaye, John, Linus Blomqvist, Stewart Brand, Barry Brook, Ruth DeFries, Erle Ellis, Christopher Foreman, David Keith, Martin Lewis, Mark Lynas, Roger A. Pielke, Jr., Rachel Pritzker, Joyashree Roy, Mark Sagoff, Michael Shellenberger, Robert Stone, and Peter Teague. 2015. 'An Ecomodernist Manifesto'. <www.ecomodernism.org>

ASSIST. 2007. 'URGENT: Don't Deport Pegah Emambakhsh', 16 August. <http://www.indymedia.org.uk/en/2007/08/378415.html>

Atkinson, Judy. 2002. *Trauma Trails, Recreating Song Lines: The Transgenerational Effects of Trauma in Indigenous Australia*. Melbourne: Spinifex Press.

Atkinson, Meera. 2018. *Traumata*. St Lucia: University of Queensland Press.

Atwood, Margaret. 2003. *Oryx and Crake*. London: Bloomsbury.

Australian Museum. 2018. 'Indigenous Australians: Australia's First Peoples Exhibition 1996-2015'. <https://australianmuseum.net.au/about/history/exhibitions/indigenous-australians/>

Awang, Sandra S. 2000. 'Indigenous Nations and the Human Genome Diversity Project', in George J. Sefa Dei, Budd L. Hall, and Dorothy Goldin Rosenberg (eds.) *Indigenous Knowledges in Global Contexts: Multiple Readings of Our World*. Toronto: OISE/UT, published in Association with University of Toronto Press, pp. 120–136.

Barnett, Antony. 2002. 'Bushmen Win Royalties on "Miracle Pill"'. *The Guardian Weekly*. 4-10 April, p. 3.

Bagaric, Mirko and Julie Clarke. 2005. 'Not Enough (Official) Torture in the World? The Circumstances in which Torture is Morally Justifiable'. *University of San Francisco Law Review*. Vol. 39. No. 3.

Bal, Vineeta. 2007. 'The Business of Sex Selection: The unltrasonography boom' in *Consultation on 'New' Reproductive and Genetic Technologies and Women's Lives*. New Delhi: Sama, pp. 20–22.

Bales, Kevin. 2000. *Disposable People: New Slavery in the Global Economy*. Berkeley: University of California Press.

Balzer, Carsten and Jan Simon Hutta with Tamara Adrián, Peter Hyndal and Susan Stryker. 2012. 'Transrespect Versus Transphobia Worldwide: A Comparative Review of the Human-rights Situation of Gender-variant/Trans People'. Berlin: TVT. Transrespect versus Transphobia.

Bandler, Faith. 1984. *Welou, My Brother*. Sydney: Wild and Woolley.

Bandler, Faith. 1994. 'Slavery and Resistance in Australia' in Susan Hawthorne and Renate Klein (eds.). *Australia for Women: Travel and Culture*. Melbourne: Spinifex Press, pp. 11–15.

Barrett, Ruth (ed.). 2016. F*emale Erasure: What You Need to Know about Gender Politics' War on Women, the Female Sex and Human Rights*. Pacific Palisades, CA: Tidal Time Publishing.

Barry, Kathleen. 1979. *Female Sexual Slavery*. New York: Avon Books.

Barry, Kathleen. 1995. *The Prostitution of Sexuality: The Global Exploitation of Women*. New York, NY: New York University Press.

Barry, Kathleen. 2010. *Unmaking War, Remaking Men*. Melbourne: Spinifex Press.

BBC World News. 2018a. 'Noura Hussein: Appeals court overturns death sentence'. 26 June. <https://www.bbc.com/news/world-africa-44614590>

BBC World News. 2018b. 'The women killed around the world on one day'. 28 November. <https://www.bbc.com/news/world-46292919>

BBC. 2019. 'Amazon forest belongs to Brazil, says Jair Bolsonaro'. 24 September. <https://www.bbc.com/news/world-latin-america-49815731>

Beale, Charlotte. 2016. 'Feminists mock Green Party young women's group for invite to non-men'. *The Independent*. 16 April. <https://www.independent. co.uk/news/uk/feminists-mock-green-party-young-womens-invite-to-non-men-a6987061.html>

Beavis, Mary Ann and Helen Hye-Sook Hwang (eds.). 2018. *Goddesses in Myth, History and Culture*. Lytle Creek, CA. Mago Books.

Behind the Wire. 2017. *They Cannot Take the Sky: Stories from Detention*. Sydney: Allen & Unwin.

Bell, Diane. 1981. 'Women's Business is Hard Work: Central Australian Aboriginal Women's Love Rituals', in Max Charlesworth, Howard Morphy, Diane Bell and Kenneth Maddock (eds.) *Religion in Aboriginal Australia*. St Lucia: University of Queensland Press, pp. 344–369.

Bell, Diane. 1983/2003. *Daughters of the Dreaming*. Melbourne: Spinifex Press.

Bell, Diane. 1998. *Ngarrindjeri Wurruwarrin: A World That Is, Was, and Will Be*. Melbourne: Spinifex Press.

Bell, Diane and Renate Klein (eds.). 1996. *Radically Speaking: Feminism Reclaimed*. Melbourne: Spinifex Press.

Bell, Diane. 2012. 'Life at the Murray Mouth: Icon and Indicator'. Submission to the Proposed Murray–Darling Basin Plan.

Bellamy, Suzanne and Susan Hawthorne. 2008. *Unsettling the Land*. Melbourne: Spinifex Press.

Bellamy, Suzanne. 2020. 'I had a phone call this morning from the Agriculture and Livestock Board'. Facebook. 17 January.

Bennett, Margaret and Jennifer Maiden. 2019. *Workbook Questions: Writing of Torture, Trauma Experience*. Sydney: Quemar Press.

Bennholdt-Thomsen, Veronika and Maria Mies. 1999. *The Subsistence Perspective: Beyond the Globalised Economy*. Melbourne: Spinifex Press.

Bergeron, Suzanne. (2006). 'Love, Sex and the World Bank: Queering Globalization and Development'. Paper presented at National Women's Studies Conference, Oakland, CA. 16 June.

Bilek, Jennifer. 2020a. 'The Billionaires Behind the LGBT Movement'. *First Things*. 21 January. <https://www.firstthings.com/web-exclusives/2020/01/the-billionaires-behind-the-lgbt-movement>

Bilek, Jennifer. 2020b. 'Arcus Foundation — "LGBT" NGO, Great Apes and the Mission of Gender Identity Equality'. *The 11th Hour*. 18 February. <https://www.the11thhourblog.com/post/arcus-foundation-lgbt-ngo-great-apes-and-the-mission-of-gender-identity-ideology>

Bilek, Jennifer. 2020c. 'AIDS and the Medical Marketing of Sexual Identity'. *The 11th Hour*. 27 February. <https://www.the11thhourblog.com/post/aids-and-the-medical-marketing-of-sexual-identity>

Bilek, Jennifer. 2020d. 'Do Parents Stand a Chance against the Trans Lobby?' Part II. *The 11th Hour*. 28 April. <https://www.the11thhourblog.com/post/do-parents-stand-a-chance-against-the-trans-lobby-part-ii>

Bilek, Jennifer. 2020e. 'Do Parents Stand a Chance against the Trans Lobby?' Part III. *The 11th Hour*. 30 April. <https://www.the11thhourblog.com/post/do-parents-have-a-chance-against-the-trans-lobby-part-iii>

Bilek, Jennifer. 2020f. 'Profits Soar for Sex Surgeries Masking Sex'. *The 11th Hour*. 5 June. <https://www.the11thhourblog.com/post/profits-soar-for-sex-surgeries-masking-sex>

Bilek, Jennifer. 2020g. 'The Stryker Corporation and the Arcus Foundation: Billionaires Behind the New "LGBT" Movement'. *Uncommon Ground*. 6 June. <https://uncommongroundmedia.com/stryker-arcus-billionaires-lgbt/>

Bilek, Jennifer. 2020h. 'Martine Rothblatt: A Founding Father of the Transgender Empire'. *Uncommon Ground*. 6 July. <https://uncommongroundmedia.com/martine-rothblatt-a-founding-father-of-the-transgender-empire/>

Bilek, Jennifer. 2020i. 'Elon Musk Dives Headlong Into Tech that Will Annihilate Us'. *The 11th Hour*. 19 July. <https://www.the11thhourblog.com/post/elon-musk-dives-headlong-into-tech-that-will-annihilate-us?>

Bindel, Julie. 2017. *The Pimping of Prostitution: Abolishing the Sex Work Myth*. Mission Beach: Spinifex Press.

Bindel, Julie and Gary Powell. 2018. 'Gay Rights and Surrogacy Wrongs: Say "No" to Wombs-for-Rent'. Stop Surrogacy Now'. <http://www.stopsurrogacynow.com/gay-rights-and-surrogacy-wrongs-say-no-to-wombs-for-rent/#sthash.bHZ7o5ve.dpbs>

Bindel, Julie. 2020a. 'I met the Cyprus rape case teenager: no one should have to experience what she went through'. *The Telegraph*. 7 January. <https://www.telegraph.co.uk/women/life/mother-ayia-napa-teen-would-woman-dare-report-rape-has-happened/>

Bindel, Julie. 2020b. 'Why do men get away with killing women — is there an amnesty on male violence?' *The Guardian*. 21 February. <https://www.theguardian.com/commentisfree/2020/feb/20/men-killing-women-cuts-refuges-legal-aid>

Blair, Jennifer. 2018. 'The Justice Gap'. 13 June. <http://www.thejusticegap.com/2015/03/lesbian-home-secretary-sets-impossibly-high-threshold-asylum-claims-based-sexuality/>

Blaise, Melissa. 2014. *"I Hate Feminists!" December 6, 1989 and Its Aftermath*. Melbourne: Spinifex Press.

Boochani, Behrouz. 2018. *No Friend but the Mountains: Writing from Manus Prison*. Translated by Omid Tofighian. Melbourne: Pan Macmillan.

Bourke, Joanna. 2000. *An Intimate History of Killing: Face-to-Face Killing in Twentieth-Century Warfare*. London: Granta.

Bourke, Latika. 2020. 'Andrew Forrest says fuel loads are primary cause of bushfires'. *Sydney Morning Herald*. 24 January. <https://www.smh.com.au/national/andrew-forrest-says-fuel-loads-not-climate-change-are-primary-cause-of-bushfires-20200123-p53twe.html>

Bradley, Michael. 2020. *Coniston*. Perth: University of Western Australia Publishing.

Bray, Abigail. 2013. *Misogyny Re-loaded*. Melbourne: Spinifex Press.

Brennan, Theresa. 2003. *Globalization and its Terrors: Daily Life in the West*. New York: Routledge.

Brewer, Kirstie. 2020. 'How do I convince the Home Office I'm a lesbian?' BBC News. 26 February. <https://www.bbc.com/news/stories-51636642>

Brodribb, Somer. 1992. *Nothing Mat(t)ers: A Feminist Critique of Postmodernism*. Melbourne: Spinifex Press.

Brossard, Nicole. 1989. 'The Killer was No Young Man' in Louise Malette and Marie Chalouh (eds.) 1991. *The Montreal Massacre*. Translated by Marlene Wildeman. Charlottetown: Gynergy, pp. 31–33.

Brossard, Nicole. 2020. *The Aerial Letter*. Translated by Marlene Wildeman. Mission Beach: Spinifex Press.

Brown-Long, Cyntoia. 2019. *Free Cyntoia: My Search for Redemption in the American Prison System*. New York: Atria Books.

Brownworth, Victoria A. 1999. 'Who Chooses? The Debate over Eugenics and Euthanasia' in Victoria A. Brownworth and Susan Raffo (eds.) *Restricted Access: Lesbians on Disability*. Seattle: Seal Press, pp. 136–151.

Brownworth, Victoria A. 2015. 'Erasing Our Lesbian Dead: Why don't murdered lesbians make the news?' *Curve*. <http://www.curvemag.com/News/Erasing-Our-Lesbian-Dead-510/> (Accessed 17/7/2015).

Brunskell-Evans, Heather. 2020. *Transgender Body Politics*. Mission Beach: Spinifex Press.

Bunch, Aaron. 2019. 'Adani bankrupts traditional owner in Qld'. *Canberra Times*. 15 August. <https://www.canberratimes.com.au/story/6331115/adani-bankrupts-traditional-owner-in-qld/?cs=14231>

Butalia, Urvashi. 2000. *The Other Side of Silence: Voices from the Partition of India*. Durham, NC: Duke University Press.

Butalia, Urvashi. 2002. 'The Price of Life' in Susan Hawthorne and Bronwyn Winter (eds.) *September 11, 2001: Feminist Perspectives*. Melbourne: Spinifex Press, pp. 53–55.

Butler, Judith. 1990. *Gender Trouble: Feminism and the Subversion of Identity*. Abingdon: Routledge.

Butler, Rhett A. 2019. 'Amazon deforestation rises to 11 year high in Brazil'. *Mongabay*. 18 November. <https://news.mongabay.com/2019/11/amazon-deforestation-rises-to-11-year-high-in-brazil/>

Cacho, Lydia. 2014. *Slavery Inc.: The Untold Story of International Sex Trafficking*. Berkeley, CA: Soft Skull Press.

Cambridge English Dictionary. 2020. <https://dictionary.cambridge.org/dictionary/english/vortex>

Campbell, Beatrix. 2020. 'Bad Dreams … Greens and Gender'. *Medium*. July. <https://medium.com/@beatrixcampbell/bad-dreams-greens-and-gender-768cde8d4e9>

Campbell, Fiona Kumari. 2017. 'Queer Anti-sociality and Disability Unbecoming An Ableist Relations Project?' in Oishik Sircar and Dipika Jain (eds.) *New Intimacies/Old Desires: Law, Culture and Queer Politics in Neoliberal Times*. New Delhi: Zubaan Books, pp. 280–316.

Cape Times. 2013. Editorial: Hate Crime. 5 July. <http://www.iol.co.za/capetimes/editorial-hate-crime-1.1542700#.VjMl1ArIcg>

Caputi, Jane. 1988. *The Age of Sex Crime*. London: The Women's Press.

Caputi, Jane. 2004. *Goddesses and Monsters: Women, Myth, Power, and Popular Culture*. Madison: University of Wisconsin Press.

Cardea, Caryatis. 1990. 'Snapshots of a Decade and More' in *On Disability*. Vol. 39. *Sinister Wisdom*. Winter 1989–90, pp. 119–127.

Carraher-Kang, Alexandra. 2019. 'Indigenous Peoples Lead the Resistance Movement in Chile'. *Cultural Survival*. 12 November. <https://www.culturalsurvival.org/news/indigenous-peoples-lead-resistance-movement-chile>

Carson, Anne M. 2017. 'Even after Breaking', in Heather Taylor Johnson (ed.) *Shaping the Fractured Self: Poetry of Chronic Illness and Pain*. Perth: University of Western Australia Publishing, pp. 18–23.

Carson, Rachel. 1986. *Silent Spring*. Harmondsworth: Penguin Books.

Cater, Nick. 2019. 'Woke folk won't even walk on the mild side'. *The Australian*. 27 December. <https://www.theaustralian.com.au/commentary/woke-folk-wont-even-walk-on-the-mild-side/news-story/07dbdeca4d3b05f6a14510ed c942d49c>

Cavanagh, Vanessa. 2020. 'Friday Essay: This Grandmother Tree Connects Me to Country. I cried when I saw her burned'. *The Conversation*. 24 January. <https://theconversation.com/friday-essay-this-grandmother-tree-connects-me-to-country-i-cried-when-i-saw-her-burned-129782>

Çetin, Fethiye. 2010. *My Grandmother: A Memoir*. Translated by Maureen Freely. Melbourne: Spinifex Press.

Chainey, Naomi. 2017. 'Not everyone with a disability wants a cure — nor should we expect them to'. *Sydney Morning Herald*. December 2, 2017. <http://www.smh.com.au/lifestyle/health-and-wellbeing/not-everyone-with-a-disability-wants-a-cure--nor-should-we-expect-them-to-20171201-gzx8ys.html>

Cho, Joo-Hyun. 2005. 'Gender and Biotechnology in Trans/National Discourse: The Case of Korea'. Paper presented at Women's Worlds 2005: Ninth International Interdisciplinary Congress on Women, Seoul, South Korea.

Christie, Jean. 2001. 'Enclosing the Biodiversity Commons: Bioprospecting or biopiracy?' in Richard Hindmarsh and Geoffrey Lawrence (eds.) *Altered Genes II: The Future?* Melbourne: Scribe, pp. 173–86.

Clarke, D. A. 2004. 'Prostitution for Everyone: Feminism, globalisation and the 'sex' industry' in Christine Starke and Rebecca Whisnant (eds.) *Not For Sale: Feminists Resisting Prostitution and Pornography*. Melbourne: Spinifex, pp. 149–205.

Cohn, Corinna. 2020. 'For 30 Years, I've Tried to Become a Woman. Here's What I learned Along the Way'. *Quillette*. 22 June. <https://quillette.com/2020/06/22/for-30-years-ive-tried-to-become-a-woman-heres-what-i-learned-along-the-way/>

Cole, Diane. 2018. *U.N. Report: 50,000 Women A Year Are Killed By Intimate Partners, Family Members*. 30 November. <https://www.npr.org/sections/go

atsandsoda/2018/11/30/671872574/u-n-report-50-000-women-a-year-are-killed-by-intimate-partners-family-members>

Coney, Sandra. 1993. *The Menopause Industry: A Guide to Medicine's 'Discovery' of the Mid-Life Woman.* Melbourne: Spinifex Press.

Copelan, Rhonda. 1994. 'Surfacing Gender: Reconceptualizing Crimes Against Women in Time of War' in Alexandra Stiglmayer (ed.) *Mass Rape: The War against Women in Bosnia-Herzogovina.* Lincoln and London: University of Nebraska Press, pp. 197–218.

Corea, Gena. 1985. *The Mother Machine: Reproductive Technologies from Artificial Insemination to Artificial Wombs.* New York: Harper & Row.

Coulter, Martin. 2018. 'Transgender Activist Tara Wolf fined £150 for assaulting 'exclusionary' radical feminist in Hyde Park'. *Evening Standard.* 13 April. <https://www.standard.co.uk/news/crime/transgender-activist-tara-wolf-fined-150-for-assaulting-exclusionary-radical-feminist-in-hyde-park-a3813856.html>

Cox, Stan. 2020. *The Green New Deal and Beyond: Ending the Climate Emergency While We Still Can.* San Francisco: City Lights Books.

Crenshaw, Kimberlé. 1989. 'Demarginalizing the Intersection of Race and Sex: A Black Feminist Critique of Antidiscrimination Doctrine, Feminist Theory and Antiracist Politics'. *The University of Chicago Legal Forum.* Volume 1989, Issue 1, pp. 139–167. <https://chicagounbound.uchicago.edu/cgi/viewcontent.cgi?article=1052&context=uclf>

Darya and Baran. 2007. 'Interview with an Iranian Lesbian in order to convey her protest to the world'. *Iranian Queer Organization*, p. 2. Translated by Ava. <http://irqo.net/IRQO/English/pages/071.htm> Accessed 17 August 2007.

Dashu, Max. 2020. Suppressed Histories Archives. <https://www.suppressed histories.net/>

Davies, Anne. 2019. 'NSW cotton grower faces more charges over water pumped from Barwon River'. 21 May. <https://www.theguardian.com/australia-news/2019/may/21/nsw-cotton-grower-faces-more-charges-over-water-pumped-from-barwon-river>

Davies, Lennard J. 1995. *Enforcing Normalcy: Disability, Deafness and the Body.* London: Verso.

de Beauvoir, Simone. 1972. *The Second Sex.* Harmondsworth, UK: Penguin Modern Classics.

dé Ishtar, Zohl. 1994. *Daughters of the Pacific.* Melbourne: Spinifex Press.

dé Ishtar, Zohl. 1998. *Pacific Women Speak Out for Independence and Denuclearisation.* Christchurch: The Raven Press.

Declaration on Women's Sex-Based Rights. 2019. Women's Human Rights Campaign. <womensdeclaration>

DemocracyNow. 2020. 'Vandana Shiva: We Must Fight Back Against the 1 Percent to Stop the Sixth Mass Extinction'. 22 February. <https://www.democracynow.

org/2019/2/22/vandana_shiva_we_must_fight_back?fbclid=IwAR2aLor_
o6ryFZGFQ62dSUoP6PY9lB-x6HnS2mPYwllCTQrLaLkvgnJPP2M>

Denham, Jess. 2013. 'Death threats force feminist campaigner out of university debate'. *The Independent*. 17 September. <https://www.independent.co.uk/student/news/death-threats-force-feminist-campaigner-out-of-university-debate-8821362.html>

Dexter, Miriam Robbins. 1990. *Whence the Goddess: A Source Book*. New York: Pergamon.

DeVille, Austin. 2020. 'Trans Rights are Men's Rights; No wonder they clash with feminists'. Women's Liberation Radio News. 19 June. <https://wlrnmedia.wordpress.com/2020/06/19/trans-rights-are-mens-rights-no-wonder-they-clash-with-feminists/>

Dines, Gail. 2010. *Pornland: How Porn Has Hijacked Our Sexuality*. Melbourne: Spinifex Press.

Doherty, Ben. 2016. 'A short history of Nauru, Australia's dumping ground for refugees'. *The Guardian*. 9 August. <https://www.theguardian.com/world/2016/aug/10/a-short-history-of-nauru-australias-dumping-ground-for-refugees>

Donym, Sue. 2018. 'Inauthentic Selves: The modern LGBTQ+ movement is run by philanthropic astroturf and based on junk science'. *Medium*. 6 August. <https://medium.com/@sue.donym1984/inauthentic-selves-the-modern-lgbtq-movement-is-run-by-philanthropic-astroturf-and-based-on-junk-d08eb6aa1a4b>

Dostoyevsky, Fyodor. 1955. *The Idiot*. Translated by David Margashack. Harmondsworth: Penguin.

Dove, Michael R. 1993. 'A Revisionist View of Tropical Deforestation and Development'. *Environmental Conservation* Vol. 20, No. 1, pp. 17–24.

Dovey, Ceridwen. 2017. 'The Mapping of Massacres'. *The New Yorker*. 6 December. <https://www.newyorker.com/culture/culture-desk/mapping-massacres>

Dow, Unity. 2002. *The Screaming of the Innocent*. Melbourne: Spinifex Press.

Dworkin, Andrea. 1993. *Mercy*. New York, NY: Four Walls Eight Windows.

Dworkin, Andrea. 2002. *Heartbreak*. New York, NY: Basic Books.

Dykewomon, Elana. 1990. Editorial in *On Disability*. Vol 39. *Sinister Wisdom*. Winter 1989–90, pp. 5–8.

Easteal, Patricia. 1995. *Voices of the Survivors*. Melbourne: Spinifex Press.

Easteal, Patricia. 1996. *Shattered Dreams, Marital Violence Against Women: The Overseas-born in Australia*. Melbourne: Bureau of Immigration and Multicultural Population Research.

Eddy, FannyAnn. 2004. 'Testimony by FannyAnn Eddy at the U.N. Commission on Human Rights. Item 14 — 60th Session, U.N. Commission on Human Rights'. <http://hrw.org/english/docs/2004/10/04/sierra9439.htm>

Ekman, Kajsa Ekis. 2013. *Being and Being Bought: Prostitution, Surrogacy and the Split Self*. Melbourne: Spinifex Press.

Ekman, Kajsa Ekis. 2014. Pers. Comm.

Elliot, Zach. 2020. 'A response to "Stop using phony science to justify transphobia"'. The Paradox Institute. 24 July. <https://theparadoxinstitute. com/blog/2020/07/24/a-response-to-stop-using-phony-science-to-justify-transphobia/>

Emberson-Bain, Atu. 1994. *Sustainable Development or Malignant Growth?: Perspectives of Pacific Island Women*. Suva, Fiji: Marama Publications.

Enloe, Cynthia. 1983. *Does Khaki Become You? The Militarisation of Women's Lives*. London: Pluto Press.

Evans, Martin and Gareth Davies. 2018. 'Transgender prisoner born a male who sexually assaulted female inmates after being jailed for rape is sentenced to life'. *The Telegraph*. 11 October. <https://www.telegraph.co.uk/news/2018/10/11/ transgender-prisoner-born-male-sexually-assaulted-female-inmates/>

Evershed, Nick, Andy Ball and Naaman Zhou. 2020. 'How big are the fires burning in Australia?' *The Guardian*. 24 January. <https://www.theguardian. com/australia-news/datablog/ng-interactive/2019/dec/07/how-big-are-the-fires-burning-on-the-east-coast-of-australia-interactive-map>

Facebook. 2020. 'Trans women are awesome ...'. 26 June.

Federici, Silvia. 2004. *Caliban the Witch: Women, the Body and Primitive Accumulation*. Brooklyn, NY: Autonomedia.

Federici, Silvia. 2018. *Witches, Witch-hunting and Women*. Brooklyn, NY: Autonomedia.

Fair Play for Women. 2019. 'Why does JK Rowling support Maya Forstater and why you should care?'. 20 December. <https://fairplayforwomen.com/ jkrowling/>

Farley, Melissa. 2007. *Prostitution and Trafficking in Nevada: Making the Connections*. San Francisco, CA: Prostitution Research and Education.

Ferrara, Jennifer and Michael K. Dorsey. 2001. 'Genetically Engineered Foods: A Minefield of Safety Hazards' in Brian Tokar (ed.) *Redesigning Life: The Worldwide Challenge to Genetic Engineering*. Melbourne: Scribe Publications.

Fergus, Lara. 2005. 'Elsewhere in Every Country: Locating Lesbian Writing'. Paper presented at 9th International Interdisciplinary Congress on Women, Seoul, Korea. 21 June.

FiLiA. 2019. 'Violence against Lesbians'. <https://filia.org.uk/podcasts/2020/4/7/ violence-against-lesbians-filia-conference-2019>

FiLiA. 2020. 'FiLiA Campaign: Support Lesbians in Kakuma Refugee Camp. We need your help'. <https://filia.org.uk/podcasts/2020/8/12/filia-campaign-support-lesbians-in-kakuma-refugee-camp-we-need-your-help>

Finger, Anne. 1985. 'Claiming All of Our Bodies: Reproductive Rights and Disability' in Susan E. Browne, Debra Connors and Nanci Stern (eds.) *With the Power of Each Breath: A Disabled Women's Anthology*. Pittsburgh: Cleis Press, pp. 292–307.

Firestone, Shulamith. 1972. *The Dialectic of Sex: The Case for Feminist Revolution*. New York: Bantam Books.

Fitzgerald, Jennifer. 1998. 'Geneticizing disability: The Human Genome Project and the commodification of self'. Retrieved 1 January 2006, from <http://www.metafuture.org/articlesbycolleagues/JenniferFitzgerald/Geneticizing%20Disability.htm>

Fletcher, Garth, Sally V. Goddard and Yaling Wu. 1999. 'Antifreeze Proteins and Their Genes: From Basic Research to Business Opportunity'. *Chemtech*, Vol. 30, No. 6, pp. 17–28.

Flannery, Tim. 1994. *The Future Eaters*. Chatswood: New Holland Publishers.

Forrester, Viviane. 1999. *The Economic Horror*. London: Polity Press.

Foster, Judy with Marlene Derlet. 2013. *Invisible Women of Prehistory: Three Million Years of Peace, Six Thousand Years of War*. Melbourne: Spinifex Press.

Fourmile, Henrietta. 1996. 'Protecting Indigenous Property Rights in Biodiversity'. *Current Affairs Bulletin* 36 (Feb/Mar), pp. 36–41.

Fraser, Janet. 2020. *Born Still: A Memoir of Grief*. Mission Beach: Spinifex Press.

Freire, Paulo. 1971. *Cultural Action for Freedom*. Harmondsworth: Penguin Books.

Freire, Paulo. 1972. *Pedagogy of the Oppressed*. Harmondsworth: Penguin Books.

Friedman, Laren F. 2015. 'IBM's Watson can now do in minutes what takes doctors weeks'. *Business Insider Australia*. 6 May. <https://www.businessinsider.com.au/r-ibms-watson-to-guide-cancer-therapies-at-14-centers-2015-5>

Frye, Marilyn. 1983. *The Politics of Reality: Essays in Feminist Theory*. Trumansburg, NY: The Crossing Press.

Gage, Carolyn. 2008. 'The Inconvenient Truth about Teena Brandon'. *Trivia Voices*. Issue 10. <https://www.triviavoices.com/the-inconvenient-truth-about-teena-brandon.html>

Gagnon, Pauline. 2016. 'The Forgotten Life of Einstein's First Wife' *Scientific American*. 19-December. <https://blogs.scientificamerican.com/guest-blog/the-forgotten-life-of-einsteins-first-wife/>

Gaika, Millicent. 2011. 'Face of Your Fears: Corrective rape in South Africa'. *Elixher Magazine*. 26 April. <http://elixher.com/tag/millicent-gaika/> Accessed 8 November 2015.

Galeano, Eduardo. 1973/1987. *Open Veins of Latin America: Five Centuries of the Pillage of a Continent*. New York: Monthly Review Press.

Gallagher, Laura. 2018. 'Review: Julie Bindel — The Pimping of Prostitution'. Bristol Festival of Ideas. 16 March. <http://www.ideasfestival.co.uk/blog/festival-of-ideas/review-julie-bindel-pimping-prostitution/>

Gammage, Bill. 2012. *The Biggest Estate on Earth: How Aborigines Made Australia*. Sydney: Allen & Unwin.

Garcia, Elena. 2019. 'Rivers in crisis: Amid drought, corporations are buying up Australia's water'. *Green Left*. 28 November. <https://www.greenleft.org.

au/content/rivers-crisis-amid-drought-corporations-are-buying-australia-water>

Garnaut, Ross. 2019. *Superpower: Australia's Low-Carbon Opportunity*. Melbourne: La Trobe University Press in conjunction with Black Inc.

Garrett, Laurie. 1994. *The Coming Plague: Newly Emerging Diseases in a World Out of Balance*. London: Virago.

Gay, Roxanne. 2017. *Hunger: A Memoir of (My) Body*. New York: Harper.

George, Katrina. 2007. 'A Woman's Choice? The Gendered Risks of Voluntary Euthanasia and Physician Assisted Suicide'. *Medical Law Review*. Vol. 15, Spring, pp. 1–33.

Ghai, Anita. 2007. 'Pre genetic diagnosis: Issues and concerns' in *Consultation on 'new' reproductive and genetic technologies and women's lives*. New Delhi: Sama, pp. 22–23.

Gilberthorpe, Emma. 2017. 'New Guinea's indigenous tribes are alive and well (just don't call them 'ancient')'. *The Conversation*. 18 April. <https://theconversation.com/new-guineas-indigenous-tribes-are-alive-and-well-just-dont-call-them-ancient-75888>

Gimbutas, Marija. 1989. *The Language of the Goddess*. New York: Harper & Row.

Gimbutas, Marija. 1991. *The Civilization of the Goddess: The World of Old Europe*. San Francisco: Harper San Francisco.

Global Witness. 1998. *A Rough Trade: The Role of Companies and Governments in the Angolan Conflict*: Global Witness. December. <www.oneworld.org/globalwitness/reports/Angola/title.htm>

Glosswitch. 2015. 'The Problem of Talking about "Pregnant People"'. *New Statesman*. 29 September. <https://www.newstatesman.com/politics/feminism/2015/09/what-s-matter-talking-about-pregnant-people>

Goggin, Gerard and Christopher Newell. 2005. *Disability in Australia: Exposing a Social Apartheid*. Sydney: University of New South Wales Press.

Goldberg, Stephanie. 2019. 'Pritzker Foundation gives Lurie $15 million for kids' mental health'. *Chicago Business*. 6 May. <https://www.chicagobusiness.com/health-care/pritzker-foundation-gives-lurie-15-million-kids-mental-health>

Gott, Beth. 2018. 'The Art of Healing: Five Medicinal Plants Used by Aboriginal Australians'. *The Conversation*. 6 June. <https://theconversation.com/the-art-of-healing-five-medicinal-plants-used-by-aboriginal-australians-97249>

Gorey, Lorrayne. 2019. 'Mparntwe Alice Springs, NT, Australia Arrernte woman'. Youtube. 1 March. < https://youtu.be/yR5DMTBNIe0>

Gorz, André. 1999. *Reclaiming Work: Beyond the Wage-based Society*. London: Polity Press.

Gould, Elizabeth. 1973. *The First Sex*. Baltimore, MD: Penguin Books.

Gqola, Pumnla Dineo. 2015. *Rape: A South African Nightmare*. Johannesburg: Jacana Media.

Graham, Claire. 2019. 'What is Dignity?' MRKHVoice. 18 December. <https://mrkhvoice.com/index.php/2019/12/18/what-is-dignity/>

Graham, Dee L. R. with Edna I. Rawlings and Roberta K. Rigsby. 1994. *Loving to Survive: Sexual Terror, Men's Violence and Women's Lives*. New York: New York University Press.

GRAIN. 2002. Farida Akhter–Founder of UBINIG. *Seedling*. July. <https://www.grain.org/article/entries/336-farida-akhtar-founder-of-ubinig>

GRAIN. 2016. *The Great Climate Robbery: How the Food System Drives Climate Change and What We Can Do about It*. Melbourne: Spinifex Press.

Green, John. 2015. 'Australian push to become the world's nuclear waste dump'. *Nuclear Monitor Issue: #808448618/08/2015*. <https://www.wiseinternational.org/nuclear-monitor/808/australian-push-become-worlds-nuclear-waste-dump>

Green, Michael and André Dao. 2017. *They Cannot Take the Sky: Stories from Detention*. Sydney: Allen & Unwin.

Greer, Germaine. 1972. *The Female Eunuch*. London: Paladin.

Greer, Germaine. 1993. *The Change: Women, Aging and the Menopause*. New York: Ballantine Books.

Greer, Germaine. 2018. *On Rape*. Melbourne: Melbourne University Press.

Grenville, Kate. 2017. *The Case against Fragrance*. Melbourne: Text Publishing.

Griffin, Susan. 1978. *Woman and Nature: The Roaring Inside Her*. New York: Harper & Row.

Guillaumin, Colette. 1995. *Racism, Sexism, Power and Ideology*. London and New York: Routledge.

Haarmann, Harald. 2014. *Roots of Ancient Greek Civilization: The Influence of Old Europe*. Jefferson, NC: McFarland & Company.

Haarmann, Harald. 2015. *Myth as Source of Knowledge in Early Western Thought: The Quest for Historiography, Science and Philosophy in Greek Antiquity*. Wiesbaden: Harrassowitz Verlag.

Haebich, Anna. 2000. *Broken Circles: Fragmenting Indigenous Families 1800–2000*. Fremantle: Fremantle Arts Centre Press.

Hanson, Pauline. 2016. 'Pauline Hanson's 2016 maiden speech to the senate: Full transcript'. *Sydney Morning Herald*. 15 September. <https://www.smh.com.au/politics/federal/pauline-hansons-2016-maiden-speech-to-the-senate-full-transcript-20160915-grgjtm.html>

Hattingh, Michelle. 2017. *I'm the Girl Who Was Raped*. Melbourne: Spinifex Press.

Havoscope. 2018. 'Prostitution Revenue by Country'. <https://www.havocscope.com/prostitution-revenue-by-country/>

Hawthorne, Susan. 1989. 'The Politics of the Exotic: The paradox of cultural voyeurism'. *Meanjin*. Vol. 48, No. 2, pp. 259–268.

Hawthorne, Susan. 1993. 'The Language in My Tongue' in *Four New Poets*. Ringwood: Penguin Books Australia.

Hawthorne, Susan. 1996. 'From Theories of Indifference to a Wild Politics', in Diane Bell and Renate Klein (eds.) *Radically Speaking: Feminism Reclaimed*. Melbourne: Spinifex Press, pp. 483–501.

Hawthorne, Susan. 2000. 'Transgender People in the Women's Circus: A discussion paper'. Unpublished open letter.

Hawthorne, Susan. 2001a. 'Wild Bodies/Technobodies'. *Women's Studies Quarterly: Women Confronting the New Technologies*. Vol. XXIX, Nos. 3–4. Fall/Winter, pp. 54–69.

Hawthorne, Susan. 2001b. 'Disability and Diversity: Challenges to Normalisation and Sameness'. *Women in Action*. Vol. 2, pp. 40–44.

Hawthorne, Susan. 2002a. *Wild Politics: Feminism, Globalisation and Bio/ diversity*. Melbourne: Spinifex Press.

Hawthorne, Susan. 2002b. 'Fundamentalism, Violence and Disconnection' in Susan Hawthorne and Bronwyn Winter (eds.) *September 11, 2001: Feminist Perspectives*. Melbourne: Spinifex Press. pp. 339–359.

Hawthorne, Susan. 2003a. 'Responsibility: Personal and Global'. *Altitude*. Vol. 1, No. 1.

Hawthorne, Susan. 2003b. 'The Depoliticising of Lesbian Culture'. *Hecate*. Vol. 29, No. 2, pp. 235–247.

Hawthorne, Susan. 2003c. 'Corporate Biotechnology: Gene patents, market dynamics versus the public good'. Paper presented at Within and Beyond the Limits of Human Nature Conference. Berlin 12–15 October.

Hawthorne, Susan. 2004a. 'The Political Uses of Obscurantism: Gender Mainstreaming and Intersectionality'. *Development Bulletin*. No. 89, pp. 87–91.

Hawthorne, Susan. 2004b. 'Post-election Blues'. *Arena magazine*. No. 74, p. 10.

Hawthorne, Susan. 2005a. 'Structural Injustice: Criminalizing the Powerless'. Paper delivered at Improving Policing for Women in the Asia Pacific Region, Darwin, Australia. August 23.

Hawthorne, Susan. 2005b. *The Butterfly Effect*. Melbourne: Spinifex Press.

Hawthorne, Susan. 2006a. 'Ancient Hatred and Its Contemporary Misuses: The torture of lesbians'. *The Journal of Hate Studies*. Vol. 4, No. 1, pp. 33–58.

Hawthorne, Susan. 2006b. 'Patriarchy, the Institution of Heterosexuality and Patriotism'. *African Safety Promotion: A Journal of Injury and Violence Prevention*. Vol. 4, No. 2, pp. 20–31.

Hawthorne, Susan. 2006c. 'Lesfest — The case for exclusion'. *Lesbiana*, October, p. 5.

Hawthorne, Susan. 2006d. 'Unbundling Water from Land'. *Arena Magazine*. December-January. Republished on Online *Opinion*. 15 January. <http://www. onlineopinion.com.au/view.asp?article=5380>

Hawthorne, Susan. 2007a. 'Land, Bodies and Knowledge: Biocolonialism of Plants, Indigenous Peoples, Women and People with Disabilities'. *Signs: A Journal of Women in Culture and Society*. Vol. 33, No. 2, Winter, pp. 314–323.

Hawthorne, Susan. 2007b. 'The Aerial Lesbian Body: The Politics of Physical Expression'. *Trivia: Voices of Feminism*. Vol. 6. <http://www.triviavoices.com/the-aerial-lesbian-body-the-politics-of-physical-expression.html>

Hawthorne, Susan. 2007c. 'Wild Politics and Water'. *Online Opinion*. 23 April. <https://www.onlineopinion.com.au/view.asp?article=5765>

Hawthorne, Susan. 2008. 'Somatic Piracy and BioPhallacies: Separation, Violence and Biotech Fundamentalism'. *Women's Studies International Forum*. Vol. 31, No. 4, Jul–August, pp. 308–318.

Hawthorne, Susan. 2009. 'bushfire four months after'. *The Age, Bushfire Special Edition*. 7 August.

Hawthorne, Susan. 2011. 'Capital and the Crimes of Pornographers: Free to Lynch, Exploit, Rape and Torture' in Melinda Tankard Reist and Abigail Bray (eds.) *Big Porn Inc: Exposing the Harms of the Global Pornography Industry*. Melbourne: Spinifex Press, pp. 107–117.

Hawthorne, Susan. 2012. 'Shades of Grey: What now that BDSM has gone mainstream?' <http://www.spinifexpress.com.au/Blog/display/id=113/>

Hawthorne, Susan. 2013. *Limen*. Melbourne: Spinifex Press.

Hawthorne, Susan. 2014. *Bibliodiversity: A Manifesto for Independent Publishing*. Melbourne: Spinifex Press.

Hawthorne, Susan. 2015. 'Lesbians: The Erasure of Torture, Rape and Murder'. Paper presented at the Australian Homosexualities History Conference. Adelaide. 13 November.

Hawthorne, Susan. 2017. *Dark Matters: A Novel*. Mission Beach: Spinifex Press.

Hawthorne, Susan. 2018. 'The Homeric Hymn to Aphrodite' in Mary Ann Beavis and Helen Hye-Sook Hwang (eds.) *Goddesses in Myth, History and Culture*. Lytle Creek, CA: Mago Books, pp. 152–162.

Hawthorne, Susan. 2019a. *The Sacking of the Muses*. Mission Beach: Spinifex Press.

Hawthorne, Susan. 2019b. *In Defence of Separatism*. Mission Beach: Spinifex Press.

Hawthorne, Susan. 2019c. 'Questions of Power and Rights in Surrogacy: Is it acceptable for gay men to exploit surrogate mothers facing poverty, racism, eugenic forces and misogyny?' Paper presented at Broken Bonds and Big Money: An International Conference on Surrogacy. Storey Hall, RMIT, Melbourne. 16 March 2019.

Hawthorne, Susan. 2020. 'You can never get enough'. Unpublished poem.

Helm, Sarah. 2015. *If This Is a Woman: Inside Ravensbrück — Hitler's Concentration Camp for Women*. London: Little, Brown.

Herman, Judith. 2015. *Trauma and Recovery: The Aftermath of Violence — From Domestic Abuse to Political Terror*. New York: Basic Books.

Herman, Todd. 2019. 'What Oregon is doing to kids who feel dysphoric is a medical, societal atrocity'. Candy, Mike and Todd Show. Kiro Radio.

7 November. <https://mynorthwest.com/1588554/oregon-children-gender-dysphoric/>

Herper, Matthew. 2015. 'Bill Gates and 13 Other Investors Pour $120 Million Into Revolutionary Gene-Editing Startup'. *Forbes*. 10 August. <https://www.forbes.com/sites/matthewherper/2015/08/10/bill-gates-and-13-other-investors-pour-120-million-into-revolutionary-gene-editing-startup/#849836663693>

Hill, Jess. 2019. *See What You Made Me Do: Power, Control and Domestic Abuse*. Melbourne: Black Inc.

Hoagland, Sara Lucia. 1988. *Lesbian Ethics: Toward New Values*. Palo Alto: Institute of Lesbian Studies.

hooks, bell. 2013. 'Dig Deep, Beyond Lean In'. *Feminist Wire*. October. <https://thefeministwire.com/2013/10/17973/>

Hopkins, Alison Julie. 2008. 'Convenient Fictions: The Script of Lesbian Desire in the Post-Ellen Era. A New Zealand Perspective'. PhD Thesis, Victoria University of Wellington.

Horacek, Judy. 1992. *Life on the Edge*. Melbourne: Spinifex Press.

Horvitz, Leslie Alan. 1996. '"Vampire Project" Raises Issue of Patents for Human Genes'. *Insight on the News*. Vol. 12, No. 27, p. 34.

Hossain, Sara and Lynn Welchman (eds.). 2005. *'Honour': Crimes, Paradigms, and Violence Against Women*. Melbourne: Spinifex Press.

Howe, Brian. 2018. 'Australians support a universal health care, so why not a universal basic income? *The Conversation*. 13 February. <https://theconversation.com/australians-support-universal-health-care-so-why-not-a-universal-basic-income-91572>

Hughes, Patricia. 2004. *Enough*. Melbourne: Spinifex Press.

Human Rights Watch. 2004. 'Sierra Leone: Human Rights Activist Brutally Murdered'. 5 October. <https://www.hrw.org/news/2004/10/05/sierra-leone-lesbian-rights-activist-brutally-murdered>

Human Rights Watch. 2009. 'Stop the Violence — Live Updates from South Africa'. 11 February.

Human Rights Watch. 2018. 'The Hidden Cost behind Jewelry: Human Rights in Supply Chains and the Responsibility of Jewelry Companies'. 8 February. <https://www.hrw.org/report/2018/02/08/hidden-cost-jewelry/human-rights-supply-chains-and-responsibility-jewelry>

Hyman, Prue. 1999. 'Universal Basic Income: A useful proposal for feminists'. *Proceedings of the 1998 Women's Studies Association Conference*, Women's Studies Association, New Zealand, pp. 112–117.

Hynes, H. Patricia. 1999. 'Taking Population out of the Equation: Reformulating I = PAT' in Jael Silliman and Ynestra Kin (eds.) *Dangerous Intersections: Feminist Perspectives on Population, Environment, and Development*. Cambridge, MA: South End Press.

Iceland, Charles. 2015. 'A Global Tour of 7 Recent Droughts'. Washington DC: World Resources Institute. <https://www.wri.org/blog/2015/06/global-tour-7-recent-droughts>

IGYLO. 2019. *Only Adults? Good Practices in Legal Gender Recognition for Youth: A Report on the Current Laws and NGO Advocacy in Eight Countries in Europe, with a Focus on Rights of Young People.* London: Thomas Reuters Foundation.

IHRA. 2011. Intersex Human Rights Australia. 3 June. <https://ihra.org.au/18194/differences-intersex-trans/#:~:text=Intersex%20is%20not%20a%20part,physical%20differences%20in%20sex%20characteristics>

ILIS Newsletter. 1994. Vol. 15, No. 2.

Ilyatjari, Nganyintja. 1983. 'Women and Land Rights: The Pitjantjatjara Claims'. in Fay Gale (ed.) *We Are Bosses Ourselves: The Status and Role of Aboriginal Women Today.* Canberra: Australian Institute of Aboriginal Studies.

Ingala Smith, Karen. 2018. 'Amnesty International and the Gender Recognition Act Consultation'. 3 October. <https://kareningalasmith.com/2018/10/>

Ingleton, Sue. 2019. *Making Trouble (Tongued with Fire): An Imagined History of Harriet Elphinstone Dick and Alice C. Moon.* Mission Beach: Spinifex Press.

Isla, Ana. 2007. 'An Ecofeminist Perspective on Biopiracy in Latin America'. *Signs: A Journal of Women in Culture and Society.* Vol. 32. No. 2, pp. 323–332.

Isla, Ana (ed.). 2019a. *Climate Chaos: Ecofeminism and the Land Question.* Toronto: Inanna Publications.

Isla, Ana. 2019b. 'Climate Change and Environmental Racism: What Payments for Ecosystem Services Means for Peasants and Indigenous Peoples' in Ana Isla (ed.) *Climate Chaos: Ecofeminism and the Land Question.* Toronto: Inanna Publications.

Jacks, Timna. 2019. '"Like losing my son": Why trees threatened by Western Hwy are so sacred'. *The Age.* 25 August.

Jackson, Andy. 2017. 'World in a Grain of Flesh' in Heather Taylor Johnson (ed.) *Shaping the Fractured Self: Poetry of Chronic Illness and Pain.* Perth: University of Western Australia Publishing, pp. 32–40.

Janssen-Jurreit, Marielouise. 1976. *Sexismus: Über die Abtreibung der Frauenfrage.* Munich-Vienna: Carl Hanser Verlag.

Jeffreys, Sheila. 1993. *The Lesbian Heresy: A Feminist Perspective on the Lesbian Feminist Revolution.* Melbourne: Spinifex Press.

Jeffreys, Sheila. 1997. *The Idea of Prostitution.* Melbourne: Spinifex Press.

Jeffreys, Sheila. 2003. *Unpacking Queer Politics: A Lesbian Feminist Perspective.* Cambridge: Polity Press.

Jeffreys, Sheila. 2005. *Beauty and Misogyny: Harmful Cultural Practices in the West.* London: Routledge.

Jeffreys, Sheila. 2009. *The Industrial Vagina: The Political Economy of the Global Sex Trade.* Abingdon and New York, NY: Routledge.

Jeffreys, Sheila. 2011. *Anticlimax: A Feminist Perspective on the Sexual Revolution.* Melbourne: Spinifex Press.

Jeffreys, Sheila. 2014. *Gender Hurts: A Feminist Analysis of the Politics of Transgenderism*. London: Routledge.

Jeffreys, Sheila. 2019. 'Men's Sexual Rights versus Women's Sex-Based Right'. Women's Human Rights Campaign Webinar. 18 April. <https://www.youtube.com/watch?v=iDM43DUT2Ic>

Jeffreys, Sheila. 2020. *Trigger Warning: My Lesbian Feminist Life*. Mission Beach: Spinifex Press.

Jeffs, Sandy. 1993. *Poems from the Madhouse*. Melbourne: Spinifex Press.

Jeffs, Sandy. 2015. *The Mad Poet's Tea Party*. Melbourne: Spinifex Press.

Jennings, Norman S. 1999. *Child Labour in Small-scale Mining: Examples from Niger, Peru and Philippines*. Geneva: ILO. Sectoral Activities Programme, Industrial Activities Branch. Working Paper. <www.ilo.org/public/english/dialogue/sector/papers/childmin/>

Jensen, Robert. 2017. *The End of Patriarchy: Radical Feminism for Men*. Melbourne: Spinifex Press.

Kagan, Julia. 2019. 'Tobin Tax' in *Investopedia*. 18 August. <https://www.investopedia.com/terms/t/tobin-tax.asp>

Kaufmann, Eric. 2020. 'How the Trans Pledge Damaged the Labour Party'. *Quillette* 27 February. <https://quillette.com/2020/02/27/how-the-trans-pledge-damaged-the-labour-party/>

Keenahan, Debra. 2017. 'The Female Dwarf. Disability and Beauty'. *The Conversation*. 3 November. <https://theconversation.com/friday-essay-the-female-dwarf-disability-and-beauty-84844>

Kelly, Annie. 2009. 'Raped and killed for being a lesbian: South Africa ignores "corrective" attacks'". *The Guardian*. 12 March.
<http://www.guardian.co.uk/world/2009/mar/12/eudy-simelane-corrective-rape-south-africa>

Kelly, Lynne. 2015. *Knowledge and Power in Prehistoric Societies: Orality, Memory and Transmission of Culture*. Cambridge: Cambridge University Press.

Kelly, Lynne. 2016. *The Memory Code*. Sydney: Allen & Unwin.

Kenobii, Ben. 2002. 'Meet Jennifer Pritzker: The Trans Billionaire Big Tech Doesn't Want You to Know About'. *Populist Wire*. 27 February. <https://www.populistwire.com/culture/how-they-rule-you/?fbclid=IwAR0Mfg8yLDOyG80IOanxpEXr3Wu9w1HsO1T2Ih9EJTvo7TmZ5MVxrDs8Ep8>

Kirkup, James. 2019. 'The Document That Reveals the Remarkable Tactics of Trans Lobbyists'. *The Spectator*. 30 December. <https://blogs.spectator.co.uk/2019/12/the-document-that-reveals-the-remarkable-tactics-of-trans-lobbyists/>

Klein, Naomi. 2000. *No Logo*. London: Flamingo.

Klein, Naomi. 2007. *The Shock Doctrine: The Rise of Disaster Capitalism*. Melbourne: Penguin Australia.

Klein, Renate (ed.). 1989. *Infertility: Women Speak Out about Their Experiences of Reproductive Medicine*. London and Sydney: Pandora.

Klein, Renate. 1996. '(Dead) Bodies Floating in Cyberspace: Post-modernism and the Dismemberment of Women' in Diane Bell and Renate Klein (eds.) *Radically Speaking: Feminism Reclaimed.* Melbourne: Spinifex Press, pp. 346–358.

Klein, Renate. 1999. 'The Politics of CyberFeminism: If I'm a Cyborg Rather than a Goddess will Patriarchy Go Away?' in Susan Hawthorne and Renate Klein (eds.) *CyberFeminism: Connectivity, Critique and Creativity.* Melbourne: Spinifex Press, pp. 185–212.

Klein, Renate. 2001. 'Globalized Bodies in the 21st Century: The Final Patriarchal Takeover?' in Veronika Bennholdt-Thomsen, Nicholas G. Faraclas, and Claudia von Werlof (eds.) *There Is an Alternative: Subsistence and Worlwide Resistance to Corporate Globalisation,* pp. 91–105. London: Zed Books; Melbourne: Spinifex Press.

Klein, Renate. 2004. 'IVF and Lesbians: Heterosexualising families'. Paper presented at Australian and International Feminisms, University of Sydney. December 12–14.

Klein, Renate. 2017. *Surrogacy: A Human Rights Violation.* Mission Beach: Spinifex Press.

Klein, Renate. 2018. 'Hope', in Susan Hawthorne (ed.) *Live Encounters: Lesbian Poets and Writers.* February. <https://issuu.com/liveencounters/docs/live_encounters_lesbian_poets___wri>

Koedt, Anne, Ellen Levine and Anita Rapone (eds.). 1973. *Radical Feminism.* New York, NY: Quadrangle.

Kolk, Ans. 1996. *Forests in International Environmental Politics: International Organisations, NGOs and the Brazilian Amazon.* Utrecht: International Books.

Koolmatrie, Jacinta. 2020. 'Destruction of Juukan Gorge: we need to know the history of artefacts, but it is more important to keep them in place'. *The Conversation.* 2 June. <https://theconversation.com/destruction-of-juukan-gorge-we-need-to-know-the-history-of-artefacts-but-it-is-more-important-to-keep-them-in-place-139650>

Krishnan, Nandini. 2018. *Invisible Men: Inside India's Transmasculine Network.* Haryana: Penguin Random House India.

Kuletz, Valerie. 1998. *The Tainted Desert: Environmental and Social Ruin in the American West.* New York and London: Routledge.

Kurtić, Vera. 2014. *Džuvljarke: Roma Lesbian Existence.* Niš: Ženski prostor.

La Duke, Winona. 2015. 'In Praise of the Leadership of Indigenous Women', in Vandana Shiva (ed.) *Seed Sovereignty, Food Security: Women in the Vanguard.* New Delhi: Women Unlimited; Melbourne: Spinifex Press.

Lane, Bernard. 2019. 'Criticism of Trans Policy Has Its Dangers'. *The Australian.* 22 November. <https://www.theaustralian.com.au/nation/criticism-of-trans-policy-brings-its-dangers/news-story/7468534d7c5eed3054a35aafe2992971>

Lane, Bernard. 2020. 'All-new female formula: just add anyone'. *The Australian*. 28 May. <https://www.theaustralian.com.au/nation/blokes-can-be-women-scientists/news-story/66daff26b5c7a886dbb9517051c1e868>

Langelle, Orin. 2001. 'From Native Forest to Frankenforest' in Brian Tokar (ed.) *Redesigning Life: The Worldwide Challenge to Genetic Engineering*. Melbourne: Scribe Publications.

Langton, Marcia. 1998. *Burning Questions: Emerging Environmental Issues for Indigenous Peoples in Northern Australia*. Darwin, NT: Centre for Indigenous and Cultural Resource Management, Northern Territory University.

Laurence, Lianne. 2020. 'Trans activist Yaniv pleads guilty to weapons charge, will be sentenced'. *Life Site News*. 17 March. <https://www.lifesitenews.com/news/trans-activist-yaniv-pleads-guilty-to-weapons-charge-will-be-sentenced>

Leigh, Andrew. 2018. 'Rising to the Challenge of Inequality'. *Inside Story*. 15 June. <http://insidestory.org.au/rising-to-the-challenge-of-inequality/>

Lerner, Gerda. 1986. *The Creation of Patriarchy*. New York, NY: Oxford University Press.

Lessing, Doris. 1973. *The Golden Notebook*. London: Panther Books.

Liddell, Henry George and Robert Scott. 1986. *Greek-English Lexicon*. Oxford: The Clarendon Press.

Liebmann, Adrienne, Jen Jordan, Deb Lewis, Louise Radcliffe-Smith, Patricia Sykes (eds.). 1997. *Women's Circus: Leaping off the Edge*. Melbourne: Spinifex Press.

Lifton, Robert Jay. 1988. *The Nazi Doctors: Medical Killing and the Psychology of Genocide*. New York: Basic Books.

Lindenmayer, David. 2020. 'Australia is losing its capacity to understand environmental recovery'. *The Canberra Times*. 19 January. <https://www.canberratimes.com.au/story/6587168/australia-is-losing-its-capacity-to-understand-environmental-recovery/>

Linehan, Graham. 2019. 'The Emperor Has No Clothes and You Should Mention It'. 1 December. <https://glinner.co.uk/the-emperor-has-no-clothes-and-you-should-mention-it/>

Listening to Lesbians. 2020. 'Argentina: Higui, lesbian accused of murder in corrective rape case to face court'. 27 January. <https://listening2lesbians.com/2020/01/27/argentina-higui-lesbian-accused-of-murder-in-corrective-rape-case-to-face-court/>

Local Memphis. 2018. 'TN Supreme Court rules Cyntoia Brown must serve 51 years before parole eligibility'. 2018. Local Memphis. 11 December. <https://www.localmemphis.com/news/local-news/tn-supreme-court-rules-cyntoia-brown-must-serve-51-years-before-parole-eligibility/1652925717>

Lomborg, Bjørn. 2001. *The Skeptical Environmentalist: Measuring the Real State of the World*. Cambridge: Cambridge University Press.

Loomis, Ruth with Merv Wilkinson. 1995. *Wildwood: A Forest for the Future*. Gabriola, BC: Reflections.

Loots, Lliane. 2006. 'The Gender Implications of Biopolitics with Special Reference to Southern Africa' in Ana Agostino and Glenn Ashton (eds.) *A Patented World? Privatisation of Life and Knowledge.* Johannesburg: Jacana Media.

Luban, David. 2018. 'Pain and powerlessness: understanding the evil of torture'. *ABC Religion and Ethics.* 1 June. <http://www.abc.net.au/religion/articles/2018/06/01/4851496.ht>

Machida, Tina. 1996. 'Sisters of Mercy' in Monika Reinfelder (ed.) *Amazon to Zami: Toward a global lesbian feminism.* London: Cassell, pp. 118–129.

Mackieson, Penny. 2016. *Adoption Deception: A Personal and Professional Journey.* Melbourne: Spinifex Press.

MacKinnon, Catharine A. 2002. 'State of Emergency' in Susan Hawthorne and Bronwyn Winter (eds.) *September 11, 2001: Feminist Perspectives.* Melbourne: Spinifex Press, pp. 426–431.

Magardie, Sheldon. 2003. 'Is the Applicant Really Gay? Legal Responses to Asylum Claims Based on Persecution Because of Sexual Orientation'. *Agenda: Empowering Women for Gender Equality. Women. The Invisible Refugees.* No. 55. Published by Taylor and Francis on behalf of Agenda Feminist Media. pp. 81–87.

Mahood. Kim. 2016. *Position Doubtful: Mapping Landscapes and Memories.* Brunswick and London: Scribe.

Mairs, Nancy. 1992. 'On Being a Cripple' in *Plaintext: Essays by Nancy Mairs.* Tucson: University of Arizona Press, pp. 9–20.

Majeke, Moyisi. 2001. 'Primageniture? A New Guise for Globalisation'. *Agenda.* Vol. 49, pp. 89–91.

Mara, Michelle. 2020. 'New Zealand is squandering an opportunity to help women in prostitution during COVID, thanks to decriminalization'. *Feminist Current.* 3 June. <https://www.feministcurrent.com/2020/06/03/new-zealand-is-squandering-an-opportunity-to-help-women-in-prostitution-during-covid-thanks-to-decriminalization/>

Market Watch. 2020. 'Sex Reassignment Surgery Market 2020 Industry Trends, Size, Growth Insight, Share, Emerging Technologies, Share, Competitive, Regional, and Global Industry Forecast to 2026'. 20 February. <https://www.marketwatch.com/press-release/sex-reassignment-surgery-market-2020-industry-trends-size-growth-insight-share-emerging-technologies-share-competitive-regional-and-global-industry-forecast-to-2026-2020-02-20>

Martinelli, Luke. 2019. 'Basic Income: World's first national experiment in Finland shows only modest results'. *The Conversation.* 22 February. <https://theconversation.com/basic-income-worlds-first-national-experiment-in-finland-shows-only-modest-benefits-111391>

Massey, Charles. 2017. *Call of the Reed Warbler: A New Agriculture, A New Earth.* St Lucia: University of Queensland Press.

Matrix Guild Victoria. 2020. <https://matrixguildvic.org.au/wp/who-we-are/>

Maxwell, Rebecca. 2004. Alan Saunders with Rebecca Maxwell and Peter John Cantrill. 'Beyond Appearances — Architecture and the sense'. *The Comfort Zone*. ABC Radio National. 6 November. <http://www.e-bility.com/articles/beyondappearances.php>

Mayor, Adrienne. 2014. *The Amazons: Lives and Legends of Warrior Women across the Ancient World*. Princeton: Princeton University Press.

McCombs, Annie. 1985. 'A Letter *Ms*. Didn't Print'. *Lesbian Ethics*. Vol. 1, No. 3, pp. 85–88.

McCoy, Alfred. 1990. *The Politics of Heroin: CIA Complicity in the Global Drug Trade*. Chicago, IL: Lawrence Hill Books.

McCurry, Justin. 2017. 'US airbase in Guam threatened by North Korea as Trump promises "fire and fury"'. *The Guardian*. 9 August.

McDonald, Hamish. 2020. 'All in the same canoe'. *Inside Story*. 30 January. <https://insidestory.org.au/all-in-the-same-canoe/>

McGuire, Amelia and Craig Butt. 2020. 'Cut off: How the crisis at Mallacoota unfolded'. *The Age*. 19 January. <https://www.theage.com.au/national/victoria/cut-off-how-the-crisis-at-mallacoota-unfolded-20200117-p53sdn.html>

McLellan, Betty. 2000. *HELP! I'm Living with a Man Boy*. Melbourne: Spinifex Press.

McLellan, Betty. 2010. *Unspeakable: A Feminist Ethic of Speech*. Townsville: Otherwise Publications.

McVeigh, Karen. 2017. 'World is plundering Africa's wealth of "billions of dollars a year"'. *The Guardian*. 24 May. <https://www.theguardian.com/global-development/2017/may/24/world-is-plundering-africa-wealth-billions-of-dollars-a-year>

Merchant, Minhaz. 2018. 'The Great Theft of India by Imperial Britain — Part 2'. *DailyO*. 18 December. <https://www.dailyo.in/politics/british-raj-east-india-company-mughals-brexit-world-war-1/story/1/28382.html>

Mies, Maria, Veronika Bennholdt-Thomsen and Claudia von Werlhof. 1988. *Women: The Last Colony*. New Delhi: Kali for Women.

Mies, Maria. 1994. 'People or Population', in Rosiska Darcy de Olivera and Thais Corral (eds.) *Terra Femina 3. The Human Factor: On Life, Love, Death and Exile*. Rio de Janeiro: IDAC (Institute of Cultural Action), pp. 41–63.

Mies, Maria. 1986/1999. *Patriarchy and Accumulation on a World Scale: Women in the International Division of Labour*. London: Zed Books; Melbourne: Spinifex Press.

Mies, Maria. 2012. *The Lace Makers of Narsapur: Indian Housewives Produce for the World Market*. Melbourne: Spinifex Press.

Millett, Kate. 1975. *The Prostitution Papers*. St Albans: Paladin.

Mix, Jonah. 2017. 'Playing the Intersex Card'. *Medium*. 9 February, p. 5. <https://medium.com/@JonahMix/playing-the-intersex-card-3d95bb29ea16>

Mladjenovic, Lepa. 2003. 'Feminist Politics in the Anti-war Movement in Belgrade: To Shoot or Not To Shoot?' in Wenona Giles, Malathi de Alwis,

Edith Klein (eds.) *Feminists Under Fire: Exchanges across War Zones*. Toronto: Between the Lines, pp. 157–166.

Mladjenovic, Lepa and Divna Matijasevic. 1996. 'SOS Belgrade July 1993-1995: Dirty Streets' in Chris Corrin (ed.) *Women in a Violent World: Feminist Analyses and Resistance across Europe*. Edinburgh: Edinburgh University Press, pp. 119–132.

Mogina, Jane. 1996. 'Sustainable Development'. Paper presented at the 6th International Interdisciplinary Congress on Women. University of Adelaide, Australia.

Moorhead, Finola. 2000. *Darkness More Visible*. Melbourne: Spinifex Press.

Moore, Michele and Heather Brunskell-Evans (eds.). 2019. *Inventing Transgender Children and Young People*. Newcastle upon Tyne: Cambridge Scholars Publishing.

Moran, Rachel. 2013. *Paid For: My Journey through Prostitution*. Melbourne: Spinifex Press.

Morgan, Jonathan, Bambanani Women's Group and Others. 2003. *Long Life: Positive Stories*. Melbourne: Spinifex Press.

Morgan, Robin. 1990/2001. *The Demon Lover: The Roots of Terrorism*. New York: Piatkus Books.

Morgan, Ruth and Saskia Wieringa. 2005. *Tommy Boys, Lesbian Men and Ancestral Wives: Female same-sex practices in Africa*. Johannesburg: Jacana.

Moschetti, Carole. 2006. *Conjugal Wrongs Don't Make Rights: International Feminist Activism, Child Marriage and Sexual Relativism*. PhD Thesis, Political Science Department, University of Melbourne.

Motsei, Mmatshilo. 2007. *The Kanga and the Kangaroo Court: Reflections on the Rape Trial of Jacob Zuma*. Melbourne: Spinifex Press.

Moulton, Carolyn. 1982. 'Editorial'. *Fireweed: A Feminist Quarterly*. No. 14, pp. 5–7.

Mullins, Greg. 2020. 'I tried to warn Scott Morrison about the bushfire disaster'. *The Guardian*. 20 January.

Murphy, Meghan. 2018. 'Why must trans activists smear those who put forth inconvenient narratives about "gender identity?"' *Feminist Current*. 19 June. <https://www.feministcurrent.com/2018/06/19/must-trans-activists-smear-put-forth-inconvenient-narratives-gender-identity/>

Ndaba, Baldwin. '"Hate crime" against lesbians slated'. *IOL News*. <http://www.iol.co.za/news/south-africa/hate-crime-against-lesbians-slated-1.361821#.VjMkGBArIcg> Accessed 30 Oct 2015.

Niesche, Christopher. 2001. 'Low Phosphate, But What a Laundering!' *The Australian*. 11–12 August: p. 28.

Nordic Model Now 2020. 'Wahine Toa Rising letter to New Zealand ministers'. 24 March. <https://nordicmodelnow.org/2020/03/24/wahine-toa-rising-letter-to-new-zealand-ministers/>

Norma, Caroline and Melinda Tankard Reist (eds.). 2016. *Prostitution Narratives: Stories of Survival in the Sex Trade*. Melbourne: Spinifex Press.

Oakley, Ann. 1972. *Sex, Gender and Society*. Aldershot: Arena.

Oelschlaeger, Max. 1991. *The Idea of Wilderness: From Prehistory to the Age of Ecology.* New Haven and London: Yale University Press.

O'Brien, Kerrie. 2020. 'Inside Truganini's Apocalyptic World'. *The Age.* 1 March. <https://www.theage.com.au/culture/books/inside-truganini-s-apocalyptic-world-20200220-p542ps.html>

O'Donnell, Rachel. 2019. 'Biotechnology and Biopiracy: Plant-based Contraceptives in the Americas and the (Mis)management of Nature' in Ana Isla (ed.) *Climate Chaos: Ecofeminism and the Land Question*. Toronto: Inanna. pp. 205–218.

Ohms, Constance and Klaus Stehling. 2001. 'Lesben Informations- and Beratungsstelle e.V.' (Hg./eds). 'Violence Against Lesbians — Violence Against Gay Men: Thesis on Similarities and Differences', in *Gewalt gegen Lesben/Violence against Lesbians: Europäisches/European Symposium*. Berlin: Querverlag, pp. 190–222; pp. 17–52.

Old Lesbians Organizing for Change. 2020. < https://oloc.org/founders-2/>

Onishi, Norimitsu. 2020. 'A Pedophile Writer Is on Trial. So Are the French Elites'. *The New York Times.* 13 February.

Orwell, George. 1976. *Nineteen Eighty-Four*. Harmondsworth: Penguin Books.

Parenti, Michael. 2002. *The Terrorism Trap: September 11 and Beyond*. San Francisco: City Lights.

Parker, Janet. 1993. 'Lesbian Space Project nears deadline'. *Green Left Weekly*. 15 September. <https://www.greenleft.org.au/content/lesbian-space-project-nears-deadline>

Parker, Posie. 2019. 'Standing for Women'. <https://www.standingforwomen.com/>

Parsi, Arsham. 2007. 'Interview with an Iranian Lesbian Couple'. Translated by Ava Iranian Queer Organization. <http://irqo.net/IRQO/English/pages/063.htm>

Pascoe, Bruce. 2014. *Dark Emu, Black Seeds: Agriculture or Accident*. Broome: Magabala Books.

Patel, Vibhuti. 2003. 'Political Economy of Missing Girls in India' in Tulsi Patel (ed.) *Sex-Selective Abortion in India: Gender, Society and New Reproductive Technologies*. Delhi: Sage Books, pp. 286–315.

Pateman, Carole. 1988. *The Sexual Contract*. Cambridge: Polity Press.

Patterson, Orlando. 1982. *Slavery and Social Death: A Comparative Study*. Cambridge, MA, and London: Harvard University Press.

Parvaz, Nasrin. 2018. *One Woman's Struggle in Iran: A Prison Memoir*. Market Drayton: Victorina Press.

Patrick. 2019. 'Detransition was a Beautiful Process' in Michele Moore and Heather Brunskell-Evans (eds.) *Inventing Transgender Children and Young People*. Newcastle upon Tyne: Cambridge Scholars Publishing, pp. 195–199.

PBS. 2019. 'Future of Food: This Genetically Engineered Salmon May Hit US Markets as Early as 2020'. 22 June. <https://www.pbs.org/newshour/show/future-of-food-this-genetically-engineered-salmon-may-hit-u-s-markets-as-early-as-2020>

Pers. Comm. 2007. 'Candlelight Vigil Honoring All African LGBT & HIV+ Heroes who have been Murdered'. This statement was jointly issued by Less AIDS Lesotho and the committee of Lesbian, Gay, Bisexual & Transgender African immigrants residing in the U.S. Email received 1 July 2007.

Pithouse, Richard. 2011. 'Only Protected on Paper'. *The South African Civil Society Information Service*. <https://sacsis.org.za/s/story.php?s=534>

Place, Fiona. 2008. 'Motherhood and Genetic Screening: A Personal Perspective'. *Down Syndrome Research and Practice*. Vol. 12, No. 2, October, pp. 118–126.

Place, Fiona. 2019. *Portrait of the Artist's Mother: Dignity, Creativity and Disability*. Mission Beach: Spinifex Press.

Polis, Jared. 2007. 'The Closet of Fear: The systemic execution of gays and lesbians in Iraq'. <http://www.squarestate.net/showDiary.do;jsessionid=4F4D21ED01EE37CF34BCFF8BF73D8C94?diaryId=4972>

Pollock, David. 2019. *The Wooleen Way: Renewing an Australian Resource*. Melbourne: Scribe.

Pybus, Cassandra. 2020. *Truganini: Journey through the Apocalypse*. Sydney: Allen & Unwin.

Radford, Jill and Diana E.H. Russell (eds.). 1992. *Femicide: The Politics of Woman Killing*. New York, NY: Twayne Publishers.

Rakova, Ursula. 2000. 'Fighting for Land'. *Horizon*. Vol. 8, No. 4, pp. 8–9.

Ranald, Patricia. 2020. 'Corporations prepare to sue over action to save lives and pandemic reveals trade flaws'. *The Conversation*. 23 April. <https://theconversation.com/corporations-prepare-to-sue-over-action-to-save-lives-as-pandemic-reveals-trade-flaws-136604>

Rangan, Haripriya. 2001. 'The Muti Trade: South Africa's Indigenous Medicines'. *Diversity*. Vol. 2, No. 6. pp. 16–25.

Raymond, Janice G. 1979/1994. *The Transsexual Empire: The Making of the She-Male*. London: The Women's Press/New York: Teachers College Press.

Raymond, Janice G. 1986/2020. *A Passion for Friends: Toward a Philosophy of Female Affection*. Mission Beach: Spinifex Press.

Raymond, Janice G. 1995/2019. *Women as Wombs: Reproductive Technologies and the Battle over Women's Freedom*. Mission Beach: Spinifex Press.

Raymond, Janice G. 2015. *Not a Choice, Not a Job: Exposing the Myths about Prostitution and the Global Sex Trade*. Melbourne: Spinifex Press.

Readfearn, Graham. 2019. 'Australia records its hottest day ever — one day after previous record'. *The Guardian*. 19 December. <https://www.theguardian.

com/australia-news/2019/dec/19/419c-australia-records-hottest-ever-day-one-day-after-previous-record>

Readfearn, Graham. 2020a. "'I'm profoundly sad, I feel guilty": Scientists reveal personal fears about the climate crisis.' *The Guardian*. 8 March. <https://www.theguardian.com/environment/2020/mar/08/im-profoundly-sad-i-feel-guilty-scientists-reveal-personal-fears-about-the-climate-crisis>

Readfearn, Graham. 2020b. 'Great Barrier Reef third mass bleaching in five years the most widespread yet'. *The Guardian*. 7 April. <https://www.theguardian.com/environment/2020/apr/07/great-barrier-reefs-third-mass-bleaching-in-five-years-the-most-widespread-ever>

Redgold, Spider. 2007. 'Sappho Gave a Party'. Paper presented at the International Feminist Summit, Townsville. July. <http://www.femininebyte.org/sapphos_party/SPI_files/frame.htm>

Reich, Michael R. 1991. *Toxic Politics: Responding to Chemical Disasters*. Ithaca, NY: Cornell University Press.

Reinfelder, Monika. 1996. 'Persecution and Resistance' in Monika Reinfelder (ed.) *Amazon to Zami: Toward a Global Lesbian Feminism*. London: Cassell, pp. 11–29.

Rich, Adrienne. 1980. 'Compulsory Heterosexuality and Lesbian Existence'. *Signs*. Vol. 5, No. 4, pp. 631–660.

Richardson, Peter and Jean Jacques Van-Helten. 1982. 'Labour in the South African Gold Mining Industry, 1886–1914' in Shula Marks and Richard Rathbone (eds.) *Industrialisation and Social Change in South Africa: African Class Formation, Culture, and Consciousness, 1870–1930*. London: Longman, pp. 77–98.

Rifkin, Jeremy. 1995. *The End of Work: The Decline of the Global Labor Force and the Dawn of the Post-Market Era*. New York: Tarcher/Putnam.

Rioja, Isabel Ramos and Kim Manresa. 1999. *The Day Kadi Lost a Part of Her Life*. Melbourne: Spinifex Press.

Rivera-Fuentes, Consuelo. 2018. 'The Copihue and the Condor' in Susan Hawthorne (ed.) *Live Encounters, Poetry & Writing: Lesbian Poets and Writers*. February.

Rivera-Fuentes, Consuelo and Lynda Birke. 2001. 'Talking with/in Pain: Reflections of Bodies under Torture'. *Women's Studies International Forum*. Vol. 24, No. 6, pp. 653–668.

Robin, Marie-Monique. 2010. *The World According to Monsanto: Pollution, Politics and Power*. Melbourne: Spinifex Press.

Rogers, Lesley. 1994. 'Not in Our Genes or Hormones: A Critique of the Latest Theories for the Biological Causation of Lesbian and Homosexual Behaviour'. *Journal of Australian Lesbian Feminist Studies*. No. 4, pp. 23–34.

Roper, Caitlin. 2014. 'Sexual Exploitation by Tom Ford'. Collective Shout. 18 November. <https://www.collectiveshout.org/sexual_exploitation_by_tom_ford>

Roper, Caitlin. 2017. 'Pleasure machines: What sex robots tell us about men and sex'. ABC Religion and Ethics. <https://www.abc.net.au/religion/pleasure-machines-what-sex-robots-tell-us-about-men-and-sex/10095118>

Roper, Caitlin. 2019. 'Better a robot than a real child: The spurious logic used to justify child sex dolls'. *Arena Magazine*. No. 163. <https://arena.org.au/edition/arena-magazine-no-163/ Available online at ABC Religion and Ethics <https://www.abc.net.au/religion/spurious-logic-used-to-justify-child-sex-dolls/11856284>

Rowland, Robyn. 1993. *Living Laboratories: Women in Reproductive Technologies.* Sydney: Pan Macmillan.

Rowland, Robyn. 2018. *This Intimate War Gallipoli/Çanakkale 1915: İçli Dişli Bir Savaş: Gelibolu/Çanakkale 1915.* Translated by Mehmet Ali Çelikel. Mission Beach: Spinifex Press.

Rowling, J. K. 2020. "J.K. Rowling Writes about Her Reasons for Speaking out on Sex and Gender Issues". 10 June. <https://www.jkrowling.com/opinions/j-k-rowling-writes-about-her-reasons-for-speaking-out-on-sex-and-gender-issues/>

Roy, Anuradha. 2008. *An Atlas of Impossible Longing.* London: MacLehose Press.

Roy, Arundhati. 2020. 'The pandemic is a portal'. *Financial Times.* 3 April. <https://www.ft.com/content/10d8f5e8-74eb-11ea-95fe-fcd274e920ca>

Russell, Diana E.H. (ed.) 1993. *Making Violence Sexy: Feminist Views on Pornography.* New York, NY: Teachers College Press.

Russell, Diana E.H. and Roberta A. Harmes (eds.). 2001. *Femicide in Global Perspective.* New York, NY: Teachers College Press.

Ryan, Lyndall. 2018. 'Partial Map of Massacres in Australia 1780–1930'. <https://c21ch.newcastle.edu.au/colonialmassacres/map.php>

Said, Edward W. 1995. *Orientalism: Western Conceptions of the Orient.* London: Penguin.

Salleh, Ariel (ed.). 2009. *Eco-Sufficiency and Global Justice: Women Write Political Ecology.* Melbourne: Spinifex Press.

Sandberg, Sheryl. 2013. *Lean In: Women, Work and the Will to Lead.* New York: Alfred A. Knopf.

Saravanan, Sheela. 2018. *A Transnational Feminist View of Surrogacy: Biomarkets in India.* Singapore: Springer.

Sarson, Jeanne and Linda MacDonald. 2019. "'A Difficult Client": Lynn's Story of Captivity, Non-State Torture, and Human Trafficking by Her Husband'. *International Journal of Advanced Nursing Education and Research.* Vol. 4, No. 3, pp, 107–124.

Scarry, Elaine. 1985. *The Body in Pain: The Making and Unmaking of the World.* Oxford: Oxford University Press.

Scarry, Elaine. 2011. *Thinking in an Emergency.* New York: W.W. Norton.

Schama, Simon. 1996. *Landscape and Memory.* London: Fontana.

Schiltz, Elizabeth R. 2006/2019. 'Living in the shadow of Mönchberg' in Melinda Tankard Reist (ed.) *Defiant Birth: Women Who Resist Medical Eugenics*. Mission Beach: Spinifex Press, pp. 182–195.

Schoppmann, Claudia. 1996. *Days of Masquerade: Life Stories of Lesbians During the Third Reich*. Translated by Allison Brown. New York, NY: Columbia University Press.

Scoop It. 2018. 'The one drop rule — La regola della goccia unica'. <http://www.angelfire.com/space/cropcircles/>

Scutt, Jocelynne. 1989. *The Baby Machine: The Commercialisation of Motherhood*. Melbourne: McCulloch Publishing.

Seifert, Ruth. 1992. 'War and Rape: A Preliminary Analysis' in Alexandra Stiglmayer (ed.) *Mass Rape: The War against Women in Bosnia-Herzegovina*. Lincoln and London: University of Nebraska Press, pp. 54–71.

Sexual Minorities Uganda (SMUG). 2011. 'Brutal murder of gay Ugandan human rights defender David Kato'. Issue 514. <http://pambazuka.org/en/category/action/70432>

Shand, Hope J. 1994. 'Extracting Human Resources'. *Multinational Monitor*. June. No. 11.

Sharma, Maya. 2006. *Loving Women: Being Lesbian in Underprivileged India*. New Delhi: Yoda Press.

Shiva, Vandana. 1991. *The Violence of the Green Revolution: Third World Agriculture, Ecology and Politics*. Penang: Third World Network.

Shiva, Vandana. 1993. *Monocultures of the Mind: Perspectives on Biodiversity and Biotechnology*. Penang: Third World Network.

Shiva, Vandana. 2000. *Tomorrow's Biodiversity*. London: Thames and Hudson.

Shiva, Vandana. 2012. *Making Peace with the Earth: Beyond Resource, Land and Food Wars*. Melbourne: Spinifex Press.

Shiva, Vandana with Kartikey Shiva. 2018. *Oneness vs the 1%: Shattering Illusions, Seeding Freedom*. Mission Beach: Spinifex Press.

Shiva, Vandana. 2020. Ecological Reflections on the Corona Virus: One Planet, One Health — Connected through Biodiversity. *Jivad — The Vandana Shiva Blog*. 18 March. <https://www.navdanya.org/bija-refelections/2020/03/18/ecological-reflections-on-the-corona-virus/>

Shrier, Abigail. 2020. *Irreversible Damage: The Transgender Craze Seducing Our Daughters*. Washington, DC: Regnery Publishing.

Simiç, Olivera. 2014. *Surviving Peace: A Political Memoir*. Melbourne: Spinifex Press.

Singal, Jesse. 2018. 'When Children Say They Are Trans'. *The Atlantic*. July/August. <https://www.theatlantic.com/magazine/archive/2018/07/when-a-child-says-shes-trans/561749/>

Sjöö, Monica and Barbara Mor. 1987. *The Great Cosmic Mother: Rediscovering the Religion of the Earth*. San Francisco, CA: Harper & Row.

Slattery, Maryanne. 2018. 'Witness Statement, Murray Darling Basin Royal Commission'. 11 July.

Solis, Raul. 2017. 'Los Vientres de Alquilar: La cara mas brutal del "Gaypitalismo"'. *Paralelo 36 Andalucia*. 25 March. <https://www.paralelo36andalucia.com/los-vientres-de-alquilar-la-cara-mas-brutal-del-gaypitalismo/>

Stark, Christine and Rebecca Whisnant (eds.). 2004. *Not For Sale: Feminists Resisting Prostitution and Pornography*. Melbourne: Spinifex Press.

Stark, Christine. 2019. 'Strategies to Restore Justice for Sex Trafficked Native Women' in John Winterdyk and Jackie Jones (eds.) *The Palgrave International Handbook of Human Trafficking*. New York: Palgrave Macmillan.

Steffen, Will. 2020. 'Scientists hate to say "I told you so". But Australia you were warned'. *The Conversation*. 22 January. <https://theconversation.com/scientists-hate-to-say-i-told-you-so-but-australia-you-were-warned-130211>

Steffensen, Victor. 2020. *Fire Country: How Indigenous Fire Management Could Help Save Australia*. Melbourne: Hardie Grant.

Sullivan, Mary Lucille. 2004. 'Can prostitution be safe? Applying occupational health and safety codes to Australia's legalised brothel prostitution' in Christine Starke and Rebecca Whisnant (eds.) *Not For Sale: Feminists Resisting Prostitution and Pornography*. Melbourne: Spinifex Press, pp. 252–268.

Sullivan, Mary Lucille. 2007. *Making Sex Work: A Failed Experiment with Legalised Prostitution*. Spinifex Press.

Swofford, Anthony. 2004. *Jarhead: A Marine's Chronicle of the Gulf War and Other Battles*. New York: Scribner.

Tankard Reist, Melinda (ed.). 2006/2019. *Defiant Birth: Women Who Resist Medical Eugenics*. Mission Beach: Spinifex Press.

Tankard Reist, Melinda. 2004. 'Do the cloning experiment egg donors appreciate their place in history?' *Online Opinion*. 11 March.

Tankard Reist, Melinda (ed.). 2009. *Getting Real: Challenging the Sexualisation of Girls*. Melbourne: Spinifex Press.

Tankard Reist, Melinda and Abigail Bray (eds.). 2010. *Big Porn Inc: Exposing the Harms of the Global Porn Industry*. Melbourne: Spinifex Press.

Tauli-Corpuz, Victoria. 2001. 'Biotechnology and Indigenous Peoples' in Brian Tokar (ed.) *Redesigning Life? The Worldwide Challenge to Genetic Engineering*. London: Zed Books; Melbourne: Scribe Publications, pp. 252–70.

Tauli-Corpuz, Victoria. 2007. 'Is Biopiracy an Issue for Feminists in the Philippines?' *Signs: A Journal of Women in Culture and Society*. Vol. 32, No. 2, pp. 332–337.

Taylor Johnson, Heather (ed.). 2017. *Shaping the Fractured Self: Poetry of Chronic Illness and Pain*. Perth: University of Western Australia Publishing.

Te Awekotuku, Ngahuia. 1991. *Mana Wahine Maori: Selected Writings on Maori Women's Art, Culture and Politics*. Auckland: New Woman Press.

Te Awekotuku, Ngahuia. 2001. 'Hinemoa: Retelling a Famous Romance' in Alison J. Laurie (ed.) *Lesbian Studies in Aotearoa/New Zealand*. Binghamton, NY: The Haworth Press, pp. 1–11.

Thadani, Giti. 1996. *Sakhiyani: Lesbian Desire in Ancient and Modern India*. London: Cassells.

Thadani, Giti. 2004. *Moebius Trip: Digressions from India's Highways*. Melbourne: Spinifex Press.

The Economist. 2018. 'Queensland is one of the world's worst places for deforestation'. 24 February. <https://www.economist.com/asia/2018/02/24/queensland-is-one-of-the-worlds-worst-places-for-deforestation>

The Guardian. 2005. 'Korean scientist resigns over fake stem cell research'. 23 December. <https://www.theguardian.com/science/2005/dec/23/stemcells.genetics>

The IQ2 Debate. 2016. 'Are some social attitudes toward gender intolerable?' The Ethics Centre, Sydney City Recital Hall. 3 March. <https://ethics.org.au/experience/iq2-society-must-recognise-trans-identities/>

The Purple September Staff. 1975. 'The Normative Status of Heterosexuality' in Nancy Myron and Charlotte Bunch (eds.) *Lesbianism and the Women's Movement*. Baltimore: Diana Press.

The Yogyakarta Principles: Principles on the Application of International Human Rights Law in Relation to Sexual Orientation and Gender Identity. 2007. <http://data.unaids.org/pub/manual/2007/070517_yogyakarta_principles_en.pdf>

Thompson, Denise. 1991. *Reading Between the Lines: A Lesbian Feminist Critique of Feminist Accounts of Sexuality*. Sydney: Gorgon Press.

Troemel-Ploetz, Senta. 1990. 'Mileva Einstein-Mariç: The Woman Who Did Einstein's Mathematics'. *Women's Studies International Forum*. Vol. 19, No 9.

Thunberg, Greta. 2019. *No One Is Too Small to Make a Difference*. London: Penguin Random House.

Trask, Haunani-Kay. 1986. *Eros and Power: The Promise of Feminist Theory*. Philadelphia, PA: University of Pennsylvania Press.

Two Hare Court. 2018. 'Gudrun Young successfully defends leading feminist and anti-racist campaigner Linda Bellos OBE in private prosecution'. 30 November. <https://www.2harecourt.com/2018/11/30/gudrun-young-successfully-defends-leading-feminist-anti-racist-campaigner-linda-bellos-obe/>

Tyler, Meagan. 2016. 'The Myths about Prostitution, Trafficking and the Nordic Model' in Caroline Norma and Melinda Tankard Reist (eds.) *Prostitution Narratives: Stories of Survival in the Sex Trade*. Melbourne: Spinifex Press, pp. 213–225.

Ugresic, Dubravka. 2003. 'Because we're just boys' in Ammu Joseph and Kalpana Sharma (eds.) *Terror, Counter Terror: Women Speak Out*. New Delhi: Kali for Women.

Uluru Statement from the Heart. 2017. *Uluru Statement from the Heart Information Booklet*. Melbourne: University of Melbourne Law School.

<https://law.unimelb.edu.au/__data/assets/pdf_file/0005/2791940/Uluru-Statement-from-the-Heart-Information-Booklet.pdf>

UNESCO. 2020. 'Wet Tropics of Queensland — UNESCO World Heritage Centre'. <https://whc.unesco.org/en/list/486/>

UNHCR. 2020. 'Figures at a Glance'. <https://www.unhcr.org/en-au/figures-at-a-glance.html>

Vanclay, Frank and Geoffrey Lawrence. 1996. 'Farmer Rationality and the Adoption of Environmentally Sound Practices; A Critique of the Assumptions of Traditional Agricultural Extension'. *Journal of Agricultural Education and Extension*. Vol. 1, No. 1.

Veevers, John J. 1999. 'Disposal of British RADwaste at home and in antipodean Australia'. *Australian Geologist*. <http://web.archive.org/web/20120410062832/http:/eps.mq.edu.au/media/veevers1.htm> (accessed 7 June 2018)

Veron, John Edward Norwood. 2009. *A Reef in Time: The Great Barrier Reef from Beginning to End*. Cambridge, MA: The Belknap of Harvard University Press.

Vertessy, Rob, Daren Barma, Lee Baumgartner, Nick Bond, Simon Mitrovic, Fran Sheldon. 2019. 'Snapshot: Independent Assessment of the 2018–19 fish deaths in the lower Darling'. <https://www.mdba.gov.au/sites/default/files/pubs/Summary-Final-Report-Independent-Panel-fish-deaths-Lower-Darling-2019.pdf>

Voices Against Section 377. n.d. *Rights For All: Ending Discrimination under Section 377*. New Delhi.

Wadrill, Violet, Biddy Wavehill Yamawurr, Topsy Dodd Ngarnjal and Felicity Meakins. 2019. *Karu: Growing Up Gurindji*. Mission Beach: Spinifex Press.

Wahlquist, Calla. 2019. 'Nuclear waste: Resident near proposed dump told to sign draconian code of conduct'. *The Guardian*. 8 August. <https://www.theguardian.com/australia-news/2019/aug/08/nuclear-waste-residents-near-proposed-dump-told-to-sign-draconian-code-of-conduct>

Wahlquist, Calla. 2020. 'Rio Tinto blames "misunderstanding" for destruction of 46,000-year-old Aboriginal site'. *The Guardian*. 5 June. <https://www.theguardian.com/business/2020/jun/05/rio-tinto-blames-misunderstanding-for-destruction-of-46000-year-old-aboriginal-site>

Wangoola, Paul. 2000. 'Mpambo, the African Multiversity: A Philosophy to Rekindle the African Spirit' in George J. Sefa Dei, Budd L. Hall and Dorothy Goldin Rosenberg (eds.) *Indigenous Knowledges in Global Contexts*. Toronto: OISE/UT, published in association with University of Toronto Press, pp. 265–277.

Ward, Elizabeth. 1984. *Father Daughter Rape*. London: The Women's Press.

Waring, Marilyn. 1988. *Counting for Nothing: What Men Value and What Women are Worth*. Sydney: Allen & Unwin.

Weiss, Margot. 2009. 'Rumsfeld!: Consensual BDSM and "Sadomasochistic" Torture at Abu Ghraib' in Ellen Lewin and William L. Leap (eds.) *Out in Public:*

Reinventing Lesbian/Gay Anthropology in a Globalizing World. Chichester: Wiley-Blackwell, pp. 180–201.

Weldon, Charmaign. 2020. 'Escaping Family Violence: How the justice system is failing Aboriginal women'. Interview with Anna Kerr. *Precedent*. Issue 59, July-August, pp. 16–21.

Wendell, Susan. 1996. *The Rejected Body: Feminist Philosophical Reflections on Disability*. New York: Routledge.

Wild, Angela. 2019. *Lesbians at Ground Zero: How Transgenderism is Conquering the Lesbian Body*. Lampeter, Wales: Get the L Out Report.

Withers, Robert. 2019. 'Be Careful What You Wish For: Trans-identification and the Evasion of Psychological Distress' in Michele Moore and Heather Brunskell-Evans (eds.) 2019. *Inventing Transgender Children and Young People*. Newcastle upon Tyne: Cambridge Scholars Publishing, pp. 141–153.

Wittig, Monique. 1970. *Les Guérillères*. London: Picador.

Wittig, Monique. 1992. *The Straight Mind and Other Essays*. Boston: Beacon Press.

Wohlleben, Peter. 2016. *The Hidden Life of Trees: What They Feel, How they Communicate — Discoveries from a Secret World*. Melbourne: Black Inc.

Wolf, Christa. 1984. *Cassandra: A Novel and Four Essays*. Translated from the German by Jan Van Heurck. New York: Farrar, Straus and Giroux.

Woman-Centered Midwifery. 2015. 'Open Letter to MANA'. 20 August. <https://womancenteredmidwifery.wordpress.com/take-action/>

Women's Aid. 2018. 'The Femicide Census'. December. <https://www.womensaid.org.uk/what-we-do/campaigning-and-influencing/femicide-census/>

Woolf, Virginia. 1966. *Three Guineas*. New York: Harcourt Brace and World.

WPATH (World Professional Association of Transgender Health). 2018. 'Open Letter: Genital Surgery Open Letter'. 4 April. <https://wpathopenletter.wordpress.com/>

Wright, Colin M. and Emma N. Hilton. 2020. 'The Dangerous Denial of Sex; Transgender ideology harms women, gays — and especially feminine boys and masculine girls'. *Wall Street Journal* (Online). 13 February. <https://www.wsj.com/articles/the-dangerous-denial-of-sex-11581638089>

Zeballos-Roig, Joseph. 2020. 'Spain is moving to permanently establish universal basic income in the wake of the coronavirus pandemic'. *Business Insider Australia*. 7 April. <https://www.businessinsider.com.au/spain-universal-basic-income-coronavirus-yang-ubi-permanent-first-europe-2020-4?r=US&IR=T>

Zhang, S., R. Zhang and G. Song. *et al.* 'Targeted mutagenesis using the *Agrobacterium tumefaciens*-mediated CRISPR-Cas9 system in common wheat'. *BMC Plant Biol*. Vol. 18, No. 302. <https://doi.org/10.1186/s12870-018-1496-x>

Index

Wild Politics: Feminism, Globalisation and Bio/diversity

Looking for a new way forward, or a different explanation of what is currently happening? Susan Hawthorne challenges the universal endorsement of global western culture with her concept of biodiversity, arguing that biodiversity is a useful metaphor for understanding social, political, and economic relations in the globalised world of the twenty-first century. She provides a visionary outlook and proposes ways forward that emphasise social justice, multiversity and an ecologically-grounded feminist philosophy.

[*Wild Politics*] is a passionate book offering a kaleidoscope of ideas, arresting ways of seeing things, and possible solutions for many of the man-contrived environmental messes across the violated globe. Its barefaced audacity is its greatest attraction. Hawthorne has blazed a trail for others to follow.
 —Alan Patience, Best Books of 2002, *Australian Book Review*

ISBN 9781876756246

In Defence of Separatism

A timely book which is an examination of the controversy around women's spaces.
 When it was first written in 1976, although it was an important subject of conversation among many feminists, it was not welcomed by academics or publishers. In this 2019 edition, through careful argument, Susan Hawthorne takes us through the ideas which are central to her argument. She analyses the nature of power, oppression, domination and institutions and applies these to heterosexuality, rape and romantic love. She concludes with a call for women, all women no matter their sexuality, to have separate spaces so they can work together to change the world and end patriarchy.

In Defence of Separatism is a powerful lesbian feminist manifesto. It was written by Susan Hawthorne in 1976, when the second wave of feminism was in full flow, as the thesis of her Honours degree in Philosophy. And now — over four decades later — it is more relevant than ever before. Her work is a must-read for any lesbian figuring out feminist politics.
 —Claire Heuchan, *A Fierce Lesbian Feminist Manifesto*

ISBN 9781925950045

Dark Matters: A Novel

When Desi inherits her aunt Kate's house in Brunswick she begins to read the contents of the boxes in the back room. She discovers a hidden life, one which could not be shared with Kate's family. Among the papers are records of arrest, imprisonment and torture at the hands of an unknown group who persecute her for her sexuality and activism.

Susan Hawthorne's dark story uncovers the hidden histories of organised violence against lesbians. She traces fear and uncertainty, and finds a narrative of resilience created through the writing of poems. The author asks: how do we pass on stories hidden by both shame and resistance to shame? A novel that is poetic and terrifying.

Dark Matters is a transformative tour de force; lyrical as Sappho and revolutionary as Wittig in *Les Guérillères*.

—Roberta Arnold, *Sinister Wisdom*

ISBN 9781925581089

The Falling Woman

The Australian Best Books of the Year 1992

A vivid desert odyssey, *The Falling Woman* travels through a haunting landscape of memory, myth and mental maps. Told in three voices — Stella, Estella and Estelle — this is an inspiring story drawn from childhood memories, imagined worlds and the pressing realities of daily life.

This book commands endless reflection, since it opens up the ontological question of being. Hawthorne's book haunts me, it won't let go. On the one hand, it journeys through an unexplored territory of mind that few apart from Dostoyevski dared look into … Let me first say that this is a perfectly structured piece of writing. Its form should help unravel the threads of signification, but we are not dealing here with the explicit, let alone the assertive, or blatant. The only certainty Hawthorne has is that nature is her cradle.

—Jasna Novakovic, *Australian Women's Book Review*

A remarkable, lyrical first novel.

—Robin Morgan, *Ms Magazine*

ISBN 9781876756369

If you would like to know more about
Spinifex Press, write to us for a free catalogue, visit our
website or email us for further information
on how to subscribe to our monthly newsletter.

Spinifex Press
PO Box 105
Mission Beach QLD 4852
Australia

www.spinifexpress.com.au
women@spinifexpress.com.au